JOYCE CARY

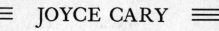

Selected Essays

Joyce Cary

SELECTED ESSAYS

Edited by

A. G. Bishop

London

MICHAEL JOSEPH

In memory of Joyce Cary's eldest
son, Sir Michael Cary, G.C.B.

First published in Great Britain by MICHAEL JOSEPH LTD
52 Bedford Square, London WC1B 3EF
1976

ISBN 0 7181 1486 8

Set and printed in Great Britain by
Northumberland Press Limited, Gateshead,
in Georgian eleven on twelve and a half point, and bound
by Hunter and Foulis, Edinburgh

Contents

Foreword by Dame Helen Gardner vii
Editor's Preface xiii

PROLOGUE
An Interview with Joyce Cary 3

I
Speaking for Myself 19
A Child's Religion 21
Horror Comics 25
Carrig Cnoc 29
Barney Magonagel 32
Cromwell House 43
A Slight Case of Demolition 66
The Meaning of England 71
The Most Exciting Sport in the World 74
Africa Yesterday: One Ruler's Burden 83
Christmas in Africa 91
Policy for Aid 97

II
Unfinished Novels 109
The Way a Novel Gets Written 117
Tolstoy's Theory of Art 130
A Novel is a Novel is a Novel 138
A Novelist and His Public 143
On the Function of the Novelist 150
Morality and the Novelist 154
Travels in a Mind 165
Including Mr Micawber 172
The Period Novel 176
The Tough World of Surtees 179

III
The Heart of England 189
Westminster Abbey 204
Britain's Liberal Influence 210
The Sources of Tension in America 220
Political and Personal Morality 227
Clothes as Expression 233
Joyce Cary's Last Look at His Worlds 239

EPILOGUE
A Great Author Faces up to Death 251

Acknowledgements 257
Notes 259

Foreword by Dame Helen Gardner

I am delighted that Professor Bishop has followed up his excellent edition of *Cock Jarvis* with this selection from Joyce Cary's occasional essays. The two books are complementary. Cary toiled over *Cock Jarvis* on and off for over a dozen years, and at last, having written some half-a-million words embodied in around thirteen versions, abandoned it. The 'main version' which Professor Bishop salvaged from a mass of papers, along with the episodes from earlier versions he printed with it, shows, as Walter Allen rightly observed, that *Cock Jarvis* contained in germ much that came to harvest in Cary's later novels, its hero being the characteristic 'Cary man'; but that, at the beginning of his career as a novelist, he was unable to solve the problems of how to render his fundamental intuitions about life in the form of the novel. These essays were written in the last ten years of his life, when he had formulated those intuitions. They are works he did not toil over, as to the very end he toiled hard and long over every novel. He tossed them off with ease out of the fullness of his mind. They give a vivid impression of the kind of person he was, and bring back memories of his lively, wide-ranging talk, his quick sympathies, his generous response to human idiosyncrasy, the shrewd and humorous eye he turned on current assumptions, the depth and strength of his personal convictions, and, above all, the faith and courage that was at the root of his being as a man and a writer.

Certain themes and ideas recur from essay to essay. There is, as Professor Bishop owns, a good deal of overlap. This was what one came to expect and love in his conversation. He was a wonderful talker, as full of ideas as an egg is full of meat; but wherever the conversation took off from, and however unexpected and lively the incidental remarks were, sooner or later one found oneself listening once more as, in his delightful, light-tenor voice, Joyce held forth again on the creative imagination as the fundamental human faculty by which man shapes and changes his world, and on freedom as the element as necessary to moral and spiritual life as air is to physical.

This 'Philosophy of Life' Joyce Cary had hammered out for himself, and he held it with passion. But nobody can miss in his novels, as nobody could miss who knew him, the fruitful tension he writes of in the essay on 'Morality and the Novelist' between the ideas a writer arrives at in his maturity and his fundamental sympathies, derived from the shaping experiences of youth. As with most great novelists, the deepest sources of his work lay in his past. I imagine many readers will find most pleasure in the autobiographical essays of the first section of this book, just as many people cherish with particular affection among his novels—as I do—*A House of Children*, with its poetic evocation of the world of his childhood. And, in spite of its obvious weaknesses as a novel, I read and re-read *Castle Corner* for its re-creation of a now-vanished world: the world of Yeats's 'indomitable Irishry', both the 'peasantry' and the 'hard-riding country gentlemen'. For all its skill and interest, Cary's second trilogy suffers from being so much based on what he called 'research', so little on memory. Along with his belief in a world endlessly evolving through the creative energies of individuals, Cary had a profound sense of the value of social bonds and a deep, instinctive love, born of his experience, for 'civilised order'. 'Cromwell House,' he writes, 'was a place of civilised order,' and he adds regretfully that he supposes it must be described as a 'feudal relic':

For it was hierarchic—from my uncle, titular head of the family since my grandfather's death, to Barney and Kate, by their own will and feeling family retainers. Everyone had his place in it, and the nephews, the nieces, even the cousins, to an English eye mere visitors, entered by patrilinear right. There were enormous pressures, as in every human society. But in Cromwell House, at that time, they were in balance. And the result was a society highly satisfying to everyone's living needs of body and soul—imagination and affection, humour and pride—a household unforgettable to all who knew it.

Cary's liberalism was shot through and through with con-
servatism. He is not only a novelist of the creative spirit. He
is also a great novelist of the affections, finding in family
affection the 'one trustworthy thing'. In his radio talk on 'Unfinished Novels', having spoken at length on the world as being,
of its very nature, a world of perpetual change, because 'the
free creative mind in action means an everlasting revolution,
everlasting change', he made at the close of the talk a sudden
volte-face:

> Of course, that world, as I see it, is not merely a flux of
> senseless change. Underneath all the turmoil there are certain
> fixed and permanent things too. In daily life there is always
> affection, family love and responsibility, ambition, the things
> people really live for ...

In his philosophy Cary did not, I think, ever manage to reconcile, or to give equal weight to, the assertion that what people
really live for are the fixed and permanent things, and the idea
that what men live for is to create their world and by creating
change it. But it is the strength of the novels that they include
both the adventurers and enthusiasts on the one hand and the
home-makers and home-keepers on the other: those impelled
to break their ties and those who live by them and for them.

The distinction drawn in the essay on 'Including Mr Micawber' is relevant here: between characters who, although condemned by some critics as types or caricatures, live in our
memory as 'real presences', and characters who impress us as
being 'real people'. The 'Cary man' tends towards the type or
caricature; Gulley Jimson, Cary's most famous character, is of
the Mr Micawber type. But the novels are also full of characters
who have the other kind of 'reality', and Cary suggests that,
although both kinds are symbolic, this latter kind are 'symbolic
of more subtle and complex situations'. It is interesting that,
except for the Red Queen, Cary's examples of the first kind of
character are all men—Mr Micawber, Raskolnikov, Sancho
Panza; but as examples of the second kind—the 'real-er'
characters—he gave only women: Tess, Anna Karenina, and
Daisy Miller. And at the end of the brilliant essay on 'Cromwell
House', after giving us those splendid 'characters', his grand-

uncle Tristram and his Aunt Doll's French-educated brother, Hildebrand Oakes, whom his childish imagination saw as models of distinction, he turns at the end to Aunt Doll, who gave to the children 'absolute security by her love':

> As a young man, I used to think I owed more to my uncle than to her; I admired him as a master in the arts of life, whose distinction was proof against every kind of misfortune. But now I am not so sure ... the uncle, with his grand head, his commanding dignity, seems like a child lost in a wilderness; the aunt, so small, so plain, with her childish cries, her sudden unexpected gestures, like a giant in strength and grasp. It was life itself she understood.

One might in the same way distinguish Gulley Jimson and Sara Munday.

Like his favourite novelist, Tolstoy, Joyce Cary was fascinated by 'the quality of women's lives'. I have often heard him quote the story he tells in the essay on 'Tolstoy's Theory of Art' of the double origin of *Anna Karenina*: Tolstoy's presence at the post-mortem on a woman deserted by her lover who had committed suicide, and the moment of revelation when Tolstoy looked at the sleeve of his dressing-gown, 'carefully stitched by some woman's hand'. Cary's novels are conspicuously masculine in their temper—they stand out for this masculine quality among the novels of his contemporaries—and it has seemed strange to some that he should have dared, not once but twice, to put a first-person novel into the mouth of a woman. His comments on the paradox of Tolstoy, 'a man of intense virility', having so profound an intuitive understanding of women are applicable to him too:

> It seems to be precisely men of this intense maleness who also have the quickest sympathy with women. And not merely because, being strongly male, they are powerfully attracted by women, and so deeply interested in women's character; but because of something much deeper and stronger, because they have actually certain feminine perceptions.... Perhaps sex is by itself a universal quality, undifferentiated except by its embodiment, as wine takes the shape of its jug, but is

still wine. So that men and women who have much of it have automatically more of what belongs to the other; and it is the very male men, the very female women, who most easily enter into each other's feelings.

His sympathy with women as understanding 'life itself', and as embodying the 'fixed and permanent' values of 'affection, family love, and responsibility' went happily along with his generous approval of the process of the emancipation of women—in his view the most profound social revolution he had lived through —and his indignation at any discrimination against women. (I cherish a letter he wrote to me, with great difficulty as he was dying, on an occasion when he thought I had been, as a woman, unfairly treated.) None of his many women friends could possibly feel they were not treated by him as fully equals; but, speaking for myself, it was a pleasure to feel, at the same time his recognition that we were different.

The same tension between his belief in change as the law of life and his sympathy with the permanent gives his African novels their special quality. In Africa he found himself in a society which, though wholly different from the world he had grown up in, was like it in that it was passing away. He whole-heartedly accepted British colonial policy and his duty, as its instrument, to assist the process by which an old tribal society was to transform itself into modern self-governing states. But he was fascinated by a society whose bonds were so different from the bonds of the 'feudal' society in which as a child he had found such happiness and security, but which were equally strong and equally based on the permanent element of all true societies, the family. His empathy with the African world, and his openness to its values, as well as to the liberal values which he himself stood for as District Officer, informs what many critics would regard as his masterpiece, *Mister Johnson*. The character of Johnson, like the character of Sara Munday, sprang out of a fascination with a quality of life that was different, but equally the difference was apprehended by means of something undifferentiated and shared: 'the needs as well as the power, the tensions and the exultations of humanity, everlastingly besieged by ghosts and devils'. The essay on 'Christmas in

Africa', which ends with these words, is well placed by Professor Bishop between two political essays: the amusing account of Joyce Cary as a benevolent dictator, but still a dictator, whose experience taught him to feel no surprise that 'Adolf Hitler, towards the end, was fighting battles with armies that had long ceased to exist', which shows a hard-headed approach to the necessities of ruling, and the closely argued defence of the policy of the African Colonial Service in 'Policy for Aid'. These three African essays not only tell us of the experiences that lie behind the African novels and of the ideas and ideals that inform them; they also provide a commentary on them and give scope for generalisations, personal opinions, and pungent incidental observations which his severe artistic conscience kept out of his novels.

The essays collected here were mainly written in the 'fifties, a more hopeful decade than the doom-laden seventies. I imagine some people reading them today may be irked by Joyce Cary's fundamental optimism and feel that in the light of the developments of the last twenty years, such an essay as that on 'Britain's Liberal Influence' can only seem ironic. This would be, I believe, a false judgement. It is only necessary to refer to his sombre picture of the probable results of the abandonment of a policy of gradualism in Africa to refute the notion that he was politically naïve. His optimism did not spring from any blindness to life's hardships and its dangers. The world of his novels is not an easy world to live in. It includes the realities of poverty and sickness and undeserved misfortune, the defeat of men's hopes and ideals, the conflicts between the imperatives of duty and the imperatives of the heart, destruction of what is good and beautiful as well as creation. But it is not a drab world. It is lit and coloured by faith and courage and loyalty. I think it is a good thing that these essays should be collected and published in a dark time, with their pride in the achievements of the past, their faith in the resilience of the human spirit, and their note of indomitable hope.

Helen Gardner

Editor's Preface

Joyce Cary (1888–1957) published over sixty essays—in addition to the Prefatory Essays for the Carfax Edition of his novels. Most of them were written during his final ten years. Established by then as a major British novelist with a rapidly-growing international reputation, Cary set out to record vivid memories of a life rich in active experience, to discuss his own novels and literary principles as well as those of writers whose work he admired, to expound wide-ranging opinions tested in long thought and lively discussion.

These are essays of impressive vigour and variety. They are also of considerable importance in relation to his longer writings, especially the novels. Yet few have been reprinted, and it is now difficult and time-consuming to locate the copies of British, French, and American periodicals in which most appeared. The main purpose of this volume then, is to make conveniently available—for the critic and scholar as well as the general reader—a substantial and representative selection of Joyce Cary's essays.

The selection has been made after consideration of the unpublished essays (now in the James Osborn Collection of Joyce Cary's Papers in the Bodleian Library, Oxford) as well as of all the published essays. Some have been excluded reluctantly, for lack of space, or (as in the case of the unpublished 'My Religious History') because they overlapped other essays very extensively; but my aim has been to include all essays of general excellence or thematic importance, while doing justice to the multiplicity of concerns reflected in the essays as a whole.

Arrangement is not by date of publication, but by topic within three groups. Written fairly close together in his late maturity, long after he had established his 'values on life', Cary's essays clearly spring from a fundamental unity of thought; and chronological arrangement would expose no significant pattern of changing opinion. Moreover, I found that when John Fischer of Harper (Cary's American publisher) had written to him suggesting that the essay 'On the Function of the Novelist', then just published, 'might serve as a section of a future book on the novel, the novelist, and the craft of writing' (7 November 1949), Cary had responded enthusiastically: 'I like your suggestion—and I'll keep it in mind' (12 November 1949). In treating all of Cary's essays as chapters in a larger, cohesive work, I have kept in mind that hint of his own possible intention when writing at least some of them.

The essays in the first group are primarily autobiographical and reflective, focusing on Cary's experiences from his affectionately-remembered Anglo-Irish childhood to his decision, in 1919, to abandon a career in the Colonial Service of Northern Nigeria and settle in Oxford as a professional writer. The central group consists of literary essays, ranging from consideration of Cary's own novels, and their idiosyncratic method of composition, to criticism of the novel as a genre and of novels and novelists he admired. Least uniform in theme are the essays in the final group: they include pieces that can be classified as political, social, historical, and regional. The retrospective 'Joyce Cary's Last Look at His Worlds', which comprehends the disparate experiences and interests of a strongly creative personality, appropriately concludes this group and the selection. Added as Prologue and Epilogue are two interviews. By all accounts, Cary was a fine conversationalist, and his essays clearly draw much of their power from their closeness to informal speech—indeed, several originated as radio-talks. In the first of these interviews, Cary is heard in discussion with two critics, at the height of his powers as a writer; in the second, he speaks movingly from his deathbed.

The essays printed here have been edited, or re-edited, conservatively. However, after collating published texts with their corresponding typescripts among the Cary Papers, I have made some changes in spelling and punctuation to achieve greater consistency and clarity; and I have rectified obvious instances of interference with Cary's style (for example, where an editorial hand has methodically removed 'And' on its appearance at the head of a sentence, I have silently reinstated it). But marks of varying editorial treatment survive, especially as some essays lack corresponding typescripts among the Cary Papers that would have guided the present editor.

Collation revealed many excisions, some of them extensive, in published texts ('Policy for Aid' and 'The Heart of England' are notable cases); and it was easy to suspect editorial pruning. Finding no proof of this, however, and recognising the possibility of authorial deletion (on galley-proofs, or on typescript-copies submitted for publication), I concluded regretfully that there was no strong case for general reinstatement: the excised passages must await a scholarly variant edition of Cary's short expository writings. But I have silently reinstated the occasional word or phrase whose omission I judged to be clearly accidental and detrimental.

Finally, I would like to record my deep gratitude to all who helped me in the preparation of this edition.

Sir Michael Cary (for the Cary Estate) and Mrs Winifred Davin (Joyce Cary's literary executrix) kindly gave me permission to undertake it. Barbara Fisher's list of 'Joyce Cary's Published Writings' (*Bodleian Library Record*, VIII, 4, April 1970, 213–228) proved a continuously useful work of reference. A Canada Council Research Grant in 1973, and a McMaster University Arts Research Grant in 1974, provided financial support that, among other things, enabled me to complete essential research in the Bodleian Library, Oxford. There the efficiency and patience of Mr Philip Bull, Mr D. W. Porter, and other members of the staff, added considerably to my pleasure in working again on the Cary Papers. In the BBC Script Library, London, I was permitted to hear recordings of radio-talks by Joyce Cary and to acquire copies of scripts. The staff of Mills Memorial Library, McMaster University, gave me much assistance, and Mrs M. Parker helped me to gather xerox copies of the essays. From these, Mrs Audrey Alexander typed the manuscript with her customary care. The Hon. Mrs Michael Joseph, Dr John Ferns, and my wife Judith were most generous in offering valuable advice on the selection and texts of the essays. And I received important help and support, in various ways, from Miss Cornelia Starks, Miss Felicity Bryan, Mr

Stephen Wall, Dr J. I. M. Stewart, Dr Douglas Duncan, Professor Richard Morton, Dr James King, Dr Maqbool Aziz, Mrs Sewell Haggard, Professor Angus Cameron, and Miss Jennifer Taylor.

This book owes much to those named above, and to many others; for any deficiencies I alone am responsible. May all who read it find in Joyce Cary's essays as much pleasure and enlightenment as I have done.

A. G. Bishop

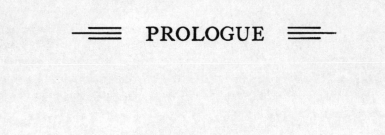

PROLOGUE

An Interview with Joyce Cary
By John Burrow and Alex Hamilton

*Joyce Cary, a sprightly man with an impish crown of grey hair
set at a jaunty angle on the back of his head, lives in a high and
rather gloomy house in North Oxford, Extremely animated,
Mr Cary's movements are decisive, uncompromising, and retain
some of the brisk alertness of his military career. His speech is
overwhelming: voluminous and without hesitation or effort.
His rather high voice commands attention, but is expressive
and emphatic enough to be a little hard to follow. He is a
compactly-built, angular man with a keen, determined face,
sharp, humorous eyes, and well-defined features. His quick and
energetic expressions and bearing create the feeling that it is
easier for him to move about than to sit still, and easier to talk
than to be silent, even though, like most good talkers, he is a
creative and intelligent listener.*

*His house, a Victorian building with pointed Gothic windows
and dark prominent gables, stands opposite the University
cricket ground, and just by Keble College. It is a characteristi-
cally North Oxford house, contriving to form part of a row
without any appearance of being aware of its neighbours. It lies
only a little back from the road, behind a small overgrown
garden, thick with bushes. The house and garden have all the
air of being obstinately 'property', self-contained and a little
severe. So we weren't really surprised at having to wait on the
porch and ring away at the bell three or four times; or to learn,
when Mr Cary himself eventually opened the door, that his
housekeeper was deaf. A very large grand piano half-fills the
comfortable room into which we were led. It has one lamp for
the treble, another for the bass. The standard of comfort is that
of a successful member of the professional class; the
atmosphere a little Edwardian, solid, comfortable, unpretentious, with no obtrusive bric-à-brac. Along one wall is a group*

SELECTED ESSAYS

of representational paintings done by Cary himself in the past. He has, he says, no time for painting now. He is the kind of man who knows exactly what he has time for. So we got down to the questions right away.

INTERVIEWERS: Have you by any chance been shown a copy of Barbara Hardy's essay on your novels in the latest number of *Essays in Criticism*?

CARY: On 'Form'. Yes I saw it. Quite good, I thought.

INTERVIEWERS: Well, setting the matter of form aside for the moment, we were interested in her attempt to relate you to the tradition of the family chronicle. Is it in fact your conscious intention to re-create what she calls the pseudo-saga?

CARY: Did she say that? Must have skipped that bit.

INTERVIEWERS: Well, she didn't say 'consciously', but we were interested to know whether this was your intention.

CARY: You mean, did I intend to follow up Galsworthy and Walpole? Oh, no, no, no. Family life, no. Family life just goes on. Toughest thing in the world. But of course it is also the microcosm of a world. You get everything there—birth, life, death, love and jealousy, conflict of wills, of authority and freedom, the new and the old. And I always choose the biggest stage possible for my theme.

INTERVIEWERS: What about the eighteenth-century novelists? Someone vaguely suggested that you recaptured their spirit, or something of that kind.

CARY: 'Vaguely' is the word. I don't know who I'm like. I've been called a metaphysical novelist, and if that means I have a fairly clear and comprehensive idea of the world I'm writing about, I suppose that's true.

INTERVIEWERS: You mean an idea about the nature of the world which guides the actions of the characters you are creating?

CARY: Not so much the ideas as their background. I don't care for philosophers in books. They are always bores. A novel should be an experience and convey an emotional truth rather than arguments.

INTERVIEWERS: Background—you said 'background'.

CARY: The whole set-up—character—of the world as we

know it. Roughly, for me, the principal fact of life is the free mind. For good and evil, man is a free creative spirit. This produces the very queer world we live in, a world in continuous creation and therefore continuous change and insecurity. A perpetually new and lively world, but a dangerous one, full of tragedy and injustice. A world in everlasting conflict between the new idea and the old allegiances, new arts and new inventions against the old establishment.

INTERVIEWERS: Miss Hardy complains that the form shows too clearly in your novels.

CARY: Others complain that I don't make the fundamental idea plain enough. This is every writer's dilemma. Your form is your meaning, and your meaning dictates the form. But what you try to convey is reality—the fact plus the feeling, a total complex experience of a real world. If you make your scheme too explicit, the framework shows and the book dies. If you hide it too thoroughly, the book has no meaning and therefore no form. It is a mess.

INTERVIEWERS: How does this problem apply in *The Moonlight*?

CARY: I was dealing there with the contrast between conventional systems in different centuries—systems created by man's imagination to secure their lives and give them what they seek from life.

INTERVIEWERS: Didn't the critics call Rose a tyrant?

CARY: Oh, they were completely wrong about Rose. She was a Victorian accepting the religion and the conventions of her time and sacrificing her own happiness to carry them out. A fine woman. And no more of a tyrant than any parent who tries to guide a child in the right path. That religion, that system, has gone, but it was thoroughly good and efficient in its own time. I mean, it gave people good lives and probably all the happiness that can be achieved for anybody in this world.

INTERVIEWERS: Are the political aspects of your work controlled by the same ideas?

CARY: Religion is organised to satisfy and guide the soul —politics does the same thing for the body. Of course they overlap—this is a very rough description. But the politician is responsible for law, for physical security, and, in a world of tumult, of perpetual conflict, he has the alternatives, roughly again, of persuading people or shooting them. In the democracies, we persuade. And this gives great power to the spellbinder, the artist in words, the preacher, the demagogue, whatever you call him. Rousseau, Marx, Tolstoy, these were great spellbinders—as well as Lacordaire. My Nimmo is a typical spellbinder. Bonser was a spellbinder in business, the man of imagination. He was also a crook, but so are many spellbinders. Poets have started most of the revolutions, especially nationalist revolutions. On the other hand, life would die without poets, and democracy must have its spellbinders.

INTERVIEWERS: Roosevelt?

CARY: Yes, look what he did—and compare him with [Woodrow] Wilson. Wilson was a good man, but he hadn't the genius of the spellbinder—the art of getting at people and moving the crowd.

INTERVIEWERS: Is Nimmo based on Roosevelt?

CARY: No, he belongs to the type of all of them—Juarez, Lloyd George, Bevan, Sankey and Moody, Billy Graham.

INTERVIEWERS: Do you base your characters on people you know?

CARY: Never, you can't. You may get single hints. But real people are too complex and too disorganised for books. They aren't simple enough. Look at all the great heroes and heroines, Tom Jones, Madame Bovary, Anna Karenina, Baron Charlus, Catherine Linton: they are essentially characters from fable, and so they must be to take their place in a formal construction which is to have a meaning. A musician does not write music by trying to fit chords into his whole. The chords arise from the development of his motives.

INTERVIEWERS: In one of your prefaces you said, didn't you, that Jimson's father came from life?

CARY: I met an old man, an artist who had been in the Academy and a success, and was then ruined by the change of taste when the Impressionists created their new symbolic school. But I didn't use him in my book, I don't know anything about his character, only his tragedy. A very common one in this world. (*Suddenly*) The French seem to take me for an

Existentialist in Sartre's sense of the word. But I'm not. I am influenced by the solitude of men's minds, but equally by the unity of their fundamental character and feelings, their sympathies which bring them together. I believe that there is such a thing as unselfish love and beauty. I am obliged to believe in God as a person. I don't suppose any church would accept me, but I believe in God and His grace with an absolute confidence. It is by His grace that we know beauty and love, that we have all that makes life worth living in a tough, dangerous, and unjust world. Without that belief I could not make sense of the world and I could not write. Of course, if you say I am an Existentialist in the school of Kierkegaard, that is more reasonable. But Existentialism without a God is nonsense —it atomises a world which is plainly a unity. It produces merely frustration and defeat. How can one explain the existence of personal feelings, love and beauty, in nature, unless a person, God, is there? He's there as much as hydrogen gas. He is a fact of experience. And one must not run away from experience. I don't believe in miracles. I'm not talking here of faith cures—but some breach in the fundamental consistency of the world character, which is absolutely impossible. I mean absolutely. (*With emphasis*) God is a character, a real and consistent being, or He is nothing. If God did a miracle He would deny His own nature and the universe would simply blow up, vanish, become nothing. And we can't even conceive nothingness. The world is a definite character. It *is*, and therefore it is *something*. And it can't be any other thing. Aquinas tells you all the things that God can't do without contradicting himself.

INTERVIEWERS: But about Existentialism.

CARY: Kierkegaard states the uniqueness of the individual and I stand by that.

INTERVIEWERS: That's what you meant, then, when you said that what makes men tick should be the main concern of the novelist? The character's principle of unity?

CARY: And action, their beliefs. You've got to find out what people *believe*, what is pushing them on ... And of course it's a matter, too, of the simpler emotional drives—like ambition and love. These are the real stuff of the novel, and you can't have any sort of real form unless you've got an ordered attitude towards them.

INTERVIEWERS: But the fundamental beliefs are not always the most apparent, or, it seems to us, the most successful of the achievements in the novel. We were expecting, for instance, a much closer analysis of the religious beliefs of Brown in *To Be a Pilgrim*. But we felt, in fact, that what came across most successfully were the emotional responses of people to people—compelling, for instance, Lucy to follow Brown.

CARY: The details were there once. That is, Brown's arguments were there, and Lucy's response. But Lucy was only one character, one motive in the symphony. And also I was up against the problem of explicit statement. I may have cut too much, but the book is long and packed already. The essence of Lucy was her deep faith. She wasn't the kind of person who can float along from day to day like a piece of newspaper or a banana-skin in the gutter. And in the book, I had her feelings expressed. But I cut them somewhere in the rewriting. I rewrite a great deal and I work over the whole book and cut out anything that does not belong to the emotional development, the texture of feeling. I left too much of the religious argument in *Except the Lord* and people criticise it as too explicit or dull.

INTERVIEWERS: Do you find in those later stages that you're primarily concerned with the more technical side of 'form'? With, for example, managing the flashback? And do you think, incidentally, that you owe that particular trick to the films? I believe that you worked on a film in Africa.

CARY: No, I don't really think it has anything to do with films. The flashback in my novels is not just a trick. In, for example, *The Moonlight*, I used it in order to make my theme possible. It was essential to compare two generations. You can't do that without a flashback contrast; the chronological run-through by itself is no good.

INTERVIEWERS: In the Preface to *Herself Surprised* you mentioned a technical difficulty you found yourself in. You wanted to show everything through the eyes of Sara, but found that to make her see everything diluted her character. This was the soliloquy as flashback. This struck us as the same dilemma that James found himself in when writing *What Maisie Knew*. Is this a just parallel? Do you read James?

CARY: Yes, but James is not very remarkable technically. He's one of our very greatest novelists, but you will not learn much by studying his technique. *What Maisie Knew*, that was one of the packed ones, wasn't it? Almost too packed. I enjoyed its intense appreciation of the child's nature, and the cruel imbecility of the world in which she was thrown about. But on the whole I prefer the beautifully clear atmosphere of a book like *The Europeans* or *Daisy Miller*—all James is in *Daisy Miller*.

INTERVIEWERS: Have you read *The Bostonians*? There was the spellbinder.

CARY: No, I haven't read that.

INTERVIEWERS: *The Princess Casamassima?*

CARY: I'm afraid I haven't read that either. Cecil is always telling me to read her and I must. But I read James a good deal. There are times you need James, just as there are times when you must have Proust—in his very different world of change. The essential thing about James is that he came into a different, a highly organised, a hieratic society, and for him it was not only a very good and highly civilised society, but static. It was the best the world could do. But it was already subject to corruption. This was the centre of James's moral idea—that everything good was, for that reason, specially liable to corruption. Any kind of goodness, integrity of character, exposed that person to ruin. And the whole civilisation, because it was a real civilisation, cultivated and sensitive, was fearfully exposed to frauds and go-getters, brutes and grabbers. This was his tragic theme. But my world is quite different—it is intensely dynamic, a world in creation. In this world, politics is like navigation in a sea without charts, and wise men live the lives of pilgrims.

INTERVIEWERS: Have you sympathy with those who most uncompromisingly pursue their own free idea whatever the opposition?

CARY: I don't put a premium on aggression. Oh, no, no, no. I'm no life-force man. Critics write about my vitality. What is vitality? As a principle it is a lot of balls. The life force is rubbish, an abstraction, an idea without character. Shaw's tale of life force is either senseless rubbish or he really means Shaw —Shaw as God's mind. The life force doesn't exist. Show me some in a bottle. The life of the world is the nature of God, and God is as real as the trees.

INTERVIEWERS: Which novelists do you think have most influenced you?

CARY: Influenced? Oh, lots. Hundreds. Conrad had a great deal at one point. I've got a novel upstairs I wrote forty years ago in Africa, under his influence. But I read very few novels nowadays. I read memoirs and history. And the classics. I've got them at my fingertips and I can turn up the points I want. I don't read many modern novels, I haven't time, but those I do read are often very good. There is plenty of good work being done, and in Britain the public for good work has enormously increased in my lifetime—especially in the last thirty years.

INTERVIEWERS: Do you find, then, that conversation with the novelists of today helps?

CARY: Conversation?

INTERVIEWERS: I mean apart from the personal stimulus, do you find that what they have to say helps to resolve technical problems?

CARY: Oh, no. Not particularly. We chatter. But you have to work problems out for yourself, on paper. Put the stuff down and read it—to see if it works. Construction is a complicated job—later I'll show you my apparatus.

INTERVIEWERS: Is there only one way to get a thing right? How close is form?

CARY: That's a difficult question. Often you have very little room for manoeuvre. See Proust's letter to Mme Schiff about Swann, saying he had to make Swann ridiculous. A novelist is often in Proust's jam.

INTERVIEWERS: You are a determinist—you think even novelists are pushed by circumstances?

CARY: Everyone but a lunatic has reason for what he does. Yes, in that sense I am a determinist. But I believe, with Kant, that the mind is self-determined. That is, I believe intensely in the creative freedom of the mind. That is indeed absolutely essential to man's security in a chaotic world of change. He is faced all the time with unique complex problems. To sum them up for action is an act of creative imagination. He fits the different elements together in a coherent whole and invents a rational act to deal with it. He requires to be free, he requires his independence and solitude of mind, he requires his freedom of mind and imagination. Free will is another matter—it is a term, or rather a contradiction in terms, which leads to continual trouble. The will is never free—it is always attached to an object, a purpose. It is simply the engine in the car—it can't steer. It is the mind, the reason, the imagination, that steers.

Of course, anyone can deny the freedom of the mind. He can argue that our ideas are conditioned. But anyone who argues so must not stop there. He must deny all freedom and say that the world is simply an elaborate kind of clock. He must be a behaviourist. There is no alternative, in logic, between behaviourism, mechanism, and the personal God who is the soul of beauty, love, and truth. And if you believe in behaviourism, none of these things has any real existence. They are cogwheels in the clock, and you yourself do not exist as a person. You are a delusion. So take your choice. Either it is personal or it is a delusion—a delusion rather difficult to explain.

INTERVIEWERS: How do you fit poetry into this? I once heard you describe it as 'prose cut up into lines'. Would you stick to that?

CARY: Did I say that? I must have been annoying someone. No, I wouldn't stick to it.

INTERVIEWERS: Anyway, at what stage of your career did you decide to write novels rather than anything else?

CARY: What stage? Oh, I've been telling stories ever since I was very small. I'm telling stories now to the children of a friend of mine. I always tell stories. And I've been writing them from childhood. I told them to other children when I was a child. I told them at school. I told them to my own children and I tell them now to the children of a friend.

INTERVIEWERS: *Aissa Saved* was the first one you published?

CARY: Yes, and that was not until I was forty. I'd written many before, but I was never satisfied with them. They raised political and religious questions I found I could not answer. I have three or four of them up there in the attic, still in manuscript.

INTERVIEWERS: Was this what made you feel that you needed a 'new education'?

CARY: At twenty-six I'd knocked about the world a good bit and I thought I knew the answers, but I didn't know. I couldn't finish the novels. The best novel I ever wrote—at least it contained some of my best stuff—there's about a million words of it upstairs, I couldn't finish it. I found that I was faking things all the time, dodging issues and letting my characters dodge them.

INTERVIEWERS: Could you tell us something about your working methods?

CARY: Well—I write the big scenes first, that is, the scenes that carry the meaning of the book, the emotional experience. The first scene in *Prisoner of Grace* was that at the railway station, when Nimmo stops his wife from running away by purely moral pressure. That is, she became the prisoner of grace. When I have the big scenes sketched I have to devise a plot into which they'll fit. Of course often they don't quite fit. Sometimes I have to throw them out. But they have defined my meaning, given form to the book. Lastly I work over the whole surface.

INTERVIEWERS: When does the process, the book, start?

CARY: Possibly years ago—in a note, a piece of dialogue. Often I don't know the real origin. I had an odd experience lately which gave me a glimpse of the process, something I hadn't suspected. I was going round Manhattan—do you know it?

INTERVIEWERS: Not yet.

CARY: It's an island and I went round on a steamer with an American friend, Elizabeth Lawrence, of Harper's. And I noticed a girl sitting all by herself on the other side of the deck —a girl of about thirty, wearing a shabby skirt. She was enjoying herself. A nice expression, with a wrinkled forehead, a good many wrinkles. I said to my friend, 'I could write about that girl—what do you think she is?' Elizabeth said that she might be a schoolteacher taking a holiday, and asked me why I wanted to write about her. I said I didn't really know—I imagined her as sensitive and intelligent, and up against it. Having a hard life but making something of it, too. In such a case I often make a note. But I didn't—and I forgot the whole episode. Then, about three weeks later, in San Francisco, I woke up one night at four—I am not so much a bad sleeper as a short sleeper—I woke up, I say, with a story in my head. I sketched the story at once—it was about an English girl in England, a purely English tale. Next day an appointment fell through and I had a whole day on my hands. I found my notes and wrote the story—that is, the chief scenes and some connecting tissue. Some days later, in a plane—ideal for writing—I began to work it over, clean it up, and I thought, 'Why all these wrinkles? That's the third time they come in.' And I suddenly realised that my English heroine was the girl on the Manhattan boat. Somehow she had gone down into my subconscious, and came up again with a full-sized story. And I imagine that has happened before. I notice some person because he or she exemplifies some part of my feeling about things. The Manhattan girl was a motive. And she brought up a little piece of counterpoint. But the wrinkles were the first crude impression—a note, but one that counted too much in the final writing.

INTERVIEWERS: A note—

CARY: I was thinking in terms of music. My short stories are written with the same kind of economy—and no one would publish them. Some of them, now being published, are twenty years old. Because each note has to count and it must not be superfluous. A son of mine, a composer, wrote some music for the BBC lately. The orchestra was small, and the Musicians' Union wouldn't let him conduct. He heard one of the players ask the conductor what the stuff was like. The conductor, no doubt intending to warn the player, answered, 'It's good, but the trouble is that every note counts.' I suppose the editors who rejected me felt like that. They wanted a little more fluff.

INTERVIEWERS: You can depend around here on practically everyone's having read *The Horse's Mouth*. Do you think that's because it's less philosophical? Or just because it's a Penguin?

CARY: *The Horse's Mouth* is a very heavy piece of metaphysical writing. No, they like it because it's funny. The French have detected the metaphysics and are fussing about the title. I want *Le Tuyau increvable*—the unbustable tip. They say this is unworthy of a philosophical work and too like a *roman policier*. I say *tant mieux*. But they are unconvinced.

INTERVIEWERS: A metaphysical work—

CARY: A study of the creative imagination working in symbols. And symbols are highly uncertain—they also die.

INTERVIEWERS: Gulley's picture on the wall then, which is demolished, is in its turn a symbol of the instability of the symbol?

CARY: That's what Mrs Hardy seems to think. But that would be allegory. I hate allegory. The trouble is that if your books mean anything, the critic is apt to work allegory in. The last scene of Gulley is a real conflict, not an allegorical one. And it was necessary to cap the development. It was the catastrophe in a Greek sense.

INTERVIEWERS: *The Horse's Mouth* was part of a trilogy. You're doing this again now, aren't you, in *Prisoner of Grace, Except the Lord*, and the third yet to come?

CARY: I was dissatisfied with the first trilogy. I've set out this time with the intention of doing better. I think I *am* doing better. The contrasts between the different worlds are much sharper. When I'd finished *Prisoner of Grace* I planned a second book on political religion, but contemporary religion. And I found myself bored with the prospect. I nearly threw in the whole plan. Then one of my children urged me to go on. And I had the idea of writing Nimmo's religion as a young man. This appeared to me as opening a new world of explanation, and also giving a strong contrast to the last book. So I got to work. And tried to get at the roots of left-wing English politics in evangelical religion.

INTERVIEWERS: And the third?

CARY: It's going to be called *Not Honour More*. In it, I deal with Jim—the lover in *Prisoner of Grace*. He is the man of honour, of duty, of service, reacting against the politician. But I'll show it to you in its present state. Upstairs.

We followed Mr Cary upstairs two storeys to his workshop. It was a room with a low ceiling. A window at the far end looked

out onto trees. *Where the walls downstairs had been covered
with pictures, up here it was all bookcases, containing, it
seemed, more files than books. Mr Cary went straight to his
desk, pulling out sheaves of paper from the shelves over it.
They were, one instantly observed, meticulously organised. The
sheaves were numbered and titled, each chapter in its own
envelope. Mr Cary explained that these were the 'big scenes'.
Clipped on the front of each envelope was a sheet of memoranda
indicating what still remained to be done within the chapter,
what would be required to give the finished scene a more con-
vincing build-up. These were the chapters of the embryonic
'Not Honour More'.* ...

Mr Cary explained that he was now 'plotting' the book.
There was research yet to be done. Research, he explained, was
sometimes a bore; but it was necessary for getting the political
and social background of his work right. He had a secretary
who did useful work for him in the Bodleian, the University
library. He was at the moment, for example, wanting facts on
the General Strike, and had given his secretary a list of
questions to work on.

We asked him if what we had heard was true—that often, as
he worked, his writing would generate another, unrelated idea
and he would thus be led to write out a block of about twenty
thousand words before returning to the work at hand. Mr Cary
confirmed this account; and it was confirmed too by the large
bookcase containing nothing but files and boxes of unfinished
work. It was an impressive proliferation of novels and short
stories, with the titles on the spines, unfamiliar titles like 'The
Facts of Life'. One file contained 'recent short stories'.

The over-all impression of the room in which he worked, as
of the novelist himself, was of a man who, much as he himself
might eschew the word, radiated 'vitality'. He rose, he said,
early, and was always at his desk by nine. We had already
used up more than the period of time he had agreed to give us.
As we went downstairs and made again for the sitting room,
he looked anxiously at his watch; but we were there only to
dig quickly among the deep cushions for the belongings that
had spilled from our pockets as we lounged.

16   SELECTED ESSAYS

Paris Review, II, 7 (Winter 1954–1955), 63–78; reprinted in *Writers at Work: The Paris Review Interviews* [I] (ed. Malcolm Cowley), London, Secker & Warburg (1958), pp. 47-62; New York, Viking (1958), pp. 51–67.

I

Speaking for Myself

They say that tensions make the artist and writer. That is certainly true of the Anglo-Irish writers, and my childhood should have been full of tensions.

Ireland was still a battleground. My own family had been almost ruined by the rent strike, and my grandfather had died of a broken heart. Yet he had been a resident landlord and a popular man. The people still tell stories of his humour, his dash, his personal beauty, his reckless, brilliant driving.

Even as a small child, therefore, I knew something of real tragedy: the tragedy of social conflict in which personal quality counts for nothing; where a man is ruined not because he has done any wrong, but because he represents a class or race.

Again, I lived between two worlds so different that they could not be reconciled: in London with my young father, who was taking a degree in engineering, and lived in a small house near his work, in the East End, among miles of streets in which all the people seemed equally drab and anonymous; and with one of my grandmothers in Ireland, where everyone, rich or poor, was intimately known, with all his family history, and where the very air was full of history, and the background was an historical war of religion and nationality.

But even in Ireland I had two different beings. With Grandmother Cary, at Clare on the shores of Lough Foyle, I was often the only child. But the house was full of old portraits and old books. I read enormously, and dreamed still more. From Clare I would wander in the old walled gardens of Castle Cary, with all the appropriate feelings of the banished heir in the romances. And the country people, with the Irish love of children and old tales, would tell me stories of my people.

But at my Grandmother Joyce's, at some holiday house

taken for all her grandchildren, I would range over the countryside with a horde of cousins. We went fishing, exploring, stealing
rides on other people's horses, sailing on the lough, often for
long journeys. We were as free as the mountain slopes, and often
in mischief.

If there were tensions I knew nothing of them, and I do not
recognise them now. All those deep, richly-felt contrasts and
conflicts remained simply as experience, the more vivid for its
light and shade. But it is possible also that they gave me, even
as a boy, a certain critical feeling (rather than judgement) about
the more complacent views of politics and history which were
then common form.

New York Herald-Tribune Book Review (8 October 1950), 10—
as 'Joyce Cary' in 'Important Authors of the Fall, Speaking for
Themselves'. The title printed here is an adaptation by the
editor.

A Child's Religion

When I was about two and a half, I absolutely refused to go to bed without a certain lump of wood which had once been a toy horse. It turned up years later in an old trunk and an aunt identified it for me.

My aunt described the fearful scene that had taken place on some occasion when this object had been mislaid—how I had howled and rejected all consolation. She had been a young aunt. There was still a note of impatience in her recollection of the affair. Obviously she had thought me spoilt and unreasonable.

I was ready to agree. I was then a boy of nineteen or twenty and I looked at the relic with little interest. All small children, I thought, had such violent fancies for toys. The thing was normal. It was not till I had grandchildren that I saw how strange this universal passion was. Yet I had been in Africa and knew something of juju.

Then I perceived all at once that I myself had been a juju-worshipper. And so I came back by this roundabout way into that strange world where, right under the noses of amused grown-ups, small children, like their stone-age ancestors, live and grapple with mysteries and demons, ghosts and monsters.

People talk about the happy secure time of childhood. After the first few weeks of life children are never secure; that is, from the time when they discover that fire can burn, cats scratch, malignant doors shut on their fingers, and even their mothers fail to drive away pain. It is from this discovery that they begin to look for affection, that they need reassurance from parents and toys.

We need not be too concerned for them. They are, for the most part, extremely tough; they have, like savages, a wonderful power of enjoying themselves amidst every kind of discouragement. The very insecurity of their lives hardens their nerve.

A small American girl of my acquaintance, Sara, at the age of three, was shown an old dry well in the garden of her new house. Her father warned her to keep away from it. She was fascinated by this place which threatened to swallow her up and kill her; she asked what it was for. Her father answered that the ground had belonged to a farm and the well had belonged to it. Sara, after gazing a long time into the ominous black pit at her feet, remarked, 'I suppose that's where they put the bad horses.'

She was three and therefore a reflective person, moving out of the world of pure impressions. She had plenty of words and an idea of law. But her law was still a primitive, a savage law; she did not falter at the notion of horses thrown down a well. At the back of her mind was the thought: 'Badness can expect no mercy.'

The child's notion of good and evil is all in extremes, terrifying dangers, ecstatic delights. He has small idea of legal justice, he hates and fears his enemies, he clings to his friends, including his pet toys. His natural religion is juju. But juju was at the beginning of all our religions and it is, after all, a reciprocity of duty and affection.

A child knows affection, by experience, in his nurse, his parents—he has complete faith in their saving goodness. That faith may have even deeper roots in his first self-centred and imperial confidence; as a baby, in his first weeks, he does not even conceive of danger in the universe. He accepts the universe as entirely devoted to him. And afterwards he trusts in affection when he can trust nothing else. He makes an emotional relation with all about him, he chooses for himself objects of devotion and creates both their devotion to him and his duty to them.

He will wrap up his horse, his bear, on a cold day, he will console a ninepin for being knocked down, he propitiates the soul of a broken mug, 'poor mug'. He feels a responsibility to those that serve him.

As a child of the old century, before I was three, I was taught to say my prayers in my mother's lap. That was a matter of course, and I was surprised, some time in the 'twenties, to find how much this casual fact shocked some modern parents of that time, parents with the most conscientious sense of duty.

They asked what prayer could mean to a child of three. And it is true that prayer then is little more than a gesture. The child kneels, puts his hands together and mutters a few routine words. But as I see it now, children much younger than three have lived already for what seems to them a lifetime in a world of powerful spirits, good and evil. They understand very well that their prayer expresses a relation with some good spirit and the relation is one of reciprocity. They are doing a duty to this spirit.

As I grew older, I added to my first short prayer for my mother and father, brother and grandparents, various relations and friends, until I had an immense list of names, such as Bridget Tobin, my grandmother's cook, Dan Kane, the gardener, and Barney Magonagel, my great-uncle's gamekeeper and dog-man.

I felt a strong compulsion to pray for everyone I loved or who loved me. It was a duty which must be performed before I went to bed. I was still, at six or seven, so much of an animist that I felt the need of propitiation towards the powerful spirits of love and friendship.

I write here 'love and friendship' because, for a child of six, the instinctive passionate relation of babyhood has long received definition. He knows what love is, by its name, and for me, at least, the animist's intense impression of living spirit everywhere about him had passed easily into the idea. God, Jesus, to me were spirits of power and love in a sense both far more potent and direct, far more ordinary and casual, than they became to my later intelligence. I was used to spirits of every size and force, phantoms that sighed along dark corridors, vast unseen presences that brooded over the woods.

I took my prayers very carelessly and I was not expected to make much of them. I gabbled them, especially that ever-lengthening list of names, and climbed eagerly into bed to hear my story. Prayers were a savage, a primitive ritual of duty, establishing a mutual bond, conciliating mysterious powers.

But they affirmed and confirmed in my mind, my idea of things, the faith with which every child is born, that there is goodness in the world, in life; that to know it is all the security, and the peace, that life can give. And this is a true faith.

Vogue (N.Y.), CXXII (December 1953), 86, 87; reprinted in *Family Doctor*, IV (August 1954), 440, 442.

Horror Comics

There has been in England this year an outcry against the horror comics and demand for censorship. It had the air of spontaneity, but it began in a newspaper article attacking the comics, and therefore encouraging all those numerous people who hate and fear liberty to express their alarm. Parents, teachers, parsons of all the different churches, wrote to the papers and got up deputations to Ministers.

This agitation had support from the press on all political sides. Everyone seemed to agree that the comics were a dangerous evil which must be stopped or they would corrupt British children.

It was only after weeks of this tumult that a few letters began to appear from people who really knew something about children and their imagination, and about the effect of their reading.

These letters, also from teachers and parents, gave good evidence to show that the comics did no harm whatever to children who read anything else—that is, to children of ordinary intelligence. And as for the minority of illiterates or mental deficients, the effect was doubtful. It depended upon factors difficult to estimate, possibly beyond estimation.

The difficulty, of course, as in all matters concerning so volatile and mysterious a force as the imagination, is to obtain any standard of reference. No one can say of any child that comics have damaged his character, because it is impossible to know what his character would have been if he had never read a comic. Child crime is as old as humanity; indeed much older. Puppies and kittens spend most of their time in mischief. It is their way of exploring the world. The puppy eats your shoes, as the baby breaks your watch or tears up your book.

And we take measures according to the circumstances. We

induce the puppy to try his teeth on a rubber bone. We teach the baby to tear only his own books. Even if the puppy is incurably destructive, the baby shows a passion to tear, we do not send for the police, we do not cry out that moral degeneracy among puppies and babies threatens to destroy civilisation. We realise that civilisation has survived worse puppies and more abandoned babies—puppies and babies which did, in fact, grow up to be vicious.

It is argued by some psychiatrists that there is no such thing as a criminal mind; no soul born to evil. The most greedy and egotistic, the most unbalanced, the most stupid, can be taught to realise his ambitions and passions in some activity which is at least harmless to society. The tough can be turned into a fearless policeman; the bold adventurer, who might be a cat-burglar, seeking the glory of danger and the triumph of skill, can become a mountain-climber or a test-pilot.

This may be so, but in practice there will always be a large stock of the maladjusted, the criminal. And no one will dare to say that some of these were not influenced by their reading. For reading is a powerful influence, especially on children.

I dare say that horror comics have been one factor in all those complex motives which can betray a child or youth into crime. So is the influence, even more powerful, of his friends, his environment, his heredity, or mere accident.

I write as one who was a gang-leader of criminal youth. As a small boy in Ireland I was quite as mischievous as other small boys, and perhaps more enterprising than some of my fellows. One whole summer I was leader of the gang that fought other gangs with stones and sods. And our proudest feat was to steal the coastguard's boat in order to make a surprise landing in enemy territory.

This was called mischief and brought down on us only an indulgent reproof from the local police. But what we enjoyed, what I enjoyed most enthusiastically, was the breaking of the law, the crime which was only not serious because no harm followed except the furious wrath of the coastguard.

And the influences which hurried me into crime were the glory of leadership among a group of other small boys, of a family tradition of leadership and enterprise, an imagination full of pirates, Robinson Crusoe, Jack the Giant Killer, and the large ration of actual villainy from the tales of country people and other children.

Children tell each other horror stories quite as savage and bloody as anything in the comics or in Grimm. It is apparently a need of the young imagination to acquaint itself with that aspect of life as well as all the rest; to realise danger, cruelty, and violence as part of the grown-up world, in which courage and endurance are at least as necessary as arithmetic. If horror comics make criminals, they are but one cause among dozens. Censorship of the most severe kind would have no appreciable effect on juvenile morals.

But even when we allow that some crime might be traced directly to the comics, censorship would be a folly and a betrayal; a folly because there is only one antidote to those instincts in the child which can make him a criminal, and that is education and example, especially in his own home.

As a gang-leader I was ready to fight and steal. I adored Father for his courage and skill as a sportsman, renowned among the people. But I admired him too as a man of quixotic honour. I had the sharpest sense of right and wrong. When, in the excitement of battle, I stole that boat, I knew I was doing wrong; that was the chief of my pleasure. I knew, too, very well, where the wrong must stop, or it would bring me shame instead of glory. Because I loved my father, I dreaded to lose his good opinion.

It is for parents to prepare their children for life in which there will always be cruelty and vice, temptation and horror. To demand censorship in any form is a confession from parents and teachers that they cannot face their job. And to give it would be to betray the basic faith of liberals that man is capable of responsibility for his own soul and his own family duty.

This is a faith, but it has also its logic. For what is the alternative? To hand over the control of publication to some committee, ultimately to the police? And why should we believe that any committee, any police authority, is wiser than ourselves in deciding what is good for our children to read? They do not even know our children.

We are to surrender the basic principle of a civilised state,

liberty of publication, at the demand of a pressure group who
are unable to grasp the very point at issue—the development
of character in a child. You do not give self-respect and self-
reliance by censorship; you can only foster ignorance or develop
hypocrisy, the blind fear that goes with ignorance, the violence
that comes from prejudice.

Spectator (18 February 1955), 177.

Carrig Cnoc

One enters childhood, the true feeling of childhood, only by
flashes, direct from the subconscious. Contact is joined over the
years, not with the memory of events but with the sense of
existence itself. This, of course, is a common enough phenom-
enon. Proust entered childhood by taste—the taste of his
madeleine cake. I knew a man who was moved only by sounds;
and certain sights, like that of fuchsia, especially when it is
being blown about in a wind, can always take me to Donegal,
where fuchsia is a wild hedge plant. But the most powerful
magic I know is smell. So, one day, at the age of fifty, lying in a
field in Wales, I smelt thrift. The breeze came my way and the
plant was within an inch of my nose or its dusty, muskish scent
could not have reached me. It is not, I suppose, a scent at all,
but a personal thing. But it must be characteristic for it carried
me instantly a thousand miles in space and forty years in time
back to a certain spot among rocks at an Irish house called
Carrig Cnoc, belonging to the Chambers family.

The Chambers were our cousins, and had been our lawyers
and agents for several generations. We had taken their country
cottage for the holidays; it was a perfect place for children,
with a private beach opening to the Atlantic, with rocks and
boats, with the mountains just behind.

Was I happy in those days at Carrig Cnoc? According to all
grown-up ideas, I was intensely happy from morning till night,
in and out of the water as I chose, sailing, fishing, playing
brigands on the hillside. We would get up at five in the morning
to lift our lobster pots, chiefly in order that no one else should
lift them first. I remember, in my mind, those green dawns, when
the horizon would be a pale water green, as if the sun, still
hidden, were shining at us through a thick piece of window-
glass; and near by the water would still be as dark as a laurel

leaf. The clumsy boat, made for rough seas and rough landings, would rock in short violent jerks, and the cold morning breeze would blow my hair while, proud and responsible, I held the thick rough loom of my oars and gave short pulls to keep our head up to the float; digging at the water in jerks with a navy stroke. The stroke that later at Oxford ruined my career as an oarsman.

The grown-ups, my father, an uncle or so, would be extremely serious, smoking their pipes (I remember vividly the glow of the pipes, probably because I longed to smoke one myself) and, as it seems to me, extremely deliberate in all their movements. My father, especially, though extremely quick of foot and eye, a famous bird-shot and an amateur boxer who might have won championships if my mother had allowed him to risk his fine delicate beak in the ring, always moved, on such expeditions, with the precision of one carrying out a ritual.

I have reflected since that this is a common manner of experienced boatmen, they never move carelessly. All their actions are balanced. But at the time I merely observed and the observation stayed in my memory of the time.

This is quite a different approach than that flash of the sub-conscious record touched off by the smell of the thrift, for it took me back into childhood itself, into a quite different world than that of memory.

For I was, in one instant, actually existing, as a child again, in a certain place among the rocks, a high place on the right side of the bay, with the sea on both sides of me. On my right it broke heavily, straight from the open sea; on my left, in the enclosed bay, it was merely lapping the shore.

I sat with my back against a rock, facing the house, which, for a moment, surprised me by appearing red. Carrig Cnoc is a brick house painted white. But at once I remembered that in my childhood it had been red.

This alone, the unexpected sight of an appearance long since removed from the present world, had a startling effect; it was not so much that the Carrig Cnoc of the past, so long departed, had asserted a claim to immortality in the subconscious world, as that the present world all about me suddenly grew insub-stantial. It too became an appearance among appearances and for those few moments the only real solid thing was my own existence, or, rather, that of my feelings.

Previously unpublished. The text printed here is from an untitled typescript among the Cary Papers in the Bodleian Library; its title has been provided by the editor.

Barney Magonagel

A thin dark man with very long arms, a thin brown face deeply creased, a drooping tobacco-coloured moustache, and a black patch over the right eye. He is dressed in black morning-coat, black trousers, and yellow leather gaiters over enormous black boots. He wears on his head a small black cap, like those worn by schoolboys, and carries on his arm a large shopping-basket while he cheapens a cabbage at a greengrocer's in a London suburb.

He is complaining passionately in a strong Irish accent about the price of cabbages. Indignation seems to choke him, so that he pronounces 'cabbages' as 'cahbaggjes', and yet he never loses a peculiar dignity that makes the grocer and some amused by-standers seem mean and cheap. His earnestness while he declares that 'there's not the heart of a fly in any wan of them' and, above all, his complete indifference to the circle about him and their stares at his outlandish gaiters, the strange cap, the long-tailed coat, give him that distinction which belongs only to those who stand so far out of the daily world that they do not even notice its whims.

This man was Bernard Magonagel, known to all our family as Barney, my great-uncle's dog-man, coachman-groom, and butler—man of all work. Often, when I was a small boy, he was also my nurse and always my favourite companion.

Barney had been with my Uncle Tristram Cary from his own childhood. As a boy in Ireland, he had gone out with other boys, from a village of my uncle's, to beat and pick up game for a shooting party. There were always plenty of volunteers for this work—the boys, like most Irish boys, enjoyed the sport as well as earning a shilling or two.

I have heard, indeed, that Barney was not chosen to beat; he went out with the rest of the boys simply from enthusiasm for the sport, an enthusiasm that brought about his disaster. For, anxious to see the effect of a shot before all the guns had fired, he put up his head from behind a wall and was hit by a pellet in the right eye. The eye was destroyed, and my uncle, being Barney's landlord as well as host to the party and responsible for his guests, promised him a life job and took him at once into his household.

I don't know what Barney thought of the transaction, but he actually did spend the rest of his life with my uncle, and became the mainstay of his family. When I knew Barney, in his forties, he had the status, almost unknown nowadays, of a family servant who is so truly part of the family that it would have been just as impossible for the family to do without him as it would have been for him to do without the family.

Such old retainers tend to become tyrants; it is hard for them not to misuse their power. Affection by itself can turn an old nurse into a cranky despot. But this was never true of Barney, even when my uncle and aunt, in old age and weakness, were almost entirely dependent on him. And yet Barney was essentially a stronger character than my uncle.

Tristram Cary was a magnificent man to see—tall, handsome. To my childish eyes, he seemed, in frock-coat and tall hat, and carrying an immense Malacca cane, at least ten feet high, a monument of power and wisdom. But he was a typical Irish landlord of the old school—a sportsman, a good fellow, hospitable to the extreme, and a very careless economist. He would have thought it disgraceful to calculate expense when he had a party to entertain or a demand of any kind to meet from a relation. His house was always full of kinsfolk, and usually they were seeking his help. Above all, he was a gambler. He did not plunge, but he loved to bet, and he slowly wasted a fortune on horses and cards.

I say 'wasted', and yet he was not a waster. He was, I think, essentially a sad man who, for all his gaiety, his love of entertaining, had little value for life. He lived at a time when his order, the Anglo-Irish of the Ascendancy, was passing; he had lost the Irish property, which he had loved; and, the greatest of his griefs, he had no children. Several were born to him, but all died in the first weeks of life.

As a younger son, he had been put to a profession and took a good degree as a doctor. But his father died young, in 1848, of typhus caught while tending victims of the famine, and my uncle inherited a fair property. So he did not practise till, his estate ruined by the land war, by his own extravagance, and by gambling, he was in his fifties.

Racing was his passion, as it is the passion, the escape, of many sad men. Even after the sale of his Irish house, and his settlement in England, first as a gentleman farmer, he still kept a chaser or two. But the farm did not pay—that is, it proved an even more expensive toy than most gentlemen's farms—and after ten years of losses he gave it up and finally took a practice, near London, on the high road to Kew. His house, called Cromwell House, was now a Victorian villa; his land was shrunk to a croquet-ground surrounded by borders and rows of pollarded limes, his out-buildings to a few garden sheds and a stable. His string was brought down to one cob, to go in the brougham or gig, and for racing he kept only greyhounds.

My father was now also settled in the London outskirts, close by, and during school holidays I visited Cromwell House almost daily. I would find Barney digging a border, or building the cob's dung into his mushroom-bed, in the left-hand yard. We would discuss the proper use of a spade or the strange disposition of mushrooms, which never grow where or when you want them. But our deepest and longest conferences took place nearly always in the high, gloomy old stable while he combed the bay or bedded down the dogs.

Their presence was not the least element in the impression, so strong in my memory, of exalted occasions. With Barney and the dogs, I entered a superior world in which the charm of the grave and lofty ideas presented to my imagination had unexpected concord with the grace and stripped power of the dogs and their peculiar attraction for me. I can't remember if I then knew my Keats, and I certainly possessed no faintest gleam of philosophical theories about coherence, but I must have had some intuition of what Keats meant when he said that beauty was truth and truth beauty. I gazed at the hounds while Barney combed and talked, now over the cob's tail, now under its nose; their beauty and their strangeness fascinated me. I was also a little alarmed by their aloofness, their sudden-fixed gaze. Their great eyes, I thought, actually gave out light in the dark of our winter evenings, while they poked their long, delicate noses from the straw in a last, nervous enquiry about events in the neighbourhood; they never seemed to be convinced that such events would agree with their refined feelings.

I was always surprised to find a hound actually asleep. I could not reconcile those restless beings with inertia, repose. And, in fact, they never did entirely relax. Even in sleep, they twitched incessantly, their pulses would be seen beating fast under their ribs, their muscles rippled, they sighed, groaned, uttered faint cries of excitement or warning. They seemed to me the most mysterious of creatures. I never knew what was going on in their heads, as I did, for instance, with spaniels or setters, simple-minded sporting dogs, or with a Donegal collie, who was as clever as you like, yet displayed all the processes of his logic as frankly as any sportsman or shepherd.

I never tired of discussing the hounds with Barney. But we passed easily from dogs to horses, religion, fairies, myth, politics, and family history. All these cognate subjects received absorbed attention from us both. A hound was regarded with the same analytic consideration as a statesman or my own grandfather, as any actor in the scenes of life. Barney saw all creation as one, a complex but significant whole, like a vast morality. His view, I suppose, was precisely that of the medieval peasant. And for the same reason: he had had the same kind of religious education and he was completely illiterate.

Barney could not even write his name. But he had, like most illiterates, a tenacious memory filled with an encyclopedia of events and facts. It was the only encyclopedia open to him. So he would give me a detailed account of how one of my long-forgotten ancestors had married a fine, handsome girl who then proceeded to ruin him. 'For she was spoilt with her face and he doted on her. Ah, Master Joyce, that Lucius was the destruction of half what should be coming to you.'

He would discuss some new hound that was as 'clever as a fox, but has he the heart within him? I tell ye, Master Joyce, cleverness is nothing without ye have the heart in it'—by which he meant something nearer enthusiasm than courage.

He would say of some Celtic god or hero and his revenge on some rival, 'Now, that was a cruel thing but ye'll mind them was cruel times. Sure, they didn't know any better.' Barney had an immense charity for all the world that didn't know any better. I dare say he included my uncle in it.

For he had no illusions about his master. He saw all his weakness with the penetration of one who has been a confidential servant for forty years. This did not affect, nothing could affect, Barney's sense of duty, because it arose not from any personal give-and-take between the two men, so different in temperament and background, but from Barney's idea of life. In that idea, every man had a place, and not only a duty but an authority corresponding with the place. His whole dignity as a man, his self-respect, depended on his understanding of what belonged to his place.

I've never forgotten his words to me when, as a child of eight or nine, I said something rude to him. 'That's no way for a gentleman to speak to a servant, Master Joyce. I thought you had more thought for your place, and mine, too. Sure, it's not that I care what you say, but you demean yourself, sir.' He then repeated this last, emphatic phrase with the strange, thick, gobbling utterance that expressed his strongest feelings, as if they came too strong and quick for his tongue: 'I say ye demean yourself.'

I did not know at the time what new impression of the world and human relations this speech opened to me, but it was certainly a striking one. Barney had a way of putting such conviction into speech, such weight of moral passion, that even trivial remarks and incidents became family history.

I say 'moral passion' because Barney was a religious man in a sense that is now growing rare. Religion entered into all his thoughts and deeds, and it was his own strongly-articulated, even rigid, kind of religion, hieratic. I must not say that in his view God, like any squire or groom, had his place that bound him to a duty, for I never heard him say so. But I do remember his discussion with one of my aunts about a sentence passed on a certain poacher. She thought that So-and-So, the magistrate concerned, had been too severe; he should have considered the delinquent's poverty and his long family. Barney answered that perhaps it was not in Mr So-and-So's place to let such a fellow off with less than a month. And I fancy he had a similar view, or at least a sense, of God's situation. It was essentially a place with duties that had to be accepted with the dignity.

Barney valued his place, but in a conflict between its duties and his principles, always severe, principle was apt to win. He was a great stickler for the truth in its most literal form, and I recall vividly his interrupting my uncle actually in the middle of a story.

This happened at one of the big dinner-parties, probably one of the earliest to which I was admitted, at least at the pudding-and-dessert stage. I seem to recall an Eton collar. Uncle Tristram, like many sad men, revelled in any kind of party. He especially loved to tell stories, an art he understood and practised with great skill and much appreciation. A dinner party, which delighted his sense of hospitality, brought out his best form, and he was, on this occasion, nearing his climax and point when Barney, handing a dish to a guest, made an odd sound, something between a strong sigh and a suppressed groan. We all looked at him, but he made no further sign, and my uncle continued his tale in a somewhat louder voice and in that tone of joyful anticipation that marked his approach to the final triumph of laughter. Barney had now passed on to the next chair—we had forgotten him—when suddenly, while still bending his head politely towards the guest, he muttered, as if to the dish, 'Ah, no, Master. It wasn't just so as ye say. Sure, it was a long time ago and ye've forgot it.'

Barney intended the words 'it was a long time ago' as a general explanation and apology for my uncle's want of veracity, but his mutter, under emotion, was an explosion of protest. It stopped my uncle in the middle of a word. And Barney then, while still handing the dish, with the same formal bow beside each chair, related the circumstance with exact truth but in the flattest kind of detail. Barney had no sense of humour, except of the grimmest kind. He could laugh at himself for falling down the cellar stairs ('Ah, I could have been kilt'), but he did not appreciate the droll. For him, life was an extremely serious business. To do the family justice, though it had, as a whole, an acute sense of humour and thoroughly enjoyed these unfore-

seen crises produced by Barney's literal and prosaic turn of
mind, it listened solemnly enough to this intervention; and my
uncle, though with some impatience, admitted that he might
have been wrong in some small detail of fact.

But he would often say, when asked about some old tale, 'I'll
wait till Barney's out of the room, or he'll spoil it for me.'

To this, Barney would make no answer. But his face would
assume a certain expression that I did not understand till many
years later. I saw it then on the worn, ascetic features of a shabby
old French monk in Normandy. He had been talking to some
friends of mine as he showed them around the monastery, and
he came up suddenly to me with the most eager gait and look.

'I hear, sir, that you have a cure for asthma—that you have
cured your own. Excuse me, sir, but I am a great sufferer. I had
to give up my mission in Africa because of my illness and now
they won't let me go back again until I am better. I should be
most grateful for your advice.'

I told him that I had had asthma in the tropics, but the only
cure I had found useful was twenty years of special breathing-
exercises. And I could not be quite sure even of that, for I had
had an attack again, quite lately, in India.

The old man's face slowly changed as the hope faded out of
him, and he said, at last, 'It's what I thought.'

He was not at all like Barney except for his dark and worn
complexion, like a peasant's, and the deep folds in his hollow
cheeks. But his look as he said those last words suddenly recalled
the old Irishman. And I realised that on those occasions when
my uncle spoke of Barney's spoiling a story, Barney's face had
had pride in it as well as resignation. Or perhaps pride is too
strong a word for the dignity of one who says, 'I know what
life is—I'm not expecting any help from it.'

Barney was a good Catholic in his own way. He deplored his
weakness for drink, and nearly conquered it. He took the pledge,
but not from his priest. He was afraid he might break it, and
for him the priest was, so to speak, God's magistrate. It might
not be the priest's place, any more than God's, to let him off a
long sentence if he broke his word. So each year he made his
oath to my aunt, signed it with his cross, and kept it rigidly for
the next eleven months and thirty days. On the last day of the

pledge year, which was Saint Patrick's Day, my aunt would warn Barney of his pledge and remind him of his danger. But he would always slip away and contrive to get so drunk that he would be brought home from the streets, or some pub, nearer dead than alive.

Luckily, at least as far as I know, he never fell into the hands of the police. Most likely, perceiving him to be an Irishman, they looked the other way. There is a general indulgence among the London police for the Irish on Saint Patrick's Day and the Scots at the New Year. Barney would take perhaps a day to recover and then reappear, grave and reserved as before, to take a new pledge and assume general responsibility for the household.

Perhaps the happiest times I spent with Barney were when we went out together to exercise the dogs. In those days, there was no greyhound-racing in the modern sense, where half-a-dozen dogs are set galloping after an artificial hare, in a prepared arena. When greyhounds were raced, they went after a real hare, in open country. They were matched in couples, and each couple was started from a single slip-leash to which their collars were attached by a spring-catch. A jerk on the spring opened the collars at the same instant, setting the dogs free. The winner—that is, the catcher of the hare—was promoted to the next heat.

It was one of Barney's duties in training the dogs to make them accustomed to the leash, so that they would start from it at full pace. He and I, after a shooter's breakfast of bread and cheese taken together in the kitchen, would set off early in the morning, with two dogs in hand. Although my uncle's house ranked as suburban and stood among others of the same type along the high road, the hinterland was still open fields. So we would make our way by quiet country paths to a certain rough meadow, lent us by a farmer friend of my uncle's. Barney would fix the dogs by their collars and hand the leash to me with a warning to take a good grip. The dogs were long and I was short. I would stand up close to them and grip the leash firmly, my hands actually over their sterns. Barney would then take off their coats and walk off, or stroll off, to a distance of sixty to a hundred yards.

I call Barney's gait a stroll, but there is no exact word for it. There was majesty as well as ease in his rolling stride—it resembled most nearly the walk of an African Emir, who, encumbered by half-a-dozen robes, and heelless slippers over his soft leather stocking-boots, combines the weighty progress of a state coach with the grand roll of a three-decker advancing into action.

It seems to me now that all our trials were in winter. I recall only cold mornings, not long after dawn, with frost on the tufted grass, wisps of fog twined in the trees, and a low white sky made of the same fog, with no very clear distinction between sky and air. I can still see Barney's dark, bottle-shouldered figure—in its black coat and the black trousers confined within the gaiters, which seemed somehow wider at the top than the bottom— diminishing and growing greyer through this fog, and leaving on the grass long, dark impressions, like those of some primitive mastodon or dinosaur in a chalky bed.

Meanwhile, the dogs and I stood shivering, as much from excitement as cold. They pulled on the leash and whimpered. The skin on their smooth, thin bodies, on which the hair shone as if it had been oiled, was in perpetual, tremulous movement. Dogs, unlike the night-walking cat, with its cold nerve, are high-strung creatures, and of all dogs the highbred greyhound is the most tense. The leash itself, pulled tight as a bowstring, came to nervous life as it vibrated between us. And Barney's pace, characteristic in its deliberation, seemed not only exceedingly slow but to grow slower as his figure receded. It drove us distracted. I not only quivered with the strained frustration of the dogs, communicated to me through the quivering leash, but I was terrified that they would drag me off my feet and prove me unfit for my job. I would drive my heels into the soft ground, actually between the dogs, and lean back till I was sitting in the air.

At last, Barney would stop, look around him as if at the fog, carefully lay down the dogs' coats, and unwind from his neck the large red bandanna that was his common wear, unless as coachman he put on a stock, or as butler a high collar and string tie. With the neckerchief in his hand, he would turn to face us, and stand quite still for a moment. Then, suddenly, the

Barney we knew vanished and was replaced by a wild, primitive creature. Tearing off his cap, he bent his knees, made a kind of leap straight upwards, and, waving the cap in one hand, the bandanna in the other, gave vent to an extraordinary scream, which resembled nothing I have ever heard before or since, though it had some of the quality of that frightful cry with which a hyena can bring one out of deep sleep literally in a sweat of terror. I call it a scream, but it had in it also the elements of the howl and the roar. It combined in one chord all their various powers of exasperating, startling, alarming, and stunning. As this sound struck upon me, my hand by mere reaction jerked the spring, and the hounds streaked away. I still remember the flick of a raised tail on my hand as a hound flew beneath it; it is perhaps the memory that, after the vision of Barney's slow recession into the fog, is most vivid to me.

And though, of course, there was no need for me to move from my place—it was on the way home—I, too, as if maddened by that fearful yell, would set off running with all my might, and would arrive, exhausted, gasping, my heart ready to burst, when Barney had already buckled one dog into its coat and was giving a last rub-down to the other.

The dogs themselves, hanging out their long, paper-thin tongues, which jerked to and fro over the sharp teeth at each side till I wondered how they were not torn, were now perfectly calm. Their fragile ribs jumped in and out, their breath panted loudly, but all the tension had gone from their nerves. Their eyes had the calm, disinterested gaze of spoilt beauties who are tended; they turned their lovely heads about with the air of bored aristocrats carelessly observing a rustic scene.

It was Barney and I who were agitated. My nerves were still tingling like pins and needles, and Barney, as after a Saint Patrick's Day, seemed to struggle with powerful and confused emotions. As after Saint Patrick's Day, too, as always when he suffered strong feelings, his voice came thick and his words tumbled out on top of one another.

'Blackie ran crooked again—his muscles arant right yet. Did ye mind how he broke step? It loasht him five yards. Dom these buckles—stand still, ye devil!—if only we could get thon near side stretched on him, he'd win the Cup. Dom it—he would, as sure as shooting. He's the shwiftest we ever pupped and turns like a shwallow.' Blackie was a dog that had been scalded, as a puppy, so that his muscles were contracted on one side. This caused him to run crooked—he would break step to get straight again, and lose impetus.

By 'the Cup', Barney meant the famous Waterloo Cup, equivalent for coursers to the Derby stakes among horse-racing men. My uncle entered for it year after year, and one year did succeed in taking second place. I don't know which hound won this high distinction—whether or not it was Blackie, whose racing-name I forget, among all the mass of names and racing-talk poured out to me, after those morning trials, by Barney. All the way home, he would talk dog. About the Cup heats, about old private matches, how the Master's Marten had beat the Colonel's Silver Arrow, for twenty pounds, and how he had lost twice as much again to 'thon English lord that shot your granda's mountain' because the incomparable Marten had put his foot on a thorn. It was only gradually that the heave, the rage of excitement, ran down in him and the thickness went out of his voice. He would not become his usual grave, reserved, meditative self till we were in sight of the yard-gate that led to the kennels.

And even then there was a kind of emotional groundswell, apt to throw up an unexpected breaker. I fancy that it was on one of these mornings, while we came home together with the dogs, both of us still a trifle unbuttoned in our nerves, that I brought upon myself that reproach, which stuck so deep in my consciousness that I have remembered for fifty years the shock and illumination of it.

New Yorker (19 June 1954), 27–31.

Cromwell House

Gavarni has a picture of an old woman, toiling along in the heat under a load of wraps, hats, balls, hoops, and toys, with the caption, 'Providence gives the aliment of nature to little birds but to little children it has given the grandmama.' To me, it sent grandmamas, and also one great-aunt who did me more than kindness and gave me more than love. I did not know it then, but I know it now.

She lived from the late 'eighties in Cromwell House. I don't know what Puritan or Republican chose the name, but it wasn't my great-aunt or my great-uncle. They were Church and King people. Cromwell House was a solid, double-fronted Victorian house at Gunnersbury, near London, on the Richmond Road, with the usual basement storey, front steps, and high, pillared porch. To one side, there was a stable and small coach-yard; on the other there were garden buildings. At the back of the house, a conservatory gave on a balcony overlooking the garden, which was just big enough for a croquet lawn. The whole place, in short, belonged to its period, when the Englishman, tied to town by business, still aspired to live the life of a country gentleman, with at least one horse, one greenhouse, and some small area of lawn under his windows. But Cromwell House, as a household, was not at all English; it was deeply foreign to England. My great-aunt herself, for all her English blood, was essentially a foreigner. She had been brought up in France. Her father, Henry Oakes, was a Waterloo captain, who, when he retired, settled in France, where his half-pay went further than in England.

Oakes had a large family, and my great-aunt was born in 1824. She was christened Dorothea Maria but was known almost invariably as Aunt Doll. She was a very little woman, always dressed in black, and she never lost her French accent or French turn of speech. With her brothers and sisters, she commonly talked French. One of her sisters, Sophie Vialls, widow of a Crimean general, lived near Cromwell House, and the Vialls household was all French, even to the fierce maid, Honorine, who detested children as much as my aunt loved them.

Her love was that special kind of love that delights in children, that can't have too much of them. And it covered not only small children like my brother and myself, but all her various nephews and nieces for whom Cromwell House was the family centre. The Cary nieces, brought up in Ireland, in the careless abundance of Castle Cary, were now, after the land war of the 'eighties and the loss of the family property, scattered about London in various jobs. And they came to Aunt Doll with all their troubles—to be scolded, to be cherished. The two things were almost one act in my aunt. She had the French volubility; she would pour out her comments at the latest folly, or mischief, in such shrill tones of horror and wrath that strangers were surprised to see the comparative indifference of the culprit. Whether it was one of us children who had broken the second window in one day, or some niece who had refused a good proposal, lost a job, or gone to the races in company my aunt could not approve, we knew that these exclamations were themselves a kind of sympathy. In them, so to speak, my aunt brought her feelings into full relation with the affair. It became her affair, and even her horror conveyed a certain guilty satisfaction to the criminal. A niece who had merely run up bills and wanted a small loan was made to feel all the desperation of ruin, a dignified state, together with the appropriate compassion given to bankrupts, before receiving a present. Aunt Doll was strongly against debts. She never lent money; she gave it.

She had the kind of generosity that is simply not aware of itself, that gives by nature, as by a reflex. Aunt Doll was so much concerned with others that she seemed hardly to consider her own griefs. Yet she had had a very sad life. Apart from the loss of her own children, who died in infancy, she had seen a continuous decline of fortune and hope.

She had married, in 1852, my great-uncle Tristram Cary, whom she met when he was in Europe on a grand tour. He was a second son, and had been brought up to a profession, as a doctor. But his father, my great-grandfather, died young, in '48, of typhus, caught while attending victims of the Irish famine, and Tristram inherited a property young, at eighteen. He did not practise medicine, therefore, till many years later. He brought his bride to Ireland, settled at Ballybrack, in Donegal, and employed himself, like his older brother, my grandfather, of nearby Castle Cary—Arthur Lunel Cary, already a magistrate—in developing his share of the estates, in a fairly leisurely way.

They were both great sportsmen, loved racing, shooting, driving-matches—tastes very much approved by their tenantry. The last time I was over in those parts, in 1940, I had a vivid account from an old man of my grandfather's habit of racing his tandem against a fellow-magistrate, after petty sessions, from Moville to Castle Cary. The Moville-Derry road along Lough Foyle is beautiful but not, even now, remarkably wide or straight. It is full of hills and fenced by stone walls. The notion of driving a tandem, even by itself, along such a road, is alarming.

Those were the days, too, of the long trace. That is to say, the traces from the leading horse went straight back to the wheeler's trace-buckles. This meant an immense length of leather, which, unless the leader was right up to his collar all the way, looped down towards the road, so that, at any check, he was extremely likely to get his leg over it. He would then kick the wheeler on the nose, the wheeler would put his hoofs through the gig, and the driver, if he was wise and lucky, jumped over the fence. Tandem-driving was probably the most dangerous road-sport ever invented. The driver had almost no control over his leading horse. A shy could tangle him up; a wagon, met at a corner, could mean a heap of kicking horses, splintered shafts, and broken wheels, all over the road.

My father has told me how my grandfather, in one race tooling along at full gallop, braced up with back well hollowed and his elbows well down, said to him, then a boy of sixteen, sitting beside him, 'Hold me together, Arthur—I'm bleeding.'

He had just had an operation for 'stone, and the wild bouncing of the gig and the pull of the reins had torn away some stitches; blood was running on the floor. My father duly put his hands up under my grandfather's coat and shirt, took a grip of his flesh on each side of the wound, and squeezed it together until the race was over.

Uncle Tristram did not drive tandem, but he kept and raced horses. And a taste for betting, combined with the Irish land war, gradually impoverished him. In the 'eighties, he went to England, and became a gentleman farmer in Kent, at a place called Holdfast. But the 'eighties were the worst times that the English farmer has known; thousands of the most practical were ruined by cheap imports of food. The gentleman farmer —that is, a man who farmed for a pastime and followed sport as a career—had no chance at all. My uncle failed to hold Holdfast, and came at last to Gunnersbury, and Cromwell House.

Gunnersbury was suburban, in its main streets, but it was still rural in its hinterland, and this was its chief attraction for my uncle. Since he could no longer keep race-horses but only a trapper for the gig and brougham, he bred greyhounds for coursing, and he needed to be near fields for their training.

Here at last he practised medicine, though by the methods of the 'fifties. He did not believe in microbes, but neither had he heard of psychosomatic complications, and, since he did not suggest them, they often failed to exist. His figure, as he walked through the streets, was itself therapeutic. In his frock-coat and top-hat, he seemed to me about nine feet high; and a certain dreaminess, which caused him often not to notice the passers-by, added to his prestige. He appeared to be sunk in reflection on the problems of his science. So, when he was greeted, he would gaze down as from an intellectual as well as a physical height, a trait that gave to his genial greeting and friendly enquiries a special gratefulness. Also, I've heard, he would always give advice on such occasions, and he never remembered, or perhaps disdained, to charge for it.

When I began to know him well, he had been already some years in Gunnersbury. After my mother's death in '97, when I was eight, my father came to live close by, to be near the Tristram Carys, partly for his own sake and partly for that of my brother and myself. As I say, theirs was the family centre and we were still foreigners in England. As a family, we clung together. And it was from this time that Cromwell House became a second home to us. We still spent our summers in Donegal with Grandmother Cary or Grandmother Joyce, but on all other holidays we sought Aunt Doll and Uncle Tristram.

So I remember several of my uncle's consultations by the wayside; one especially, when I was honoured to be included in a party of three—my uncle, myself, and Barney Magonagel, who was my uncle's dog-man, as well as butler and groom—to try a couple of hounds. They were always tried in pairs to make them used to starting with another dog and to accustom them to being bumped into by one.

The training-runs were managed in this manner. One person held the leash, to which the collars of both dogs were fastened by a spring-catch, until Barney had walked off to a suitable distance; Barney would then throw up his cap and utter a yell; the leash-holder would pull the spring-catch and let go the dogs, who would race to Barney. On this occasion, my uncle intended to take his stand half-way along the course, and I was to start the dogs. I was already aquiver with excitement and nervousness. Barney, who had unbuttoned the dogs' coats and was about to hand the leash to me, was saying, 'Now, Master Joyce, mind what you're about. They're fresh the day. Be quick on the spring, or they'll pull you over,' when a serious-looking, middle-aged man, from one of the terraced villas across the road, started towards us. He had on his top-hat and he tipped it to my uncle as he approached. I had the idea he had put it on for the purpose.

My uncle acknowledged the salute by raising the gold top of his big Malacca cane towards the brim of his own hat and saying, 'Well, Mr Smith, and how are we this morning?'

I don't remember what the man's name actually was, but I recall his great red face. He at once began to pour out a long tale of his symptoms.

My uncle interjected, speaking to Barney, 'Blackie, there— he's shivering this morning.'

'Sure, sor!' Barney exclaimed in an explosion of wrath that made his moustache shake. 'Why wouldn't he be? They'll both be catching their death.'

His voice and look accused my uncle of neglecting the dogs to attend to Mr Smith's idle chatter. Actually, of course, the dogs were not stripped, their coats still hung on their backs; and greyhounds, the most high-strung of creatures, are always shivering. But Barney had a standing grievance against my uncle—indeed, against the whole world—that they did not give sufficient consideration to his dogs.

My sympathies were all with Barney. I looked indignantly at the red-faced man, and he, realising his mistake, began to apologise. But my uncle would not allow him to reproach himself. 'Not at all, Mr Smith. Not at all. It's the east wind; it plays the devil with dogs and men. We all have to look after ourselves in a wind like this. Now, what you need is to go home to bed, and Barney'll bring you a bottle of medicine. Then in a few days you can send and tell me how you are.'

The man stooped to pat one of the dogs, and asked, 'How many days?' He was clearly a hypochondriac.

My uncle paused a moment to reflect, and answered, 'Three days, unless the wind holds longer. Yes, three for a start.'

The red-faced man thanked my uncle profusely, apologised again for breaking in upon him, shook hands, tipped his hat, and went away. His very back expressed self-deprecation and gratitude. My uncle turned once more to the serious business of the morning.

I'm not going to say that my Uncle Tristram cared more for his dogs than his patients. On the contrary, there was something in his voice, his face, as he looked down upon some interlocutor over the long slope of his chest, that expressed both the warmest kind of sympathy or fellow-feeling, and a certain resignation in the face of human ills. The whole man seemed to say, 'We are but mortal—but let us at least die like men.' And I believe it was this courageous sympathy, combined with his majestic presence and his prestige as a sportsman, that made him so popular with his patients.

Next to my aunt and uncle, Barney had my devotion. He was then about forty, and he had been with my uncle from the age of twelve—one might say from birth, for he had been born in a village on the estate in Ireland—and his imagination had been brought up largely on the family history, centred in my uncle himself. He had, I dare say, after thirty years' close study, as deep a knowledge of my uncle as any man can have of another, and treated him with what, to an Englishman, would have seemed like the rudest frankness. He would question his orders, and criticise his judgement, on anything from the care of dogs to the management of a mushroom-bed. But what to an Englishman would have seemed like insubordination was, in fact, the mark of a relation profounder than any ordinary personal loyalty. To Barney, my uncle was the master, and masters had their place by appointment of Heaven. On the other hand, Barney had *his* place also, a place of responsibility and dignity. And as with any Prime Minister to an autocrat, it was his duty to criticise, to state his own point of view, to propose the right policy, even if it was to be rejected, and to remind my uncle of past failures, if the reminder could lead to wisdom. He had also, as a good Christian, a direct duty to Heaven—that is, to truth—so he would interrupt my uncle's stories to correct him in any detail that, to Barney's recollection, was not exact.

With Barney, I entered, without knowing it, into a social idea, a form of existence, now extinct in the West. For instance, Barney did not divide his life into work and play. He always had a task and he always gave to it special and appropriate attention; he carried it out with the pleasure that an artist takes in technical accomplishment. I never remember him except as being on duty. When at times I found him sitting down, he would be cleaning harness in the stable or silver in the pantry, or, seated on a bucket in the yard, sorting a box of spring bulbs, early windfalls, or winter potatoes. I especially enjoyed these times. It was then I had with Barney some of my best and most philosophical talk, about the nature of man, the nature of the world, the strange ways of horses, the traits of different hounds, and the odd character of Carys generally. Barney knew the family history for three or four generations back, and in his view Carys formed a special race, admirable but foolish, mysterious in its crotchets, wild and rash in conduct, but, all the same, of a unique and valuable quality.

This quality consisted almost entirely in the fact that the Carys were, in Barney's words, old stock. At one time, this seemed to me an odd title to distinction in a family of otherwise quite undistinguished squires. But now I see that it is one that includes everything old—old coats, old books, old chairs, old trees, old houses. Man lives by his imagination, and his imagination is deeply engaged in history—the human drama. An old chair, an old house, carry with them the idea and the marks of a long concern in the affairs of men, their struggles, hopes, desperation, follies, and glories. Barney, who could not read, had exercised a great deal of imagination on Cary history. He would say suddenly, 'Ah, it was thon Lucius that ruined himself with marrying that Miss Ray.' 'Thon Lucius' would turn out to be a Cary who had flourished half a century before Barney was born.

He dwelt on the Carys' follies and disasters rather than on their successes as resident landlords who had three hundred years of reasonably good development work behind them. Yet he held them in honour above all others. For instance, in spite of his deep respect and affection for my aunt, he thought nothing of her own family, the Oakes, with their far more obvious distinction. He would say of my aunt's brother Hildebrand Oakes, one of the finest, handsomest men I've ever seen, 'Thon Master Hildy, ye only have to look at the poor fella to see he's a wanderer,' expressing in the last word both pity and a mild scorn.

Hildebrand, in fact, was a great traveller and, at that time, possessed no settled home. His headquarters were a room kept for him at Cromwell House, where he would suddenly arrive from some distant port, to spend a month or two with his sister, of whom, in his undemonstrative way, he was very fond. For Barney, the want of a home, above all the want of land, was a prime defect, amounting to a misdemeanour. There was a certain amount of malice in Barney's view of Hildebrand. He knew that Hildebrand thought little of the dogs, and he suspected that he did not sufficiently admire and respect his brother-in-law, Tristram, or even the Cary family generally.

This, I may say, was certainly true. To Hildebrand, brought up in Paris and Brussels, we were wildly provincial. It was with consternation that he had seen the tall young Tristram from Donegal—a place as remote and barbarous-sounding to him as

Kamchatka—carry off his small, neat, delightful, and highly-cultivated sister to his native mountains.

For Barney, France was the remote, barbarous land, and his remarks about Hildebrand were a favourite part of the Barney canon, as treasured by the numerous Cary male relations, known commonly as 'the nephews', who frequented the house. They would repeat in Barney's tone of commiseration, 'Ah, what would the poor fella know of dogs? He's nothing but a Frenchman.'

This, as I say, was thought a joke, one of Barney's sayings. But I think it was more true than we realised. Hildebrand, as I see now, was intensely French in mind. He was a man of logic and method, with the highest standards of private and family duty, and deep but extremely narrow sympathies. He had absolutely nothing in common with my Uncle Tristram, who was as intensely Anglo-Irish as the Oakes were French. The Carys were, to Hildebrand, impossibly vague and careless, and indifferent to the ritual of social life. I have seen him point out, with the end of a cigar, on a picture of Castle Cary, the mistake made in extending the house to the rear instead of at the sides. The house should, in his view, have had wings with roofs at a level lower than that of the central block. My grandfather, rebuilding the house in the 'fifties from the ruins of the old semi-fortress—a real castle—had produced simply a plain Victorian house, and this in Hildebrand's view was a betrayal of family duty. He acknowledged that in France the squire's house was always the *château*, but declared that, however modest, it at least asserted itself in some lordly pinnacles on the roof-ridge, a high mansard, or conical extinguishers over the attic windows. Even if it were no bigger than a weekend cottage, it had a flavour of Chambord or Azay-le-Rideau about its sky-line. But Castle Cary had no pretensions at all. It was simply a family house.

Hildebrand had, in fact, something of the prejudice against us that you find in Proust, among the society nobles, in their amused disdain for the country gentry of Brittany or the deep French South. His attitude was not at all Irish or even English. A society lord from Dublin or London visiting a country gentle-man would be very happy to tramp the fields with him and talk of drainage or turnips as if he understood them. There is, I dare say, a lot of British and French history in this distinction. And Hildebrand was French of the old style, to the last degree —to his beautiful linen, his manner with ladies, at once gay and formal, his quick and alert mind, his sharp gaze. I have seen this look fixed on Barney when Barney, waiting at table, entered into our conversation, and I felt rather than knew that he regarded Barney as a comic Irish character, almost a joke.

Hildebrand always treated Barney with courtesy. The rest of us, however, would chaff him—a process that Barney much enjoyed if he was not too busy. But, unlike Hildebrand, we never thought of Barney, or Kate, the cook, who was rarely quite sober after six o'clock and usually roaring by bedtime— we never thought of them as comic. They were part of the family, in the old sense of the word. We were an Irish household; everyone under the roof was a member of it, and, in some respect, concerned in all its family affairs.

Barney was expected to remember the names and even the ailments of my uncle's patients. This enabled my uncle to give them occasionally what some of my younger uncles, the nephews, called the 'absent treatment'. Uncle Tristram would be sitting in the back parlour, a combined library and smoking-room, in mid-afternoon, entertaining a party of these nephews, and also cousins, at conversation. Barney would appear at the door, and say gruffly, 'Mr So-and-So, sor—in the surgery.'

Surgery hour was six, and Barney objected to patients at any other time. They interrupted his routine of work. Thus on such occasions he would appear always, not only in working dress— stable jacket and gaiters—but carrying some implement from the task of the moment. He would hold a trowel in his hand, or, if he had been grooming, a curry-comb or water-brush. My uncle, checked in full anecdote, would turn his head slowly and gaze at Barney as if he had come up by a trap.

'Mr So-and-So,' my uncle would say. 'Ah, Mr So-and-So. He has a pain. What sort of a pain, Barney?'

'Why, sor, he didn't say. But sure, sor, he never has but the one.'

'Never mind that, Barney. Haven't I told you always to ask

what's wrong with 'em? Go and ask him, Barney. Go and ask him what sort of a pain.'

Barney would disappear with a slight wave of trowel or brush as if to say, 'This is what I ought to be doing.' After a moment's pause, my uncle would resume his tale. At Barney's reappearance, he would again gaze round with surprise.

'It's what I telt ye, sor. It's the same pain,' Barney would say, more gruffly than before.

'The same pain—ah. The *same* pain. Well, Barney, what did he have the last time?'

'Why, sor, I didn't think for to ask him.' Still more gruffly.

'Ah, Barney, you'll never make a doctor.' And here, my uncle, realising that he had been interrupted for the second time, would straighten his tall back and say, 'Bless my soul, Barney, go and ask him. Go and ask him.'

Barney would turn round and clump away. The surgery was downstairs in the basement, and every thump of his boots up and down was a protest against this foolish affair. He would reappear once more with abruptness and stare at my uncle in silence until one of the attendant nephews would say, 'Here's Barney, Uncle.'

My uncle would stop again, gaze at Barney for a moment, and collect himself. 'So it's you, Barney. Well, what is it now, Barney?'

'It's Mr So-and-So, sor. In the surgery.'

'Ah, yes. So he was. And what's wrong with him now?'

'It's thon pain, sor. And we gave him some of the red. But it didn't shift it, sor. It's there yet.'

'Then give him some of the blue, Barney. Give him some of the blue.'

The red and the blue were two of my uncle's favourite medicines. I've heard that he ordered them by the barrel, but this is probably a family legend put about by some nephew.

The surgery was forbidden to us children, and therefore we would always slip in when the coast was clear. But we never stayed long, or went far beyond the door. My recollection of the room is still full of a special awe. It was essentially a brown room. Everything in it seemed to lie in a brownish shadow— its two dusty mahogany bookcases, one full of brown books, the other of dim bottles; a fog-browned ceiling; a brown carpet; a brown desk covered with dun-coloured papers; and what I can only call a brown smell, compounded of ancient chemicals and a cold, earthy damp like that which rises from a lately-opened tomb. There was a fearful stillness in it. All its associations— the idea of dangerous poisons, sudden agonies, sinister knowledge of people's insides, and that brown earth smell—combined to produce a horror in my veins delightful to any child, and probably as necessary to me as salt to wild animals. In those quick, nervous visits, I seemed to go into another world—a lower world—and even now I can't imagine my uncle in it. I never saw him as a doctor, but only as a sportsman who had patients.

All this gives the impression of a harum-scarum place. Nothing could be further from the truth. Cromwell House, like other Irish households of the time, had a very definite order, even a rather elaborate routine. Meals were punctual. The cake and Madeira always appeared in the morning room at the same hour, eleven. Everyone and everything had an acknowledged time and place. But the whole atmosphere, the whole effect, was quite different from that of an English household. There was room, within the stout framework of routine, for more individual whim. Two nephews would borrow the kitchen for a boxing-match, and the spectators would build a gallery with chairs on the kitchen table. My brother and I would organise an aerial railway with string, down the main staircase, by running a cord from the top landing, to a picture nail at the half-landing, and so to anchorage on a hall chair or door-handle below. A small box or basket slung to this stringway by a cup-hook would take one dive to the half-landing and, with luck, jump the fixing there and fly on down to the hall. If the hook stuck, as it often did, at the nail, it could still be sent forward on the last leap. But often it simply jumped off the string and crashed down the stairs.

This game might be condoned, even by the servants, for a whole morning, or it might end in two minutes, even before the first big crash, by offending one of the nephews, who, possibly depressed by the morning's racing news, would suddenly demand, in passing, what the devil we were playing at—giving to the verb a meaning so different from ours that I can remember a certain perplexity with my consternation while I dismantled the string.

A visiting niece, full of some private distress, would stalk about the house with a cigar in the midst of the morning—all the Castle Cary girls, to my aunt and uncle's high disapproval, had smoked from childhood. But the niece risked meeting my aunt, who, if she were in the mood, would denounce her in a speech of twenty minutes, without a single pause, for poisoning herself and the house, for ruining her complexion, for throwing away all her chances in this world and the next, for being a reproach to her sex, her name, and her generation. It was my aunt's very force of affection that made her so angry with this young thing who thus imperilled her happiness by a shocking self-indulgence. She would literally throw up her hands in despair of these girls; she had probably no hope of making any of the Castle Cary nieces respect the conventions of Victorian England, much less of Bourbon France. All the same, wild and independent as they were, they did not smoke in her drawing-room.

And though the boxers in the kitchen had Kate's permission and probably her invitation, they must bundle out as soon as she needed her table or suddenly took the whim to resent their presence.

Cromwell House was a place of civilised order that must, I suppose, be described as a feudal relic. For it was hierarchic—from my uncle, titular head of the family since my grandfather's death, to Barney and Kate, by their own will and feeling family retainers. Everyone had his place in it, and the nephews, the nieces, even the cousins, to an English eye mere visitors, entered by patrilineal right. There were enormous pressures, as in every human society. But in Cromwell House, at that time, they were in balance. And the result was a society highly satisfying to everyone's living needs of body and soul —imagination and affection, humour and pride—a household unforgettable to all who knew it. I suspect, though, that its solidarity, so resilient and so tough, owed something also to outside pressures, to the fact that we were all, except the English housemaids, who came and went, in a sense exiles and refugees. We not only gave way more freely to imagination, to dreams, including my uncle's dream of winning the Waterloo Cup, the blue ribbon of coursing, but we had richer sources to feed on, of regrets, of memory. Even the children, ourselves, were never without the sense of a special fate, renewed every year when we went back to the countryside where we were native, proscribed, and yet honoured for our name.

The imperturbable Hildebrand Oakes, too, as I realise now, was an exile and a dreamer. His room, a big front bedroom, was reported to us children, by way of the housemaids, through Barney, to be a regular Aladdin's cave of wonders; that is to say, of battle pictures, soldiers' portraits, weapons. There hung on the wall, so we had heard, his father's Waterloo medal and, above, the Waterloo sword. The idea of the room was, of course, fascinating to us children. We had never seen inside. When Hildebrand was away, the room was locked; when he was at home, it was taboo. I don't know why this taboo had so much effect when we took lightly the prohibition of the surgery; the reason was probably in the difference between the two uncles' characters.

We admired Hildebrand immensely. He was not only a very handsome man, with a great white moustache, an eagle beak, and fine blue eyes, but he was almost as tall as Uncle Tristram. He carried himself superbly in his frock-coat. His glance, when he looked at us, was penetrating and shrewd. Uncle Tristram, on the other hand, with an equally superb presence, had the abstracted gaze of one who sees visions. You could always hope, when in mischief, that he didn't notice you at all. Children are highly sensitive to such distinctions; they feel and respond to the subtlest degrees of personality. So though our Uncle Hildebrand's eyes, unlike our Uncle Tristram's, acknowledged our existence, we were uneasy with him—on our guard. He was essentially from outside, and his taboo had great force.

But by the dialectic of children the strength of the taboo added to the attraction of the room. I knew that Hildebrand, when he went out, often stayed out for the day. Besides being a traveller, he was a great man of affairs, a company director, an executor of important estates. And on days when he went out early, the housemaid would often attend to his room last;

until she did so, it would still be open. One day, I watched carefully and darted upstairs at the very second when the front door closed behind Hildebrand. The room was better than any expectation. I was, for a moment, quite astounded and stood gaping just inside the door. The walls were covered from top to bottom with pictures and trophies. Tiger skins lay on the floor and were draped over a sofa; Uncle Hildy was a sportsman himself, and had shot tigers in India. Then I heard the stairs creak, and, fearing the maid, I shut the door behind me. I looked round and saw what I knew must be the medal—a gold medal in its glass case—and over it the sword. But both were far up on the wall, out of my reach, and this was a fearful disappointment.

Swords were a good deal in my imagination at that time. I was destined for the Navy, by my own choice. I had played about in boats from early childhood, and fancied that to spend my life at sea would be the most delightful and romantic of occupations. Only short sight prevented my going into the Navy. It was my brother who became the sailor, and his first appearance, at twelve, in blue and gold, made him my hero. Sailors, indeed, had been my highest admiration from the age of three, but I respected soldiers also as men whose business was glory, whose uniforms were distinguished, and who—above all —wore swords. And a Waterloo sword had supreme quality. Thus the sight of old Sir Henry's Waterloo sword, the first of its kind I had ever seen, had a powerful effect on me. I had an irresistible desire to touch the relic—more than a desire, an urge, an obsession. I could not leave the room without putting at least a finger on it. The risk of being caught was now enormous; footsteps had reached the landing and seemed to be turned towards this very room. But I did not care. After all, the housemaid would only scold, or at worst report me to my aunt. There was no chair near the sword, so I seized a large carved upright and desperately pushed it across the carpet. The door-handle was actually rattling as I climbed up and reached for the sword. And then it was Hildebrand himself who walked in. Terrified, I clutched the sword and pulled it off its nail; it fell across the chair with a tremendous clatter. But Hildebrand showed neither surprise nor indignation. He lifted me down from the chair and said, in his deep voice, full of French gutturals—the richest voice I ever knew—'Ha, I thought so! Don't you know you're not allowed in my room?'

I was too overwhelmed to be able to answer.

'Of course you know. You've been told often enough. It's no place for children. You've no sense—you just break things. Don't you do it again, you understand. Or I shall have to go away and live somewhere else.'

He then led me to the door by the ear and left me outside. He did not hurt me. And later that day he took a half-crown out of that same ear. He was an accomplished conjurer, and though he did not give me the half-crown, I dare say he chose to make me his subject as a mark of reconciliation. But I was not fully reconciled. The idea that a grown-up, and especially a grown-up of such dignity and prestige, should change his habit of life because of anything I could do gave me a frightening sense, not of my power, but of my responsibility. I scarcely dared to look at the door of that room again. I would pass it on the far side of the landing to avoid all suspicion of lingering within temptation.

I did not exactly dislike Hildebrand for putting this anxiety upon me. I couldn't dislike a man so distinguished, and so favoured by my aunt, but I felt that he was, in his calm way, the most formidable as well as the most mysterious of all my relations. I did not understand him at all. And yet Uncle Hildebrand, as I came to know him later, when I was at Oxford and he had settled in a house of his own, was essentially a very simple man—simpler, I think, than any of the Cary clan. He was, like all the Oakes that I knew—my Aunt Doll, my Aunt Sophie—a very strong person, and the strength of them all was in the simplicity of their values and the black-and-white clarity of their judgement.

Even Uncle Hildy's dream was simple. Although he was at that time over ninety, he still wanted to inherit the family baronetcy. He had already inherited from various quarters a fine collection of family portraits, which he hung in a row on a wall of his house. But there were gaps in the row, and he would point to a gap and say, 'Regy has that one.' His nephew Reginald, the reigning baronet, was then about sixty. And yet Hilde-

brand's dream was not unreasonable. He was still perfect in
wind and limb, a man of energy and health. He had been a
great cigar-smoker. Lately, the doctors had forbidden him to
smoke, and he obeyed them: he still carried a cigar in his
mouth but he did not light it; he only chewed it. In this way,
he would eat four or five cigars a day. And it is pleasant to
record that this habit in some degree reconciled the Carys, and
even Barney, to Hildebrand in his old age. The fact that he
risked his health, and the baronetcy, to eat cigars, approximated
him, all at once, to their idea of what befitted a man. For them,
one who cosseted his health, like one who took too much care
of his money, had something ungenerous in his soul, and want
of generosity was for them a fundamental vice.

It was, in fact, made almost a crime in Hildebrand that he
kept and improved his small fortune, while Uncle Tristram
consumed his, as much in gifts as in bets. All the nephews,
except my father, came to Uncle Tristram for money; if they
did not borrow, they won it from him at cards. He was a careless
player and he had lost so much already that he did not particularly mind losing more, especially if it stayed in the family.
As small children, my brother and I were allowed to attend the
card table, hear the bets made, see money pass. There was
nothing of that separation between grown-ups and children
which obtained in English households of the same standing.
Except into bedrooms, we penetrated everywhere and at all
hours. We were, much oftener than our English cousins, allowed
to stay up to dinner. I was put up, at eight or nine, to propose
some family toast. I don't recall the toast, but I remember
vividly standing on a chair to speak, and afterwards the sour
taste of the wine and water in which, in the French style, I
drank the toast. And after such a dinner, though I was always
supposed to be hustled to bed, no one noticed me if I kept quiet
in the background of the room. Only Barney, that stickler for
routine and good behaviour, would protest. 'Now, Master Joyce,
you know you ought to be in your bed. Ye'll never grow to be a
man like the Master if ye wear down your legs in your growing time.' But on party days he was too busy clearing the tables,
hustling the maids, and attending to coffee in the drawing-room

and the gentlemen's whisky in the back parlour to harry me further.

I would slip into the drawing-room, where I would find the ladies sitting around the fire in upright chairs, gossiping about family affairs, in a style at once lively and formal. This assembly, in full dress, was like a committee of ex-Ministers or State Secretaries; they had the manners of the old bureaucracy. Barney, coming in to gather coffee cups or make up the fire, would be appealed to for a detail. And, like some chamberlain to the court, some gold-stick in waiting, he would address the party, poker in hand, with all the circumstantial particulars of the court memorialist.

But even the entrancing analyses of these acute social observers could not keep me long with them; I would soon steal away to the back parlour. Here Uncle Tristram, in a black velvet skull-cap shaped like a small pork-pie, would be playing poker with half a dozen of the nephews. The cap was to keep the smoke out of his hair, still thick and curly. He himself did not smoke, but all the nephews and cousins—comrades of exile and old wars—smoked like veterans. The room always comes to me in a mist of smoke, blue as a Donegal haze, through which I watched the players, tense and wary as duellists, play their hands in silence broken only by a bid or a demand for cards. After each hand, there was an explosion of talk and laughter. One heard the echoes of triumph as well as of grief and frustration. My uncle would recall some pertinent incident. But some young nephew would already be shuffling. The nephews enjoyed my uncle's stories, but for them the game was the serious occupation of the evening. And in a moment there would be silence again, the tension of the battle.

The pictures on the walls were of horses, dogs; the shelves were full of the *Gentleman's Magazine* and the sporting novels of Nat Gould; racing and coursing trophies stood on the mantel-piece. The atmosphere, especially my uncle's grand gestures as he laid down a broken-backed flush or a couple of low pairs, had the charm of the raffish combined with a certain distinction. For, in spite of the bursts of laughter and the stories and lively talk, all these men, but especially my uncle, had manner—manner as distinct from manners—a certain poise, genial but always extremely self-possessed; above all, dignified.

While Tristram played cards in the evening, Hildebrand would often sit with the ladies. He considered our habit of keeping the sexes apart after dinner till a late hour—when they united, in the old style, for tea before the bedroom candles— uncivilised, savage. Yet Hildebrand, himself foreign-bred, without a local seat, was essentially out of his time. He preserved from his youth, unmodified by new social neighbourhoods, the tradition, the aristocratic poise, of an old France. As one Cary nephew, always critical of Hildebrand, said of him, he would have been just right for a tumbril in 1793.

He was, in his way, as much an anachronism as the whole household, as Tristram, who himself had brought from the Ireland of the 'fifties, itself fifty years behind the times, the grand manner. Tristram's distaste for smoking dated from the period when smoking was regarded as a dirty and blackguardly vice. He had the Byronic attitude towards sport—that it behooved a gentleman to be skilful in all the athletic arts. He was an authority on boxing and delighted in the exploits of a nephew who won many matches, and of my father, who was good enough to be considered for the amateur lightweight championship of England. He had strong moral judgements and scorned the pretentious and the sentimental, both in things and people. He heartily scorned the Prince of Wales' circle at that time—Queen Victoria's time—the Marlborough House set.

My Aunt Doll had moral views equally definite. But she did not despise anybody. Her distinction was that of a perfectly understanding soul. She was something of a genealogist, like her brother Hildebrand—the French are great on family records —and, like so many thousand others, French and English, she could show her Plantagenet descent. But that consciousness of blood did not serve her for pride. It gave her only a closer relation with history, and history for her was the whole troublesome tale of humanity, doomed to insecurity, injustice, and the everlasting revolution of politics.

Aunt Doll's affection for us had a special quality; love was for her the only constant, the only dependable thing. Her devotions were passionate. She not only forgave us for mischief;

she seemed even to be fonder of us when we were under a
cloud. For if she could scold us, she compensated us immediately afterwards in direct proportion to the severity of the
scolding and the badness of our crime. A broken window might
be worth a shilling; a hole in a portrait, made by an air-gun
bullet, rose to half a crown. In short, she spoilt us. In any
trouble, my brother and I flew to her, as did all her troubled
and troublesome nieces and nephews.

She had no attraction in looks or grace. She was not only very
small, but plain, with a very long nose, a prominent chin, and
pale-grey eyes. Her hair was parted and swept back over her ears
in two cone-shaped protuberances, a mid-Victorian style. She
wore always a little black apron with twelve pockets in it—
three rows of four. Here she carried her keys, her handkerchief,
her *bonbonnière*, her *vinaigrette*, any letters from poor relations
that needed attention, her small money, and usually some slabs
of chocolate for any child who might want it. She not only
spoke all her life with a French accent, her intonation was quite
un-English. Her scolding was histrionic, like a recitative from
Offenbach. I suspect that some of its want of effect, its total
failure to hurt, was due simply to this brilliant effect. It was
difficult for a niece, even in the greatest default, to believe that
such a star performance was serious. For, though my aunt
meant every word, she was always so deeply convinced of the
difficulties of life for young people, especially Cary nieces in
this English world, that she used the words in a special sense.
When she said, as I have heard her say, 'You are a very *silly*
gel. I don't know *what* will become of you,' the word 'silly'
meant 'innocent', 'unprotected'. And a certain lamenting emphasis on the 'gel', combined with the despair of the last cry,
conveyed strongly her sense of the pathetic helplessness of the
victim in a bad world.

And as her reproaches were in dramatic form, so she would
express admiration—for instance, when my brother and I had
summoned her outside to see us ride our bicycles without hands
—in loud birdlike cries. She also had a special scream, like that
of a parakeet, when, at dessert, my uncle would bombard her
down the length of the dining-room table with sweet biscuits
or Carlsbad plums. But 'bombardment' is the wrong word. It

calls up pictures of Edwardian horseplay, so scorned by them both. What happened was that the decanter, in going round the table, would come to a stand at my aunt's elbow, and my uncle would call out, 'Doll, the port sticks with you.' My aunt, deep in vigorous conversation, would not hear, and then my uncle would lob a biscuit over the centrepiece and onto the cloth in front of her, and she would utter her scream, not so much of protest as of ritual, to please the marksman.

Uncle Tristram and Aunt Doll were essentially sad people, and had that devotion to each other of those who have shared tragedy. In my uncle's case, the sadness came not only from the loss of his property but the realisation that his order had been thrown aside and was about to suffer the slanders of history. My aunt was sad for him, for the loss of her children, for us all, who seemed to her deprived by no fault of our own. No wife could be more loyal; loyalty was the very centre of her nature. Yet for children, for us, she would even conspire against her husband. My uncle loved croquet. How often have I seen him play that immensely dignified game, and watched, fascinated, for the last, the winning shot. For, as the ball struck the stick, it caused a fountain to shoot up—a fountain of silver and even gold—the stakes of the game piled upon the winning-post. And then it was my duty to run and pick them off the grass for the winner, and probably earn a sixpence. My brother and I, when we got our first bicycles, discovered that polo could be played on bicycles with croquet mallets and a croquet ball. The result of our game was one broken bicycle, two broken mallets, including a favourite of my uncle's, and a good deal of broken skin—also immense holes in the croquet lawn. Like all children, when we came to perceive the enormity of our conduct, we simply couldn't understand how it had all happened. In horror and panic, we rushed to find our aunt, to confess at once. And she did not even scold us. I suppose the crisis was too grave. She immediately sent for Barney and organised our defence. The broken mallet was purposely mislaid for three days. By that time, my uncle was half reconciled to another. I don't know how Barney explained the patched turf, but when the old mallet reappeared, with a new handle, he told my uncle what had happened to it. Indeed, as we heard from Barney, who took a serious view of our bad conduct, our uncle heard the whole story from our aunt as well. This news, as Barney no doubt intended, caused us extreme anxiety. My uncle, however, did not even mention the matter to us. He did not much notice children; possibly this was his personal reaction to the loss of his own. And he never punished or even reproached us for any mischief.

Uncle Tristram accepted all misfortune, large and small—the loss of his estate, the failure of a horse, a dog, or a hand at cards—with the same melancholy calm, and the remark: 'We were born in a bad time.' He did not bewail his luck; he regarded it as his special fate. But for my aunt luck was part of the larger, the universal, tragedy—that world history in which family disasters are of very minor consequence. But these disasters, as I realise now, played a very important part in making our background as children entirely different from that of our English compeers. The perpetual gambling, the sense of chancy finances, the general indifference to the future, which so shocked Hildebrand—all this was part of an atmosphere not so much of anxiety as crisis, natural to a generation ruined in a land war, the cruellest, most tragic and unjust form of civil strife. For it is precisely the resident landlords, who have been born in the country, who have lived and worked all their lives in it and put all their capital into it, who suffer most. To us, from earliest childhood, in England or Ireland, the fundamental injustice and instability of things, the cruelty of blind fate, was as natural as the air we breathed, and, as I think now, probably as important to our health. Cromwell House and the Irish households of my various relations had a sense of life both older and more modern than that of our English cousins. We lived more intensely, and we set a far higher value on what we had of secure happiness. We were more eager in our attachments. We knew, more consciously than other children, what family affection meant, as the one trustworthy thing among so many treacheries.

And it was, above all, my Aunt Doll who gave us that absolute security by her love. Even to be in her neighbourhood, to know, if only subconsciously, that she was somewhere in the same house, in the same world, provided a solid foundation to our enjoyment of life. As a young man, I used to think I owed more to my uncle than to her; I admired him as a master in the arts of life, whose distinction was proof against every kind of misfortune. But now I am not so sure. Looking back from my own sixties, the uncle, with his grand head, his commanding dignity, seems like a child lost in a wilderness; the aunt, so small, so plain, with her childish cries, her sudden unexpected gestures, like a giant in strength and grasp. It was life itself she understood.

New Yorker (3 November 1956), 45–52, 54, 56, 58, 61, 62, 64, 67.

A Slight Case of Demolition

Oxford is a turning-point for most people, especially if they take Philosophy. For me, certainly, it was a turning-point when I met Prichard, Philosophy tutor of Trinity. Philosophy dons start always with destruction. They clear the site.

Prichard had a high reputation as a destroyer. At a first tutorial he would reduce a man's ideas, that is, his assumptions, to confused ruins, obscured by clouds of dust, in about twenty minutes.

My case was slightly different because I was not taking Philosophy. Prichard greeted me as a friend, as a member of his own school, Clifton, and asked me to his house. But here, probably in pure benevolence, and for the logical salvation of my soul, he did subject me to a short course of demolition. The subject was art. This was appropriate because I had studied art for the last three years.

The dialogue went something like this:

P. 'Ah, you don't think much of So-and-So as a painter.'

C. (*Relieved at this choice of subject, so nice and easy. He has been alarmed in case Prichard might start on philosophy.*) 'Good heavens, no. Did you see his Academy stuff this year—Highland Sunset? Awful colour, like mud and glue, awful texture, like lincrusta, no composition.'

P. 'Why do you think they made him an R.A.?'

C. 'They would—he's just their style.'

P. 'You mean they thought him good?'

C. 'I suppose so—unless he had a pull.'

P. 'Does he sell—do people generally think him good?'

C. (*Still imagining that he is being asked for information on account of his special knowledge.*) 'People buy him because he's an R.A. They think that's a guarantee that he's worth the money. He makes plenty. But the scandalous thing is that really *good* painters are practically starving.'

P. 'What would the Academy think of them?'

C. 'They hate 'em—because they're original. They don't like good living art of any kind.'

P. 'So the painters you think good, the Academy thinks bad, and *vice versa*?'

C. 'Absolutely.'

P. 'Is goodness just a matter of opinion?'

C. (*Hastening to correct a misunderstanding.*) 'Oh, no. It's a thing you recognise—you know it at once.'

P. 'But other people know differently about the same picture?'

C. 'Oh yes, oh certainly.'

P. 'Then how can you be so sure? How do you know you know?'

C. (*Still confident but aware that an interesting point has been raised. After all, how did one get an eye for pictures?*) 'Well, I suppose it comes from looking at a lot of pictures—in a special way. Just *as* pictures. You sort of expose yourself to pictures. And of course you get something by drawing and painting on your own account, handling materials, studying anatomy, modelling, etc.'

P. 'Don't the Academy Committee look at a lot of pictures in a special way?'

And so on, until I was completely confused and much humiliated. But I was also indignant. Because I had already noticed Prichard's pictures. And seeing nothing but sepia reproductions of popular sentimental works I thought to myself, 'But what does *he* know about *art*?'

I was too polite to say, 'But after all, I've studied art—and you know nothing about it. So what is the good of all this nonsense?' I was too polite but I was very much aggrieved. And when I met my friends that evening I complained bitterly. 'And you'd only got to look at the stuff he hangs on his walls to see that he knows absolutely nothing about art.'

My friends were mostly philosophers and they were greatly amused. And the more I was annoyed, the more they were amused. I discovered, in short, that, like Prichard, they looked upon me as an innocent, whose ideas were as naïve as his reactions.

This surprised me very much. I had been talking art for years with other art students, and I had not found any difficulty in the use of terms. We might differ, but we could usually agree on why we differed, and we had no doubt about the really good and the really bad.

Of course, when we thought we were explaining our judgements, we were really paraphrasing them. Statements like, 'It means something all over,' or, for a drawing by a certain famous but unequal master, 'He's been slinging his hand again—just waving a pencil. A cheap job—he didn't feel or think a single line,' were not really, as we supposed, explanations, but only enlargements of a first impression.

Later on I should not have been so confident in damning the whole of traditional academic art. But I was still sure that the quality of a picture was something known directly. Prichard hadn't shaken me there.

But, so far as I remember, I only once again, at Oxford, raised the question of aesthetic judgement. I asked one of the usual after-dinner gatherings in my rooms why Beethoven's Ninth was considered better than a music-hall song.

The only one who bothered to answer used words like 'depth', 'richness of conception', which, as even I could perceive, were analogues of 'It means something all over.' But I didn't go any further. The man was a brilliant scholar who took a double first; I didn't dare to accuse him of innocence and naïvety. And I was probably right. He is now an international financier.

I read some philosophy at Oxford, but nothing in aesthetics. It was not till long after that I opened Croce, whose system would have so strongly supported my naïve intuitionism.

The only positive philosophical discoveries of any importance that I made were in Kant. I realised what he meant by the autocracy of the moral will, implied in the word 'ought'; and also found a plausible solution of the free-will problem: that all action is determined, but a man's action is at least partly self-determined. If he has power to frame his own ideas, those ideas enter into the stream of causation, as cause, to determine his action.

But even here I knew that the argument could be refuted, in logic, by the statement that a man's ideas are themselves entirely determined. I *believed* in the free mind, but I knew the belief was logically open to attack. Kant's *Critique of Practical Reason* merely added to my unconscious confusion.

It was only afterwards, alone in the wilds of Africa, when I began to write, that I found how large and vital a problem Prichard had offered me. What and how did I know?

My trouble was the common one of the time. I had lost my faith, the naïve faith of childhood, and believed in 'science'.

I lost my faith at school when I was prepared for confirmation. In class my form-masters were urging me to ask questions; they were irritated if I learnt simply by rote. They were always jumping on me with, 'Well, *why* do you think that?' But when I asked the tutor who prepared me for confirmation questions about the problem of evil, miracles, and so on, I was fobbed off with an *ipse dixit*. I saw very plainly that questions were not in order.

I was duly confirmed, with great emotional effect. But soon afterwards my faith began to wither like a plant whose root has been cut, and when I went to Oxford I was calling myself an agnostic and, in fact, existing in a cheerful muddle. I accepted the world as science described it, a complex kind of machine; I also admired poets, painters, as great creative minds; and deeply respected goodness, courage, wherever I saw it.

It did not strike me till I began to write that these views were in conflict. I perceived at last that, when I had so innocently fallen into Prichard's trap, I was using 'know' in a special sense, quite different from that of the scientist who says, 'I know that H_2 plus O will produce water.'

And it did not take me long to see that the judgement of goodness in a man belonged to the same type of knowing. I recognised unselfishness in the same way as I felt beauty; by direct experience of a datum, not mediated by reason or judgement. Thus my faith returned, with all the enormous force of confidence which comes with a personal discovery.

I perceived that my old difficulty with miracles, as one who accepted scientific results, was unimportant. Miracles were a secondary question. But knowledge of God was as direct, as certain, as knowledge of beauty, as the experience of love.

As for the old charge of dualism, so popular with scientists— the rationalist's favourite gibe about the ghost-in-the-machine, which had impressed me so much, which still impresses students —I realised to my surprise that it was quite unscientific. It is founded simply on a *metaphysical* notion. Scientists are assuming, against all the rules of the scientific approach, that the world must be, somehow, a unity, a whole. The basis of their assumption is a dogma stolen from the Fathers of the Church.

Science relies not on intuition of reality, but on observation of phenomena. And the scientific evidence for a dual world in which thought and thing, emotion and nerve-cell, values and reflexes, exist side by side in chance juxtaposition, often in violent conflict, is just as strong as that for a unified world in which everything, including humanity, is composed of certain fundamental elements, and humanity everywhere displays a fundamental character—with emotions of love, beauty, and truth.

Personally, in spite of the formidable evidence for a duality in my own self, the conflict between mind and body, between will and physical incapacity, I could not accept it as fundamental. I could not believe in a ghost that inhabited the bodily machine as a hermit crab occupies a whelk shell. The problem bothered me for years.

But I realised that it was a dilemma of reason, and that it could wait. What was of basic importance to me first was the certainty of truth without an arbitrary rejection or falsification of any part of experience. Other problems were incidental.

But I would not have reached this point if Prichard had not made me feel, so deeply, the problem of knowledge. He taught me once and for all that there were realms of aesthetic experience beyond the reach of verbal logic. From that, in due course, it was a short step to the discovery that religious experience lay outside the scope of scientific analysis. It can neither be weighed nor measured.

Sunday Times (20 May 1956), 6—in the series 'A Turning-Point in Life'.

The Meaning of England

A man's country is the home of his imagination, and men live by their imagination. A friend of mine from Somerset, touring in the next county, Devonshire, had a motor accident. He was taken up unconscious and sent at once to a cottage hospital where he finally came to. He looked out of the window and was greatly distressed, saying over and over again, 'Take me home.' It was explained to him that he was in a hospital near Chard.

'Chard,' he muttered; 'that's Somerset.'

'Yes.'

He took another look at the fields and settled down peacefully to sleep. The scene, which he had taken, very reasonably, for Devonshire, had become Somerset—in Somerset he felt at home.

Not a twig or leaf was changed in the fields, but they were different, and this all-important difference was in the name and the associations attached to the name: not only my friend's childhood memories but the history of Somerset towns, battles, loyalties, and disasters.

So, for good or evil, the name of a country becomes one of the most powerful symbols in the world; men will die for its glory who do not care in the least for their own. They will also commit the worst of crimes if some dictator can persuade them that the name has been insulted.

Many people have come to hate patriotism as the seedbed of hatred and war. But you can't abolish so fundamental and primitive an attachment as the love of home. You can only pervert it. Neither is patriotism necessarily an evil or a weakness. Its quality depends on the values embodied in the symbolic name.

My feeling about England is especially deep and conscious because I was born in Ireland to an Anglo-Irish family, long settled there. My earliest memories are of Donegal, its wild hills and the great sea loughs of Foyle and Swilly. I loved the country and the people, spoilers of children. But my heroes were the great men of English history, many of them Anglo-Irishmen like myself; and English history is world history. My imagination played on a world stage. I was engaged for England; I triumphed in her glories and suffered in her defeats and shames.

I was, like my family, sharply critical of the English and often of English policy, but my anger was that of a lover. I could not bear that England should be betrayed by her own children or by party politicians with narrow views and mean aims. I had, that is, a far more definite and romantic idea of England than the average born Englishman.

Of course, the early 1900s, when I was at school, was everywhere a time of romantic patriotism. If there is ever again a great war I don't suppose any nation will enter upon it in our mood of 1914. Men will still fight and die for freedom but only as a bitter necessity. The soldier's duty, so far as fighting is concerned, has lost its glamour. There is nothing romantic about a bomb.

But apart from the spirit of the time, I had a special feeling about England, because, for my family, she was the mother country and not merely the homeland.

She was for me, as a young man, not only all the riches of English literature and art but the long history of its free institutions. As the U.S.A. for an American does not suggest conquest or domination, even within the American Empire, but responsibility, especially to the ideal of freedom, so the British Empire for me was the liberal and liberating power which had begotten the free states of Canada, Australia, New Zealand, South Africa, and was preparing many more to govern themselves.

This was not mere fancy on my part. I knew from friends in the Indian Service that the British governing staff were being replaced by Indians—those trained and devoted servants of state who now alone make Indian self-government possible. And when I myself joined the West African Service and found myself responsible for law and general welfare among primitive tribes, I was given the fundamental rule, 'Act always so that the local native government, however primitive, can carry on without you.'

I was to develop the beginnings of representative government, if only by persuading chiefs to have consultative councils, but I was not to break their authority. Native government at every stage of development must remain native so that when the time came for local independence the British staff could go without causing a breakdown in the machine.

The results of this policy are now being tested in Africa where the first free African states of the Commonwealth are now being formed. And this development is keenly interesting to me, as a test and proof of the English colonial policy that I helped to administer.

People think of me as a writer but my years in the African Service, given to that England of my youthful imagination, are richer to my memories than any of my books.

Holiday, XXIII (April 1958), 117.

The Most Exciting Sport in the World

There's no reason why polo should be a game for millionaires. And it's a great pity that it has become so, because it is the most exciting game in the world, at least for the players. I played my first polo with two ponies, of which one had cost ten pounds and the other six. Neither did I pay for the second: I borrowed it from a friend who wanted it to learn the game. I did not mind playing on an inexperienced pony because I was also learning; I did not expect my mount to follow the ball closely, or always to put me in the right place for a stroke. I was satisfied if it did not swerve when my stick flew past its nose, and turned quickly when it got the signal.

In Africa, our method of training our ponies was first to hang a polo-stick in their stable, or in the dry season, when they were not stabled, near their food. So they got accustomed to the look of the thing. Then we took them out and swung the stick gently alongside them, first on the right side, until they were used to this swinging object. After they had also got used to it on the left side, we would begin to dribble a ball.

We carried out all this preparation at a walk and in the laziest fashion, as if we were simply wasting time. Horses are innocent but sympathetic creatures; they catch their riders' moods. So in polo training, one should, if possible, not only pretend to be bored and indifferent but actually be so. The pony will then take things so easily that at the first click of the ball it will barely turn one ear. Of course there are ponies who are stick-shy from the beginning, and others who will go right through the training and then balk at the game; swerve away the first time they see an opponent galloping towards them head on, dodge the ball, or rear when it flies between their legs.

We considered such ponies incurable. But then, in Africa in the 'twenties, ponies were cheap and plentiful, and most of them were quite ready to play the game. It was a waste of time to take much trouble with the nervous or vicious.

As for our own training, we began in the pit. This was constructed cheaply by digging an oval hole about ten feet wide by fifteen long in a sandy spot and lining the sides with palm planks, cut thin enough to have plenty of spring. In the middle of the pit stood a wooden horse complete with a wooden head. The head was important. In making any left-side shot you have to swing your right hand, holding the polo-stick, across and over the left hand, which is holding the reins. This puts you in an awkward position to start with. Added to that, the pony is galloping forward and you must keep him on the line, that is, just so far from the ball that you can hit it without hitting yourself on the boot instead—a very humiliating shot. But your rein hand is pressed close to your stomach and it is very easy, as you swing down for the stroke, to jerk, or at least to move, the rein without noticing it, so that the pony changes direction just at the wrong moment. Also in the follow-through (which is extremely important) after a forward shot on the left side, an excited amateur may easily hit his pony on the nose. The player's body, coiled like a spring to the left, is pulling him round, and the shot itself, which is done backhand, tends to the right.

That's why our wooden pony had a large wooden head complete with two tent-pegs for ears. A bad left-side shot would skin our knuckles on this head.

For training you simply put saddle and bridle on this dobbin, and banged a ball about in the pit. It came at every kind of angle, and ten minutes of pit practice gave you more odd shooting than half-a-dozen chukkers.

Polo is not a difficult game in itself and need not be played with full teams. At Nafada, in Northern Nigeria, where I learnt the game, we often played three to a side, and, if there was no game, two of us would go out with a ball and have a practice, both for ourselves and the ponies. Polo practice is better exercise than hacking and much more amusing. If no one was available to pass the ball, you could dribble it up and down the ground and teach your pony to turn at each end. A pony should be able to recognise a backhand shot on either side and prepare for a quick turn.

One of my ponies, a black, learnt to spin so fast, getting back on his haunches and coming round with something like a jump, that he sometimes took a pursuer by surprise. I had a fine crash one evening while being pursued by a tall fellow called *A* on a powerful and fast pony. *A* was reaching over to hook my stick, when I made a backhand stroke on the right side (after the forehand drive, it is the easiest of all polo shots).

My pony saw my stick fly past his right eye in the backhand direction, heard the click of the ball and promptly whirled round to the right. Whether I had given the signal or not, I don't know. To turn at once when you have someone galloping on your tail is not always wise, but at Nafada we played a very hot game and my hand may have signalled before my intention, and more sharply. In any case, we spun as on a coin, in a cloud of dust, simultaneously with the click of the ball, and *A*'s pony took mine full tilt just behind the shoulder.

All four of us, men and ponies, turned somersaults and *A* broke a rein and went off the ground. My reins held, they were still in my hand when I landed on my back, and my pony was on his feet again almost before I knew what had happened. I still remember the jerk of the reins as he tossed up his head as if to say, 'Come on.' And we went on. At Nafada the game never stopped for ordinary falls. Besides, I was then Officer Commanding Company and most of my company were looking on. My men would have bitterly resented their loss of face before the civilian population if their O. C. had failed to go on with the game, after any number of crashes. A broken collar-bone or leg would have ruined my prestige with these pagan fighting-men. O. C. of troops among pagans has to be unbreak-able and unkillable, he has to have the most powerful kind of juju or some local juju-man will run his company.

I say that my pony turned in a cloud of dust. We had no grass at Nafada. Grass grounds in West Africa have to be sown with special grasses that were far beyond our means. Our ground was therefore bare earth, which looked so alarming to some of our visitors that they presumed we played at a canter. But in fact the ground was not nearly so dangerous as it looked. It was covered with several inches of dust, which seemed to cushion the ground almost as well as grass. Certainly none of us was ever badly hurt by a fall. The only concussion suffered, a mild one, was from contact between a player's head and the ball. At Nafada we made our own balls out of palm-tree root. This is a light wood, but on a dust ground the ball gets up easily, and a solid wooden ball flying through the air, eight feet from the ground and twenty or thirty miles an hour, is something to be dodged. This man did not see it coming and did not dodge. But he was knocked out of the game only for two or three days, and afterwards I made a rule that all players must wear polo-hats or tropical-helmets.

This rule is even more necessary to avoid damage from the sticks. It is quite easy to get a knock over the head from a stick; or a kick in the skull, when thrown, in the midst of a *mêlée*.

For other amateur captains of polo, starting to found clubs. I may say that this rule, about hats or helmets, is surprisingly hard to enforce. The trouble seems to be that no one likes to begin with a precaution that means he is afraid of getting damaged. The members of the Nafada Club thought me fussy when I insisted on hats, but I still insisted. And when I advanced the argument that we were short of players anyhow and one casualty spoilt the game, I had less opposition. This put the case on a basis of public duty instead of private self-regard.

Our chief casualties apart from that concussion, a few pulled riding muscles and a good many bruises, were horse-bites. In West Africa ponies are stallions. I only knew of one gelding in my whole service. It belonged to an old doctor who had gelded it himself because he wanted a quiet mount. As far as I remember, he never rode it, but it looked well being led behind his litter. All mares are, of course, kept shut up, and so, normally, one has quiet riding.

But stallions will fight anyhow, whether there are mares about or not. The greatest curse of those days in Africa were the horse-fights. We would just be sitting down to dinner about eight o'clock when the air would be split by screams and squeals from some neighbouring hut and an excited horse-boy would come running: 'Judge's horse fight 'em Captain's horse,' or, 'Little Judge's horse and Big Judge's horse and Doctor's horse all fight 'em.' And the diners, cursing, would throw down their

napkins and rush to the spot. There we would find two or three
stallions standing on their hind legs, battling at each other
with their forehoofs and stretching out their necks to catch
each other in their teeth. All the time they would utter the
screams that seem so much more blood-curdling than any other
animal noise, except perhaps the yell of a hyena. And one gets
over the hyena yell at the first impact; the horse scream goes
on being alarming.

Grooms were always hopeless in these battles. They would
pretend to grab at headstalls or leg-ropes, but took care to keep
out of range. If you cared for your pony and didn't want it to
be lamed, or to have an eye knocked out, it was up to you to
rush into the battle.

Our problem at polo was that the ponies, if they weren't kept
on the move, and pretty fast, would stand up and fight. And
there are moments in every game when ponies can't be kept
on the move, when three or four players are circling round the
ball, each trying to hook it away from the others and to prevent
the others from hooking it. The ponies are jostling, sticks are
rattling together, the men are swearing, everybody is in a fret.
At such a time, our ponies were very likely to go up on their
hind-legs and start a free fight on their own account.

I remember once when my Colour Sergeant, an enthusiastic
player but not very firm in the saddle or confident with his
stick, overrode the ball and sat shouting, 'Where is the b—
thing?' The ball was under his pony's belly and three of us at
once tried to hook it out. His pony (the battery pony and a
keen fighter) could not stand this and went straight up with
his mouth wide open and his lips curled back showing teeth
like a crocodile. And, of course, all the other ponies went up
too and began to box.

The Colour Sergeant then slowly slipped over his pony's croup
and fell to the ground. This gave his pony a great advantage
and it took the District Officer's pony by the neck—the District
Officer, a large and dreamy man always preoccupied with public
affairs, merely laid his left hand on the enemy's nose as if to
remonstrate. The captain on the other side, a visiting soldier
used to the European rules, was horrified by the whole spectacle
and kept shouting, 'Man down—stop—stop.' But our rule was

never to stop. Besides, I had had the good luck to profit by the District Officer's distraction—I had got the ball and went away to score.

There was a protest once when my black, always the keenest of players, bit the Doctor. He had the ball and I was galloping after him. He was a first-class horseman and well mounted but a bit heavy in the saddle, and in a long chase his weight told. My black gradually came up to him until I, by leaning forward, could hope to hook his stick when he swung it back for a drive. But just then, my pony, wildly excited by the chase, made a tremendous spring forward, stretched out his long neck and bit the Doctor in the behind. He stood up in his stirrups with a yell of pain, I got the ball, and sent it to one of my forwards, who scored.

The whistle blew almost at the same moment, it was the end of the chukker. But as I made my way to the club seats where we assembled at the end of a chukker to take a drink and change ponies, if we had a change, I saw an indignation meeting in progress. The Doctor had found support. It was pointed out that my black had now bitten every officer in the station at least once, as well as the Sergeant Major's chief wife, who had merely been standing on the sidelines talking to a friend.

I answered that the black had bitten me dozens of times, he bit me almost every time I mounted. But the meeting was not impressed. In the end, I had to point out that I was president of polo and the black, at the moment, was my only pony; no black, no polo. But I would play him in a muzzle.

I duly carried out my promise, at some cost to my game. I did not get the ball so often after the black was muzzled. For though the muzzle did not prevent his biting, it did prevent his opening his mouth to its full extent as we rushed to battle. And this gave other players more confidence than was always justified.

Polo is a wonderful game. I have played it on bicycles with croquet-mallets but one bicycle barely lasts a game—even millionaires could not afford the expense of this variety. I have played it on every size pony from twelve hands up, and in games where every size was playing, and if I had put my head down I could have ridden right under the bellies of some of the other monsters. My advantage on such occasions was that I could turn twice while the monsters were only thinking how to stop themselves. My disadvantage was that they would push me off the ball.

Riding off, as it is called in polo, is the equivalent of a charge in football. It is a very important part of the game. You lay your pony alongside the enemy, both going after the ball, and then press against him. This is highly effective in spoiling his shot. It is even possible to throw him off his horse. Indeed, once, as I was riding off an opponent, he came round on a sharp curve and my right boot got under his left stirrup, so that, as we straightened out on the line of the ball, my foot came up beneath and I put him clean out of the saddle. This accident, it is said, has not always been accidental, and I was under suspicion for that evening. But I was able to clear myself on the grounds of my inexperience. And it was true that I had never even heard of such a trick. But in riding off it was very easy, by quite legitimate pressure, so to rock any but the tightest seats that a man might miss his shot, or lose control of his pony.

You need a tight and backward seat at polo, in order to have complete control with the one hand. You ride therefore very short. One of my subalterns, who joined in mid-season, told me he could not ride. I explained that every man was needed at polo to make up a game, and, as for riding, there was no better way to learn than to play polo. The young man agreed and I lent him the battery pony. But he insisted on letting down the stirrups as far as they would go.

His idea was obviously to wrap his legs round the pony's belly. At the start of the game, the battery pony gave a mild buck, which threw the rider forward on his neck. And the pair then disappeared into the jungle at full gallop. We did not see them again till sometime after dark. I might say that this young man became a very good player, and also a good horseman.

I'm not going to pretend that a man can learn to ride, playing polo, but I do think that riding, apart from a few elementary rules, is largely a matter of practice and confidence. And polo is a fine school of both. It is hard fast work, at every possible angle, and it needs good hands as well as a firm seat. A man who jags his pony's mouth at polo will ruin his pony and always be out of the game. For the pony must play too; it must not be thinking all the time, 'This clumsy brute is going to hurt me again,' but, 'Where is that ball?'

The rider must not jag his pony's mouth but neither must he ride with a slack, hopping rein. He must feel his pony all the way; there must be the closest rapport between the pony and the man. For there is something to communicate every half-second, and the rider's signals must be given without thought, by a mere reaction of the hand.

A polo player hasn't time to attend to his riding, that is, to his rein. He is about as much occupied with the game as a man can be anywhere, he has about forty things to think of all the time.

All this is good riding practice. Every riding school ought to teach polo and run a practice game. Why then do they not do so? Why is there no way for people of moderate income to enjoy this most delightful and exciting of games? The reason, at present, is simply that the ponies do play the game and so a rich man, able to afford thousand-dollar ponies, will always be able to beat a poor one on a local hack.

This difficulty has been met by clubs owning all the ponies. But such clubs, again, tend to become ambitious and expensive. They want to put out a team able to play first-class polo, and so they spend their money on expensive ponies; too expensive to be trusted in the hands of any but first-class players. And so most of the subscribers never get a game. Rules can be made limiting the price to be paid for ponies, but if the club is in the hands of real politicians who mean to break that rule, or any other rule, it will be broken.

But this is no reason why a few people anywhere, who own or can buy some cheap ponies, should not start a club and play polo. They will be well rewarded. And when some one of them becomes crazy about the game, as will surely happen, and gets hold of the president, and blackmails the secretary's wife, and wangles the chief supporter, and suborns the owner of the field, and turns the club into a conspiracy to buy high-priced ponies so that he can lead a local team to victory against the next state, let them resign and start another club, with cheap ponies, second-hand sticks, home-made balls and a cow pasture for

field. I'm not sure that this is not the most enjoyable form of
the game and, if so, it is certainly the finest game in the world.

Holiday, XXI (June 1957), 42, 44, 47, 48, 155, 157.

Africa Yesterday: One Ruler's Burden

It is a great pity that some of our political theorists can't enjoy a short spell as dictators. Nothing is more instructive in the problems of actual government. I have always thought myself lucky to have had such a spell when I was sent, in 1917, to take over Borgu, a remote district of the British colony of Nigeria which at that time had not even a telegraph office. Letters took anything from a week to ten days, according to the state of the Niger and the morale of its ferrymen, for an answer.

I was told, therefore, by my Provincial Resident, Hamilton Brown, that I should have to act on my own in any crisis, and rely on him to back me up.

This was not an idle or conventional promise. Some months earlier there had been a rebellion in Borgu. The people had risen, murdered sixty members of their own native administration, and then rushed off to find some British magistrate and state their case.

A friend of mine, Diggle, was sent down to look into it. He found plenty of reason for grievance: extortion, stealing of women, blackmail, corrupt judgements. He turned out the worst offenders and handed over a peaceful country to me. But he warned me to keep my eyes open. 'You can't get rid of corruption in these parts, you can only hope to stop it from going on the bust.'

Then he went off on leave and left me with my first independent civil command, in a country of about twelve thousand square miles. My staff consisted of one clerk who could not spell (we had no typewriter); twelve police with single-shot carbines and ten rounds apiece; a Political Agent—a Hausa Negro who spoke the local languages and was supposed to be an expert on local affairs; and a couple of office messengers to sun themselves on the court veranda.

Government has been called a relationship. This is a misleading half-truth. The essence of government, the nub, is rule.
That is the hard part. But it is true that to rule efficiently, a
relationship has to be formed: one of confidence, or fear, or
hope, often all three. And in forming such a relationship the
first need is knowledge. My relationship with Hamilton Brown
was one of mutual confidence based on knowledge of each
other. Any other would have made my job in Borgu impossible.
But in the other direction I had neither knowledge nor
confidence.

William the Conqueror understood very well what he needed
when he ordered the Domesday Book compiled. It gave him the
foundations for his system. But I am pretty sure that it gave
him no more. He had to rely for the really important question
(not what things people have in their possession, but what those
people are doing with them) on what he was told from day to
day, on opinion, on reports from spies, on his own guesswork
and knowledge of human nature. And I am sure, too, that the
success of his rule was not due so much to his system as to some
method by which he did get reliable information about the
working of the system, and the men who worked it. Systems,
ultimately, are men.

My first, immediate discovery, quite unexpected in its force,
was that I could not trust anybody or anything—that is, any
appearance. All information was vague, contradictory, palpably
false (like the news of a shipload of Negro nationalists just
arrived from the United States to drive the British into the sea),
or trivial. The Waziri (Vizier) to the Emir came up every day
on his official duty to give me the news and consult upon it; but
the Political Agent had different news, and each implied,
deviously but resolutely, that the other was a liar. Each gave
broad hints of the other's plots to benefit himself at the expense
of a 'new judge'—that is, myself.

My secret-service men, a few ragamuffins recruited by the
Political Agent, either gave wild reports like that of the Negro
invasion from America or told me solemnly that some chief
had cursed me, which I could guess for myself and which did
not matter. (As a dictator I could not pick my own men. Every
action of a dictator is watched and known immediately, and if

I had chosen an informer he would have been corrupted or beaten up within the same day.)

No one not placed in such a position can fully realise the sense of blindness and distrust which took possession of me in those first months of solitude in Borgu. I say 'took possession' because it was at once like a foreign invader seizing on my mind, and a kind of demon. I would wake up at night and feel as if the dark itself were an immense black brain, meditating, behind its thick featureless countenance, some deep plan for a new and still more surprising outbreak.

I could not forget that the last rising had been caused by nothing but the failure of the District Officer, in exactly my own position, to know what was going on under his very nose—and that officer had had much more experience than I, and besides had done nothing but his duty. It was the rule then in the Nigerian Service, and has always been one of the guiding principles of British colonial policy, to preserve local law and custom as far as possible, and to do nothing that might break the continuity of local government. Tribal chiefs and tribal councils were to be maintained, and progress made by educating chiefs, by improving their administrative machine, and by a general development of trade, roads, public services—which (as experience shows) by itself modifies the whole situation and can (if that end is kept in view) quite quickly build up a class capable of some share in the government, on the first elementary representative committees.

But the first principle was absolute: Do not break the continuity. Do not attempt to force a constitution on the people. However good it may seem, however suitable to the place and time (and this is granting a lot), it will be hated and sabotaged. So it will serve only as a bar to all constitutional development.

My predecessor (let's call him Smythe) had done no wrong in supporting the Emir who provoked the rising. He was, I learnt, not only astonished but aggrieved when, having been sent on leave in a hurry with acute fever, he heard in England that his people, of whom he was so fond, had burst into revolution as soon as they were left to themselves. He felt that he had been badly treated by fate. I dare say every dictator feels the same in the same case. And in fact Smythe's only fault had been trustfulness and ignorance. He had simply failed to know in time how badly the native administration had been behaving, and to use his powers to keep the Emir in order. For a political officer, though he must stay in the background, has great power over a chief. He can always warn him, either through his Waziri or at a private interview, that if he does not behave himself he will be reported to the Governor or fined, or even deposed in favour of some other member of the dynasty. On the other hand, a good chief can be rewarded with a rise in pay or some special honour.

Smythe thought that he had a good Emir, a really progressive man. And so, I believe, he had. The Emir was a clever fellow who supported all Smythe's favourite schemes. He perceived that they were actually to his advantage. They cost money, and the more money there was floating about, the more he could steal. In fact, it is just the clever, the active, the really valuable chief who can be most dangerous. How was I to discover that the new Emir, a very distinguished and reserved old gentleman, who had been a slave-raider in his time (he had been passed over for the succession partly because of his conservative background and was now brought in as a popular choice to restore public confidence), was not another more sedate and conservative crook?

I remembered the casual remark of an old official that, in Africa, even an honest and loyal subordinate never told all the truth to a District Officer, because he never knew what use would be made of it.

I realised that the man in absolute power is not only dangerous to all his subjects; he is also a mystery to them. And this, I think now, is true of *all* men in power. Even the foreman of a labour gang or a senior office clerk is, I suspect, so far as he has power, an uncertain quality to those below. That is to say, the uncertain element in all human relations becomes, in power relations, a source of mistrust. All subordinates say to themselves, 'I'll tell the boss no more than I need to—for no one knows what he'll do with it.' Everyone in authority has seen in the face of the most trusted subordinate that peculiar look of discretion which means, 'How much need I give away—how little will satisfy him?' And the greater the power, the more the discretion that surrounds it, even in the stooge, who seems to be within the iron curtain but in fact chooses his words so cunningly.

The way I escaped, simply by good luck, from this invisible gaol that shuts off every dictator from the sense and sound of the actual world was still more illuminating. An old friend, my first commanding officer, meeting me by chance on trek and hearing of my difficulty, said that for his part he had found only one method of getting some independent news. He slept always as far as possible from his guard and staff, in a shelter, or, during the dry season, alone in the bush. 'Your people will never come out into the bush at night, unless they have to—they are much too afraid of ghosts, lions, hyenas, and so on. And as for you, no lion, however hungry, will ever attack a mosquito net. Lions simply don't understand such things.'

I took this advice, put my bed under a tree about thirty yards from camp, and after some disappointing weeks suddenly began to have results. I was waked up about three one morning by a voice whispering out of the dark, an urgent voice full of bitterness. I don't remember what it said, whether a trivial complaint (one man talked half the night about a deer into which, he claimed, he had shot the first arrow and of which he had been cheated of the share due to the first arrow) or one of the really important ones, such as the revelation (by an aggrieved petty trader) that a certain chief had closed up fifty miles of the international frontier with Dahomey. Or, more important still, that my Political Agent was in league with this same chief, to get him special privileges.

But I did in fact, perhaps on a dozen occasions in any one year, get news. Much of it, of course, was false; all of it needed careful checking. But what was valuable was such that I could not have got it by any other method; and all of it was sufficiently important to some native to make him take the risk of hostile ghosts, as well as the ordinary terrors surrounding a dictator.

You may think that this plan, really that of the anonymous letter, should be beneath the dignity of government. I can only say that a man with real responsibility for other people's lives and happiness has no scruples about dignity. And I knew no other way to get the same results. I saw too that the Lion's

Mouth of Venice, via which the Doges received anonymous denunciations, was not (as the books say) the wicked device of despots to keep their people in terror; it was an essential organ of their government, to preserve their own peace of mind. Of course it was an instrument of terror also. But that is an unavoidable factor in the whole form of government, in dictatorship itself. Dictators are always alarming.

This, then, was the first discovery of my dictatorship, that even the most elementary truths were difficult to come by. The second was that they suffer a special kind of distortion. Subordinates to any absolute power have a special irresponsibility. Over and over again intelligent men—sub-chiefs, headmen in charge of road or bridge construction—broke out in the stupidest fashion. They suddenly went on the spree, or, having done half a job in a careful and responsible manner, abandoned or botched the rest. One of them, with a long and good record, a steady family man, suddenly robbed the pay account in so careless a way that he was at once detected and brought up for trial. I asked him what had persuaded him to such a folly, and his only explanation was that gesture, a slight horizontal movement of the hand to and fro, which means, to the Moslem, 'As Allah wills,' otherwise, 'Anything can happen.'

What I think is that the fear and uncertainty that pervade every such régime, as with an atmosphere, breed fatalism. A soldier recognises the same thing in himself during war service. You have the paradox that men in daily fear of their lives are therefore more reckless than those in safety, and that subordinates under a police state, who can be gaoled or shot for a very small fault, are therefore more open to sudden corruption. The enormous corruption of the Nazis and Fascists should not amaze us, and it is easy to understand why the Communists need such frequent purges.

But a still more subtle cause of the treachery infecting every relation in absolute government is the irresistible desire, even among its loyal supporters, to keep things sweet. No one ever gives his immediate boss bad news in its bare form. I can't say how many times I was taken in by reports that seemed, even to my suspicious dictator's mind, clear and exhaustive, but proved to have left out the vital point. The most exasperating and comical was the detailed news of 'damage' to a bridge that, when I arrived two days later, was found to have disappeared totally. It was too late to take another road. I had to swim the river, in flood among rocks, and the old chief whom I had brought with me had to be left behind, at the risk of wasting a long, careful negotiation, in which he was to have been the peacemaker, with certain troublesome villages about district boundaries.

I cannot be surprised that Adolf Hitler, towards the end, was fighting battles with armies that had long ceased to exist. And this disease of absolute government extends in a lesser degree throughout all government hierarchies. There is a fatalism in the old bureaucrat that comes not so much from fear as the thought: 'This damned set-up is so unpredictable anyhow that no one knows what it will do next,' and so does not trouble too much about details that will probably be misunderstood or be lost in some pigeonhole. And again there is the tendency to keep things sweet.

I don't know the real basic reason for the Labour Government's groundnuts disaster in East Africa, but plainly it arose in the first place from bad information. And I have watched at least one process by which information is regularly falsified, in what we might call the chain-report. I used to report twice a year on the economic position in Borgu, suggesting possible developments. I would write something like this: 'The export of shea butter would be greatly increased by simple improvements at the river port of Leaba, such as a market building. The chief expense would be on the Leaba road, which for over forty miles has neither any water nor any settlement. At least two villages with wells would be needed, and there are no local welldiggers. I could find hunters ready to settle if wells were provided and three years' tax exemption were offered. Estimate for such a road, complete, with wells and huts for ten families, can be put at x pounds.'

In the Provincial Report for the half year, this would read: 'D. O. Borgu reports that a new river port and market at Leaba would greatly increase the export of shea butter. A new road would be required from Leaba to the capital.' That is to say, the qualifications would have been left out to save space and give an encouraging effect. If the suggestion ever reached the Secretary of State for the Colonies, it would be in this form: 'A general development of ports on the Niger promises excellent and immediate returns. This could be achieved with local labour.' 'Local labour' to the Secretary of State in London would mean merely African labour.

The report writer has to condense. But in the act, he tends, unless he is careful, to leave out more of the drawbacks than the advantages. And if otherwise, he runs the risk that some energetic politician on the lookout for positive opportunities will think him a knockover, a Blimp, a stick-in-the-mud, even a secret enemy.

Now I realise why dictators, and even democratic heads of government—Wilson, Chamberlain, Roosevelt, Churchill—tend to have confidential advisers, favourites, to send them on private missions of enquiry, and to lean heavily on them for information and advice. This, of course, is only to shift some power to the favourite; to surround him also with walls and distrust. Power does not so much corrupt the ruler as the whole world in which he is compelled to work. It becomes for him, the moment he reaches power, a kind of Castle of Otranto, full of uncertain noises and vague threats, in which the very servants edge away from him as if he had the evil eye. And his friends become favourites, and therefore his closest friends can become his most dangerous enemies. For they, above all, have power; the power to deceive.

Reporter (15 May 1951), 21–24; reprinted in *The Case for African Freedom and Other Writings on Africa by Joyce Cary*, Austin, University of Texas Press (1962), pp. 201–209.

Christmas in Africa

Christmas in West Africa comes in the dry season, the time for feasts. The ground is too hard for working—the harvest has long been gathered, and yet there are still corn and yams in store. The time of scarcity, in our summer, when old stocks are low and the new crops are not yet ripe, when women starve themselves to keep their men fit for work, is still months away. There is nothing for the farmer to do but hunt, gossip, and dance. Whole villages go hunting together with bows and spears and sometimes a few old muzzle-loading guns; the dry grass, six or eight feet high, is set on fire to drive the game and there is plenty of meat for the feast. Beer, often very strong beer, is brewed from millet or corn and so there is plenty to drink—the celebration will last all night. Christmas with the African, as with us, is a time of family rejoicing, but the family is a whole village, even the whole tribe. For a primitive African tribe is still essentially a family to its own idea of itself and local feeling—and the hunters' feast is a time when men and women whose lives are full of hard work take a return for it.

It was supposed to be a matter of sympathy when I, already overdue for leave, had to spend Christmas in the remote bush. But now I am glad of that unique experience. A whole week before Christmas Day my sergeant of police came to salute me 'for the holiday'. I gave him a sheep and beer-money and leave to entertain friends in the police lines, the *bariki* about fifty yards behind my bungalow.

Just after sundown on Christmas Day, I took my bath in my top storey as a file of women in their bold, flowered prints, and in separate groups their men in their best, but still dusky, white gowns, streamed past the corner of the office below with that continuous babel of African talk and laughter which always seems more gay than any other in the world—and with a special kind of gaiety. A children's treat is excited, noisy, but it has not the same tone of purpose. Children do not know so well when or how they are going to celebrate, to invoke a spirit. That is to say, in spite of common talk, Africans are not children, they are a shrewd and hard-working peasantry with the natural feelings and limitations of an illiterate peasantry wherever you find it. The only element of truth in the comparison is that both children and illiterates are highly dependent. That is why the ruler in Africa, white or black, is, so to speak, elected by the people themselves to a father's place, and often addressed as a father.

A friend of mine, District Officer to a cannibal tribe on the Naraguta plateau, used to resent this title. He was a man of small sentiment, fonder of sport than files, and indifferent to power. He would answer the greeting of 'our father' with a snort and the question: 'Who have you been eating now?' He was not going to be got round by flattery.

But he kept a pack of hounds for his pagans (or, as he called them, his blackguards) and he would hold a special meet on every important festival, especially at Christmas. They would go, or some of them would go, to a Mission service and then join the hunt, led by my friend in beautiful boots and a velvet cap. And the solemn dignity of this appearance was not at all impaired when he opened, as the sun grew hot, an immense carriage umbrella, in alternate red and white stripes, labelled on the white sections in red letters eight inches long, 'STOLEN FROM J. FINCH'. A state umbrella in Nigeria is the mark of a king. Finch was the master of those cannibals and I've no doubt of the reason—both he and they loved hunting and he made the hunt for them.

He stood no nonsense in the field. He would shout at some pagan stuck to his bare-back pony by mere dirt, 'How dare you ride over my hounds, sir? Do you want me to take them home?' The very threat was worse to that man than seven years' imprisonment. His life would have been in danger if Jimmy had indeed taken his hounds—that is, his collection of pie-dogs, outcast mongrels rescued from some pagan cooking-pot—back to the kennel.

Not that Jimmy ever did send his beloved pagans to gaol—

he did not need to. His prestige was too great, his mere indignation too much dreaded. It was under that immense prestige, the discipline of the Master of Fox Hounds, that stray tin-prospectors were reasonably safe from murder, and missionaries could preach, and even the telegraph wire (much valued for bangles, anklets, etc.; every good husband was expected to provide it) was left uninterrupted for as much as three months at a time.

Finch's rule, of course, was paternalism, now so much decried. But paternal rule where it is still possible, that is, among primitive tribesmen, has two great advantages. It is flexible and its reasons can be explained. The police state with its cruelty, its indifference to the individual, and bureaucratic democracy with its complications and its bylaws, defeat and discourage simple people till they rebel or simply lose the wish to live. What they want is an actual ruler to whom they can state their special case. Finch did not need to impose a liquor law. If there was too much drinking anywhere, he could say, 'No more hunting' and explain his displeasure. I did not need a special act to let my people in Borgu drink all night or to declare them for that night a family party and the stars their family roof—the Sergeant Major had leave to celebrate and that was enough.

And I on my side knew that even if regulations had forbidden such a feast in barracks, it was time to set them aside. For the mood of the people and the police (and no one can follow such moods unless he is on the spot and close to the people) was more than usually restless. They needed a break. Drums had been bursting out into exclamations for a week past, and on Christmas Day they were warming up in the town from earliest morning. There were also at least three amateurs in the barracks. Eight were playing when, half an hour after the first arrivals, the dance began in earnest. Scores of hard feet in rhythm made a sound that came to me on the other side of the house, the quiet dark side, like the steam that used to jet out of my toy engine as it worked up power—the very noise of mechanic passion.

It made the quietness still more sensible when, dressed formally in clean pyjamas and mosquito boots, I sat down to dinner. I was alone in that station, Kaiama of Borgu, and I had been alone there for nearly a year. I was beginning to think and even to dream native, and in consequence, I suppose, I had a deeper sense of Europe. I read the English classics; I was, for the first time in my life, punctilious, tidy; I kept up all the ceremonies of parade, drill, and courtroom. When I sat in court, for an important case, I put on uniform, at least down to the waist (what I wore beneath the table fell, I considered, into my private domain), and I dined by candlelight.

My dinner that year consisted of the same meal that I ate at least ten times a week—soup from the tin and roast chicken with sweet potatoes. But I had pudding and I opened a bottle of champagne, brought for the celebration.

My mail had not arrived—mails to Borgu were extremely erratic and there was no wire to ask what had happened to the runner. Probably he had stopped somewhere in his five-day journey to enjoy a Christmas party.

Champagne is a wine that goes with the mood—but enlightens it. It makes a man alone more keenly aware of his aloneness, but as a vantage-ground instead of an exile. As I found myself ready to enjoy the mere expectation of letters, so I began, like any of my police outside, to be glad of idleness in which to follow the music.

By this time the drumming had reached a high point of virtuosity. The symphony was so complex that one had to listen with the closest attention, as to Beethoven, only to follow the rhythms.

And they were strange rhythms, of a furious ecstasy of exhortation as well as triumph—two drums especially, in the middle register, would grumble and argue together like a couple of old warriors behind the fire, then suddenly break out in shouts of menace and warning, defying some enemy of the feast, some ghost in the dark. One could understand the note of excited challenge in Borgu, a solitary and desolate land where the very night seems to have a special quality of threat. At my first coming, I had hated it. I had left an Emirate of the North with its desert traders, its pageants of horsemen, and got in exchange this twelve thousand miles of waste. I did not mind the solitude, but I felt deprived, I had not even a wire; there was no news of the real world outside this limbo.

Now all that feeling had changed. I saw how lucky I was in

an exile that made me my own master. Just because Borgu was remote and cut off, just because I had no wire, I had been given free leave to make quick decisions, in fact to do what I liked. And there was always interesting and practical work at hand: mapping, road-making, bridge-building, the founding of markets and towns, the training of native staff; work I preferred very much to the endless minute-writing and form-filling of a big station in a rich province. Besides, when most of my colleagues were living in mud huts, I had a bungalow on a hill, a house of two storeys, with a broad balcony all around it.

True, it was falling into ruin, and in one of my two upper rooms most of the floor was hole. But this too was an advantage. I could see from my bath right down into the office and know at once what I was in for that morning: a visit from old chiefs anxious to get up a war on the French frontier, hunters quarrelling about the correct division of a deer, one of my road gangs complaining of evil spirits who turned the edge of their best tools, or a witch murder with about twenty-five witnesses, all utterly convinced of the existence of witches and the expediency of killing them.

Another advantage of my tall house on its hill was that it gave me command from my balcony of a long stretch of that same desolate Borgu bush which had once so disgusted me. For that very desolation, the want of all romantic airs, had now become its charm.

Borgu is an ancient land whose antiquity stands over it as history broods over Europe. But in Borgu the history is not of mankind but of primeval nature, of beasts and trees in their eternal battle for life, and I had discovered the special fascination of such a scene.

And now I was not surprised by this attraction—I had asked myself why the traveller likes to find even a single valley that no one has ever seen before, what thrill he receives from being first at the Pole, a bare ice-field like any other ice-field. Certainly it is not the pleasure of discovery.

There is nothing to be discovered in most of the places 'explored' by explorers. And well they know it. The spell is quite different. It is to look on something that no human eye has ever seen before and above all on a piece of nature that has never submitted to man. And looking now outwards, over the bush stretching in the bright steel starlight up to the sky, a lazy ocean of blue-black waves, I felt again that savage indifference which was at once its attraction and its estrangement.

It was true that the people in common greeting called it my land and themselves my people, but it was only as Jimmy's cannibals saluted him as their father and their mother; I was as far from them in time as from the bush in spirit. And yet as the difference between the children and the parents brings them together, as the greater difference between the grandparents and the grandchildren gives them, often, a more immediate sympathy, so I felt joined to the unseen dancers in the barrack-yard.

I was like a man in a tower. He is so high that he is cut off from the people below, he can't understand what they are saying to each other, he can barely guess at what they are thinking by their gestures and the sound of their cries.

But as he climbs, the horizon lifts about him—the higher he goes, the further it sinks him down into that vast ring of the savage earth, more foreign to him than any creature. I was cut off from the dancers by a thousand years. But now, surrounded by the untamed bush, we were brought together in a common solitude which was a fellowship—the community of travellers in time. And their dance, their drums expressed for me, as well as themselves, the needs as well as the power, the tension and the exultations of humanity, everlastingly besieged by ghosts and devils.

Esquire, XL (December 1953), 101, 208; reprinted in *The Case for African Freedom and Other Writings on Africa by Joyce Cary*, Austin, University of Texas Press (1962), pp. 211–217.

Policy for Aid

My orders, when I joined the African Colonial Service forty-two years ago, were to develop native institutions and native economy, with the final aim of producing an African state that would govern itself on more or less democratic lines. Indian policy had shown the way and Indian examples were quoted. But in Africa, as in India, I was instructed, it should be the particular care of officials to make necessary changes and to carry on the daily work of government in such a manner that, should the British for any reason suddenly withdraw, native local authorities would be able to carry on.

The idea behind this was shrewd and subtle. It was not prompted by the fear of an Imperial collapse, but by a sound knowledge of official psychology. It gave the officer on the spot a day-to-day rule for his general policy, and a remarkably comprehensive one.

For instance, we hesitated to get rid even of an inefficient native official if no immediate substitute was available. We sought opportunities to increase the responsibility and scope of native administration, even if clumsy and short-sighted, instead of trying to cut it down. We took care not to damage the prestige of native chiefs even when they behaved badly; the practice was to deal with them in private and to use all possible courtesy. We were extremely careful of offence to local law and custom, however troublesome, or to local prejudice; and to avoid any sudden revolutionary change in local economy.

The rule was not always very easy to carry out. I had an early experience of that. In my first weeks of service, my immediate superior officer was involved in a problem of crucial difficulty. Some women had been flogged for theft and prostitution and the case was reported in a coast paper. It had reached the London press and there was an outcry. Orders came down for an enquiry.

This demand, telegraphed from H.Q., was the first we had heard of the floggings. They had been ordered, as routine, by the Mohammedan Court, under Mohammedan law. And we had guaranteed that there would be no interference with religion or native law, in this case Mohammedan law.

We sent for the Chief Justice, a learned and distinguished Mohammedan lawyer. He was astonished to hear of our objections. He said, 'Quite apart from our laws, what am I to do with these very bad women?' 'In Britain,' we said, 'they would go to prison.' But now he was really horrified. 'You can't send women to prison,' he said. 'That would be an abominable cruelty as well as a wicked act. A woman sent to prison would die of shame and grief. And what prison? We have no prison for women here.'

A long argument followed. In the end we compromised. Women sentenced for theft would not be flogged; but they would have their heads shaved. In bad cases, they should be put in the stocks.

But these were mild deterrents compared with a flogging. The Chief Justice agreed to the change with reluctance, and shook his head over the possible consequences. And, in fact, they *were* bad. We had an influx of unsavoury characters from parts of the country not yet closely controlled.

Throughout all Nigeria, in those days, the British were accused of undermining both religion and morality. We had, for instance, stopped the punishment of thieves by cutting off their right hand, and so, it was said, theft was encouraged.

I think the charge was true. There *was* more theft. It was certainly true about crime in general. As soon as we stopped the slave raids, put down inter-tribal war and opened the roads to traders, court cases increased everywhere and prisons had to be enlarged. This was not only because we had mitigated the Koranic severity of punishment; it was a natural result of the King's peace, which permitted a new and unprecedented liberty of movement. Crooks and thieves made their way into the most primitive tribal lands, where theft was unknown, where the only crimes had been murders of passion and inter-tribal raids.

The educated native from the coast found it very easy to cheat pagans who had never seen money and knew none of the tricks of the swindler. His very dress, like that of the white man, gave him prestige.

That is to say, every reform we brought also caused dislocations or evil of some kind; and this was inevitable. One of my experiments in Borgu, in the first attempt to push an autocratic chief towards some degree of democratic organisation, was to attach to him economic advisers representing various local interests. I was opening up trade roads and markets. I had built a hostel, or *zungo*, in the town to house traders safely and cheaply. This had bigger and more immediate effects than anyone had expected and I pointed out to the chief how important it was to find out exactly what these effects were. What classes would suffer from a rise in prices? Who was making the big profits?

But the chief hated the whole development and blamed me, fairly enough, for the trouble it had caused. His people were better off, but increased incomes and security only made them insubordinate. Alien traders did not salute him, and spread revolutionary ideas. He did not want change. What I called progress, he saw, again quite fairly, as a backward step into social confusion, crime, political strife. And it was no good telling him that these things must come, in any case, from forces which neither of us could control, from world movements of power and opinion; he couldn't grasp such a notion. He had no idea of such forces.

He himself was a gentle, wise old man, deeply religious, and indulgent to his people; but he had the inescapable limitations of his age and education. And religion itself, the Mohammedan religion, meditative and world-rejecting, austere and puritanical, urged him to hate the new régime. If he had known the word, he would have called it materialistic.

His opposition did not surprise me; but I was startled to find that my trade representatives were even more unmanageable. They were all making money out of the new prosperity, but they complained bitterly of the foreign traders; they wanted to keep them out of the markets, to raise taxes on them. As for village chiefs, several of them complained that I was breaking up family life because the women could now sell food at good prices to the traders, and were neglecting their home duties. What is more, as my Political Agent informed me, the Emir and chiefs imputed the whole new economic policy simply to an anxiety on my part to get in the taxes. Nothing would persuade them that a large proportion of tax did not go into my own pocket.

All this, of course, is only to be expected in backward and primitive societies, accustomed to autocratic rule and plenty of corruption. I had been warned to expect little co-operation, no gratitude; and, above all, not to worry too much about local rackets; to push on in spite of local dislocations and complaints, always with the proviso that the dislocation should not go so far as to cause a breakdown in native government.

These trivial details about elementary administration in a primitive country may seem beside the point in 1955; I give them because, in varying degrees of complexity, they could be paralleled in the records of every practical official, and because I think British experience in the administration of backward or underdeveloped peoples, extending over centuries, is worth more attention than it gets.

The essential points of emphasis in our administration were continuity and balance. We were not to destroy native rule and economic custom, but to develop them on their own roots; we were to aim at a general advance on all fronts, including education.

It has been said that the Nigerian administration gave the native society about two centuries of ordered progress in the forty years between 1900 and 1940. That is to say, its plan worked. But it could be added that in 1940 the country still needed at least another forty years to be ready for self-government. For what was organic in African society, the tribe, was not only primitive, it was extremely fragile; it was liable to break up at the smallest contact with new ideas, at the first attack from the destructive critic.

But now there is no more talk of gradualism, of balance; what is demanded everywhere is popular education. There is no more talk of continuity, but of revolution, of immediate democracy, of votes and elections, caucuses and parliaments. The turmoil and instability which, forty years ago, were the consequence of our first careful and tentative reforms, are magnified a thousand-fold; the whole African polity, and most of the Asian, is in danger of a complete breakdown. Central Africa, Indonesia, Indo-China, Burma, may well follow China into social chaos and final totalitarianism. For dictatorship is the only cure for a general collapse, and in backward states dictatorship has to take the most ruthless form.

This situation has been accepted everywhere by the British Colonial Office and you hear it said that the old plan of balanced and measured social progress has been abandoned entirely. I have heard an American announce joyfully that it was a good thing too: it was time for Britain to get a move on.

Britain has been forced to get a move on, but whether it is going to be a good thing is not at all certain. I suspect that in twenty years the same young critics who now urge speed will be accusing her of panic, of running away from her job. But she is still trying to do that job. She has not abandoned her principles of continuity and balance. What has been given up is the hope of a gradual and therefore safe development, of an approach to full democratic self-government along the course which history has shown to be natural and rational; a development which might be hastened by experience learnt from history, but not beyond certain limits set by human nature.

Men still take twenty years to grow up and are not, even then, fully educated. And African villagers, even at forty, belong mentally to a world as primitive as Nineveh or Sumer.

These adults are the parents of your school children and have the most powerful influence upon their ways of thought. That is to say, the education of a race does not begin to take hold, in essentials, until you have the second generation at school.

But it is fully realised by officials that this ideal scheme is now impossible; that the radio, the cold war, have abolished all possibility of a scheme of education keyed to economic and political progress. The people demand the vote before they can read, and independence before they can either staff or pay an efficient administration. Tribal chiefs are driven from power and tribal systems broken up by demagogues who have nothing to offer in their place but half-understood slogans borrowed from nineteenth-century anarchists or modern Russia. Day-to-day politics are a succession of crises which have to be solved on the spot, often at an hour's notice.

And often it seems that the decisions of the man on the spot are those of pure expediency, mere devices to get out of a jam. Administrators are criticised, even by their own countrymen in Parliament, for acts described as surrender to violence, appeasement. They work under a continual fire from both sides, one lot saying, 'Get on and get out, in the name of all that is reasonable and right, that is, nationalism and the people's will'; and the other crying, 'Hold fast in the name of all that is good and sensible, that is, justice, honest administration and the people's welfare.'

But the first are living in the dream world of anarchist catchwords, the second in the past.

It cannot be said too often that politics is the science of the possible. It is from forgetting this hackneyed maxim that the world spends so much of its time battering its head against stone walls; or alternatively, and just as stupidly, throwing dust on its head and saying that liberal civilisation has lost its way, and must simply trust to luck to bring it out of the wilderness.

If it does trust to luck, that is, if administrators and committees of aid look only to the immediate problem, then it is true that civilisation is done for. But the British Commonwealth is not trusting to luck; it is still holding to its principles of continuity, of balance, even of gradualism. And these are the only principles worth consideration by U.N. committees, by the various commissioners of aid.

It may not be possible to apply them in any given crisis. It is often necessary to do things at once, to make decisions on the spot which are obviously dangerous and may lead to disaster. No one pretends that Africa and Asia are not in extreme danger all the time; no one would dare to bet that they won't crash. But the only chance of saving them lies in sticking to the one course which can bring them through.

Government nowadays may be compared with navigation in uncharted seas, among perpetual typhoons, without radar and with worn-out engines that may blow up or seize at any moment. But all the more it needs a course laid down and a port to aim at. The course, even if it cannot be taken straight, is balanced development, and the port is democracy as we understand it in the West.

There is no alternative. Western democracy in its developed form is the only stable, moderately secure, and peaceful form of government known to the world. And there is a good deal of evidence to show that it is a natural consequence of modern industrial society; that is to say, that its stability is due to internal causes, and that if any given democratic state should collapse, it would nevertheless gravitate, after a certain period of confusion, back to the democratic order.

We have to aim at democracy, in spite of all the dangers by the way. And these dangers seem more formidable every week. Revolutionary enthusiasts look more irresponsible; and old conservatives fall into despair and would cheerfully accept reaction anywhere, so long as it did not actually carry the Fascist or Communist label.

Enthusiasm and despair, I think, both arise from a failure to ask what democracy really is, how it works, how it comes about. We see at once that it is not a formula, to be applied by proclamation, as so many liberals imagine. No blueprint for freedom has ever worked in practice. It is not even a constitution; it is more like a condition, a situation, which has arisen slowly from economic and social development. And because it has arisen in different nations, at different times, and by different courses, it varies greatly in aspect even when fully developed. The most advanced and stable democracies are the monarchies of Western Europe; the most troubled and insecure is republican France. But all show certain common characteristics: a complex industry, educated and organised workers; organised professional bodies; a high degree of freedom for opinion, for publication, for religion, and a strong ideal sense of the value of these freedoms. They show always a balance of powers between forces, each of which is capable of standing up to the central authority, but held in some kind of unity by common ideals and self-interest.

It follows that there are degrees of democracy. Such a complex development, even under the best circumstances, does not take place in an orderly form. Wealth may grow more quickly than education; one class may hold on to authority much longer than is good for it or the state; another may make too quick an advance into political power. The balance is continually broken, and has to be adjusted. The very adjustments, if they take place at all, are rough and crude. A neglected class of workers goes on strike; a set of employers, out of step, is driven into bankruptcy; political parties fight desperately and unscrupulously for power, seek support among the discontented or ambitious.

A growing democracy is always restless and disturbed. And nations on their way from autocratic and theocratic government to popular control are much more turbulent and unstable than those at the two extremes. Every variation between these extremes can be found and studied on the American continent. And there is no quiet and smooth course from one extreme to the other. Democracy in Western Europe took centuries in development; and passed through every kind of vicissitude.

Turmoil by itself, in a backward country, is not a proof of failure in progress, or a reason for despair and a refusal of democratic forms.

As we saw, the forms must be granted even when they enormously increase the confusion of administration and the danger of a general breakdown, a deadlock.

And this is another point that must be firmly laid hold on. The democratic machinery—votes, elections, parliaments— except in a developed industrial state with literate workers and a responsible middle class, are merely forms. They not only increase confusion and turmoil, they are dangerous to the unity and continued progress of the state. Nevertheless these dangers must be accepted. The catastrophe of the Russian Czardom lay primarily in its refusal to accept turmoil and danger as the price of representative government.

For, though representative machinery, votes and so on, among an illiterate people, open the way to every kind of political crook and industrial exploiter, they are probably the only means by which a people can now be turned towards the democratic line of progress and away from the totalitarian. They are a gamble but a necessary one.

It is perfectly true that in a real democracy such as Britain, development was so slow, autocratic government was so gradually transformed, that the final revolution, that is, the Reform Bill of 1832, produced little disorder, and not more corruption and chicanery than the state could bear. Dickens's Eatanswill election, based on an actual post-reform election at Norwich, can be set off against dozens of others in the newly-enfranchised towns where candidates appealed to voters with more or less reasonable argument. And the United States began with an educated people, professional orders; above all, with the democratic tradition. Would the tradition have been useless without the education, the economic organisation—as merely the ideal or memory of a few leading men? Many people would say yes; I am inclined to think, or hope, that an ideal of any kind has more force in human life, that, by providing a frame of reference, a concept of direction, it can have powerful influence in the actual course of history, in the life of a state as well as a man.

And in any case the only answer to the Communist agitator is the liberal idea, the democratic forms. However illusory among primitives, they open the way towards representative government. By introducing democratic machinery, though in the crudest shape, they make the idea of liberty known; they produce the rudimentary groups and organisations which may, with luck, grow into the responsible societies and unions that give full democracy its organic, but flexible and manageable, body.

They will not do much to hasten real progress, for that, in the final resort, depends on education in the fullest sense; not only of children but of a whole population, not only by books, radio, schools, but, even more importantly, by a long course of social and economic experience: an experience which, to produce its final value in administration, must have sunk deep enough to become a tradition.

A high European official only last year confided to me, 'The trouble with us is that our administrative class has only two generations behind it. You, in Britain, have had such a class for centuries and your public schools continually support its ideals. France is saved by its administrative families which date from

Napoleon. Though no one ever hears about them, they give France all the unity and solidity she still possesses, and provide her with the means of a recovery, which, at any moment, could surprise the world. But we have barely started in the tradition and so our administration is uncertain, confused, often irresponsible. It has not yet acquired the self-respect, the sense of honour, which makes it a vocation rather than a career. And unless it is a vocation it will not get the brains and integrity it needs, not even if it pays the price of big business.' And the development of such a class of men who are content to devote their lives, often on bad pay and with very small recognition, to the public service, is but one step in the complex and difficult advance of a nation towards real democracy.

Three generations are not enough to accomplish it. Twenty have not produced, among ourselves, any very dignified or rational polity.

But it is the freest yet known to the world and, therefore, the most dynamic, the most placable, the most creative and enterprising, ultimately the most stable and enduring.

Confluence, IV, 3 (1955), 292–301.

II

Unfinished Novels

I have more unfinished novels than published ones. There is in the attic an enormous work running to at least half-a-million words, as well as half-finished or quarter-finished books in box files lying about in my study. The vast work upstairs was unfinished for a special reason. I simply lost control of it. It was about a District Officer in a remote part of Nigeria, among primitive pagans, usually alone there, a dictator in a small way but also very fond of his people. I had been all these things myself, and knew the life extremely well. I had got stacks of material and any amount of first-hand description. The man was called Jarvis, the book was to be called *Cock Jarvis*.

I don't mean to say I was Jarvis. Jarvis was rather a Conrad character, in a Kipling role. He was sensitive, intelligent, and thoughtful, like Conrad's heroes, but he was also a strong imperialist, like Kipling's. He had a high sense of honour and duty like Kipling's soldiers, but he was also essentially liberal in sympathy. He believed in the Empire, in fact, as the only liberal civilisation in the world, and he would say that the fall of the Roman Empire before the tribes of nationalist barbarians had wrecked civilisation for a thousand years. And would do it again if they could smash the British Empire.

My problem was to show that though Jarvis was right in principle he was wrong in fact because the Empire couldn't last —it was up against powers that would certainly destroy it, and the problem was therefore to dissolve or transform it in such a way that it wouldn't be succeeded by a thousand years of barbarism, war, and misery. What I had on my hands was a study of an honest and honourable man who didn't understand what politics was about, that it has to deal all the time with new problems, with an everlasting revolution. And that it hasn't any final answer, any blueprint. The best state in the world must change; there isn't such a thing, and there never will be such a thing, as a perfectly just, reasonable, and peaceful world. For the simple reason that the majority of human beings are not primarily interested in justice, peace, and reason, but in satisfying their passions and ambitions, good and bad. Look at any newspaper for proof.

I had started in fact on a big subject, but I couldn't manage my material or my characters. I had actually too much material and I could not manage it. Neither my ideas of life, nor my technical experience, were well enough established to handle even a small and simple tale. I wasn't yet sure of what I thought about a lot of things and so I had difficulty in character and dialogue. If you set people talking you have to know their minds. Even if you are representing stupid people you have to know exactly in what their stupidity consists, and why you think them stupid. Nothing is more instructive to a writer than novel writing, because he is always creating people who talk and who often say things he didn't expect them to say. If you set two people arguing in a novel you must let them argue their best, according to their characters. So it is quite possible that the wrong person may win the argument and ruin your plot. Then you have to decide whether to have a new plot or throw that person out of the book. In any case, you have to do some hard thinking yourself about the arguments so unexpectedly advanced by the characters.

I had to re-educate myself as a novelist and it took me more than ten years. Nothing I wrote during nine of those years was published—most of it was unfinished, and what I finished I didn't like. I grew out of my books as fast as I wrote them. My first published novel, *Aissa Saved*, which looks so simple a job, took three years to do and is full of technical mistakes. But it was the first that didn't raise questions I couldn't answer and didn't want to dodge them.

And that, as I say, was the big trouble with this novel *Cock Jarvis*. It was far too ambitious. It took on too big a subject. It went on raising fundamental questions about religion and politics, to which, very much to my surprise, I found I hadn't got the answers.

I did, however, realise that to fake dialogue in order to avoid giving away my own ignorance or uncertainty would be fatal to the work. It is often done, you can see it being done, but it ruins a book. I tried to find the answers while I was writing, and the result was a most tremendous muddle. But I was so interested in my chief character and my problem that I went on struggling—that's why the thing reached that enormous length. I worked at least three years on *Cock Jarvis* before I had the sense to give it up.

But this was a rare case. Most of my novels have been unfinished for quite another reason, that I never know how I'll like a book or a story until I've done some work on it; that is, until I have got some of it written and can read it over. This, of course, is common practice among painters—they don't just knock off a picture right away—they make sketches, compositions. Manet would scrape the whole thing off over and over and over again before he had decided exactly what he wanted. Painters' studios are full of sketch-books, drawings, unfinished pictures. And I had had my first serious artistic training at an art school.

Even if I do decide to go on with a book I may drop it at any moment in the first six months. And these novels themselves grow out of sketches and notes made at odd times which are not meant to turn into anything. They are made like a painter's, for my own interest, and most of them are never used—in fact, the majority are lost. But when I want to write a story or novel, I browse among the old notebooks and always find something of interest. I don't think I've ever begun a novel right off, from scratch. All my published books have been based on stories or notes that have been lying about in notebooks or jackets for a long time.

A Fearful Joy began from a story of a young girl who went to a dance and could not get any partners, a truly fearful position for any girl. She was, in fact, rather plain and prim, and a step-mother without taste had dressed her in a very unbecoming frock. Also her family had not had the sense to make sure that she went to her first dance with friends capable of seeing that she enjoyed it. They were busy with other things that seemed to them more urgent. No one in fact had been unkind to the girl, the point was simply how much young people can suffer, simply because no one of taste or intelligence happens to be about to give their sensible help and advice. Her failure at the dance was simply a piece of bad luck.

But it is a real misfortune for the girl, a disaster. And she is too proud to run away and hide in the cloakroom, at least till the supper interval, and then she can't stand any more. And just when she is making her escape, the young man who is easily the most popular success of the evening comes up and asks her for a dance. After that she has a wonderful time. But the young man's reason is not that he has suddenly seen the charms of a rather plain and very badly dressed girl, but that he has been told she is an heiress. And afterwards she finds this out.

I don't know why I abandoned this story but, years later, when I wanted to write a novel with a background of economic change and dealing especially with the role of the imaginative man in business and in invention, I remembered it. One of my characters in the novel was to be an ambitious young man, full of ideas for making a fortune and I said, 'Why shouldn't the young man at the dance be a man of enterprise and imagination looking for some capital to start his schemes? And this would suit me down to the ground because the girl in that story is a decent girl with decent standards but not much imagination and therefore not much grasp of the world in which she has been placed. She has never realised, for instance, that freedom itself, the free creative mind in action, means an ever-lasting revolution, everlasting change. She belongs, that is, to the kind of person who cannot accommodate herself to change, who begins to say in middle age that the world is going to the devil.' We all know the academician who says that art is finished because people don't like his pictures any more, or the critic who says the novel is finished because he doesn't like any novels written later than those he read about forty years ago. This nice, intelligent decent girl belonged to this type and would bring in just the right element of contrast to the lively imagination of the man.

So I made the story my first chapter and throughout the book I showed the girl perpetually overwhelmed by what I call the revolution in ideas, by new situations that she couldn't cope with, new ideas that shocked her, perpetually running aground on some conventional mudbank.

The man in the book turns out a bit of a crook. But even when he is only after the girl's money he can float her off the mudbank, back into the stream of life, simply because he has no conventions, he creates his own schemes.

However, the last thing I did when I had finished the book was to take out the first chapter containing the story. I saw that the book needed a solider, more historic, first chapter, and the story remains somewhere in the house. It is still an unfinished story and it might even start another novel.

Another book of mine, or rather a whole trilogy, the last trilogy, dealing with the political scene in this same world of the imagination, began in a dialogue between two women, written in a notebook, I rather think somewhere in a train. There were two women, one called Aunt X and the other Niece Y. Niece Y has been proposed to by an ambitious young man in the village. She has refused him, she takes the whole thing as a joke and tells the Aunt about it. But the Aunt says, 'You are a very silly girl, that young man is going to have a future and you haven't got any future as you are. You think you are so pretty and clever but your looks aren't going to last and your cleverness is simply in amusing yourself and dodging responsibility. As you are going now you will make a complete waste of your life, but that young man would make something of you and give you a real career. What's more, he is very fond of you and will never let you down if he can help it.'

I had no recollection of this dialogue or when it was written; I say it was written in a train only because there were some notes next-door in the same notebook about cloud effects and field colours as seen from a train behind the jump of the telegraph wires, but it turned up while I was browsing among various notes and I said at once, 'Here is a good situation for my political novel. The ambitious young man will be my politician, the clever girl shall tell the story. What's more, since she does not love him and is pushed into marriage with him by Aunt X, she will have on her hands a real political job, in handling a husband so different from herself in ideas, in character, and in taste.'

Now this is important to my idea, because all human relationships have what I can call a political aspect, they have to be managed. Every lover, every parent, knows that, and if you listen to children in a nursery you will hear them entering into political relations with each other all day long. One says to the other, 'If you leave my horse alone, I won't knock down your fort.' Here you have an elementary social contract and we all know how much questions of justice and its opposite, special consideration, both crop up every day in handling children. I wanted in my political trilogy to have a completely political atmosphere, both in domestic and social relations; both in politics, strictly speaking (that is to say, the politics of my politician), and also the politics of marriage and the nursery. And the germ of them all was in that little piece of dialogue which stopped in the middle, which had no explanation or description to it, and which had not even developed into a short story.

Of course, a vast number of notes have never had any use and most of my stories and novels have never been finished. Some of them have a beginning and end, but no middle; one, about artists, ran to about thirty thousand words and has most of the big scenes written or sketched. It could easily be finished in a few months. And it has a fascinating subject, the revolution of taste, of what is called fashion. It shows the old academician in a rage at what he calls the cult of ugliness, that is to say, of an art that he doesn't understand and couldn't understand if he tried. It shows the young artists studying abstraction under a modern master and quite convinced that every other kind of art is out of date. And it shows the indignation of their master the abstractionist at this new fashion just beginning to appear of pictures that are far from abstract, pictures like Francis Bacon's, pictures that tell a story. True, a new kind of story. But what a shock to all the schools for fifty years back—especially the abstractionists. And the Victorians themselves are coming back. Even Frith of 'Derby Day'. Yes, Frith. People will soon be collecting Frith and paying big prices for him. And artists who think themselves modern today will find themselves right out of date. For the trouble is that artists live much longer than artistic fashions. So that you often have about three generations of artists all furious with each other and despising each other's art, and only united in rage and hatred against the very latest school.

All artists live in this world of the revolution of taste—in fact, we all live in it and it affects us all. It is always producing new ideas in art, or industry or politics, and breaking somebody's heart; and very often ruining him and his family on top of that. And it's never going to stop. Even Russia is moving, Russian writers want to write something new, Russian women want the new fashions.

This novel about the change of taste was unfinished because it began in a cut out of *A Fearful Joy*, a cut of about fifteen thousand words. I cut them because they introduced new episodes and characters which I realised were off the main line of the theme of *A Fearful Joy*. And when I had finished *A Fearful Joy*, I went back to this material and did some work on it—not meaning, however, to make a complete novel yet, because I had decided some time before on the political trilogy. The political scene in this world, dominated by men of imagination, good and bad—men like Lloyd George, men like Churchill, men also like Hitler—by spellbinders, propagandists, and fanatics, was one I had not tackled. And yet it was a very essential part of my general plan to show the complete world of the creative revolution.

Of course, that world, as I see it, is not merely a flux of senseless change. Underneath all the turmoil there are certain fixed and permanent things too. In daily life there is always affection, family love and responsibility, ambition, the things people really live for; and on the other hand you have always the same anxieties, loss, bitterness, and danger, the everlasting dilemmas of life. And so, in spite of changing fashion, the great art of the past in our galleries is still great: it expresses something that is eternal and not subject to fashion at all. Fashion is simply a new way of saying an old thing, of putting over something important that has been overlooked and forgotten.

This is a book I want to finish. I meant to go back to it last year, but alas, when I was looking for the MS. I found another, and the other interested me so much that I looked no further. I'm working on it now.

Radio-talk broadcast on the BBC Third Programme (14 October 1956). The text printed here is edited from a typescript among the Cary Papers in the Bodleian Library, and Cary's studio-script in the BBC Script Library.

The Way a Novel Gets Written

You ask me how I write a novel. But I do not in fact write one novel at a time. The process is more like collecting. I begin, that is, not with an idea for a book, but with a character in a situation. Then, if both seem to me useful and significant, I write a few pages to show that character in that situation.

Of course, every character in every situation is significant to some degree, because all of them are part of the one real world in action; but there isn't time to deal with all of them. To take an example, every family shows the everlasting situation of authority and freedom; or, as I see it, of older people who have grown attached to a certain kind of existence because they have made it, and younger people who, in their turn, are anxious to make a new existence for themselves. This situation produces a great variety of tension, comic or tragic, but it is usually confused, muddled, and therefore insignificant. Or, if you like, it signifies only muddle. A writer for whom muddle is the chief characteristic of life would no doubt be interested therefore in a man or woman for whom the muddle of his family relations was incurable, who was defeated by it, or grew resigned to it, or escaped from it into some bolt-hole of juju.

But muddle doesn't interest me except as a necessary accident of life, like the weather. It is part of a background, and so I should not be concerned with a situation of muddle, or a character who illustrated it.

But a character like Rose in my novel *The Moonlight* fascinated me, because she tried with all her soul to make order in the world, to make her sisters live what seemed to her good, dignified, worthy, and happy lives. With one sister she succeeded; with the other she failed. And her success and failure were both due to the nature of the world, of a reality shot through and through with creative freedom, with imagination.

Therefore I had Rose in my mind and in various notebooks for years before the book was written, or rather I had about six different Roses. Because every woman, more or less, is tackling Rose's problem, and it takes thousands of different forms. I had notes, years old, not only of Rose's character, that of the responsible parent, teacher, ruler; but of the younger sisters, the taught, the governed, struggling not so much for liberty as for freedom to make their own lives, for power of every kind, knowledge, jobs, money, a place in the world.

Sometimes this description of a character and a situation grows into a book. It gathers to itself other characters and incidents, until one day I realise that it is at least the matter of a book.

But *The Moonlight* did not arise in that manner. It started in a violent reaction against Tolstoy's *Kreutzer Sonata*. I thought that great novel not merely unfair to women, but stupid about them, and stupid about the world in which they had to create their lives. I made notes then for a parallel book in which a woman just out of gaol tells the story of a murder, exactly as Tolstoy's hero in *The Kreutzer Sonata* tells how he has murdered his wife from sexual jealousy. I wrote a good deal of this story, perhaps fifty thousand words, and then for some reason abandoned it. Three years later, I came across the other notes on Rose and her sisters, and the two separate conceptions ran together and interested me so much that I set out to write *The Moonlight*.

But this new book was quite different from the old. In the old, the narrator was the equivalent of Ella, one of Rose's sisters. I did not dare even to read the old manuscript, which is still in the attic, in case it should overwhelm the new scheme. I knew that it had a power which might well draw me back to it and away from my new conception—so that neither would be achieved.

The advantage of the new plan, as I knew, was to give a larger background, to show the woman's special dilemma in different generations, and the means by which, in different social periods, it might be solved. And I wanted also to show the relation between these devised expedients, or moralities—

what are often called the conventions of a time—and the fundamental quality of a woman's life, imposed upon her by her sex, her natural powers, and her natural place in a society which contains, like herself, both primary elements from nature and a secondary social and political form.

Thus *The Moonlight* exists in two different states, with different characters and, as far as I can remember, different incidents. And whether the one that was published is the better, I cannot tell.

I have a great number of similar manuscripts in every stage of development. Some of them are almost complete books, abandoned because I was dissatisfied with them. Two or three are complete, but I don't publish them because I don't care about them any more. Others consist of only a few pages, often cut out of a finished book. I cut the best chapter out of *The Horse's Mouth*, and some day I shall enlarge it and finish it. I cut fifty thousand words out of *A Fearful Joy*, a novel I have just completed, because, though they belonged to the theme, they developed it at an angle from the main line, and brought in new characters when I had already as many as I could deal with.

Thus a finished book of mine starts usually, perhaps ten years before, as a character sketch and a bit of description; it goes on to an incident or so, it gathers subsidiary characters, and then perhaps I grow interested in it, and set out to give it form as a book. I sketch a plan; I may write the end, the middle, and the beginning, and very often in this order. That is, I decide how and where the book shall end, which is just as important to a book as a play; and then I ask myself where are the most difficult turns in the book. Then I may write one of these difficult passages to see if it is viable. And if, as often happens, it does not work, I may stop there. But if it does work, then I may devise a beginning and finish the book.

But the chief problem still remains, which is to decide what I shall express in the book. All my books suffer large cuts, even in the last draft. This is largely because they are all statements about a single reality, in which every part is related to every other part.

It is impossible to show this whole in one book. James Joyce has tried in *Finnegans Wake* to give his notion of reality in depth; for that purpose, he devised a special language, and still he had to leave out nine-tenths of what is significant even by his own scheme. The very fact that it takes time to read limits the field of a novelist. Feelings that should be simultaneous in a reader have to be invoked in succession, and therefore become ineffective or false. Joyce's attempt to pack the effect of three or four different symbols into one word often has a brilliant success but, if it should fail, fails disastrously: I mean, it breaks the spell for the reader and jolts him out of pure experience into bewilderment or anxious enquiry.

And it is my first rule that the reader must not be confused, must not be jolted. I'm told that I have a style, but I am not aware of it. I try only to be clear, to avoid, especially, provoking in the reader ideas which have nothing to do with the theme; above all, to keep out of sight. An author has no more business in a book than the microphone on the screen. It is hard enough for him to give a clear coherent impression without unnecessary distractions.

There are two versions of *The Moonlight* because I wanted to give a larger picture, but I suspect that I did so at the cost of definition and power. My gains were paid for.

To Be a Pilgrim, for instance, deals with a man of strong religious and affectionate character, suffering the moral changes of seventy years, the inevitable and continuous revolution which goes on all the time, everywhere. I had to show, therefore—I had to make the reader *feel*—the fundamental power and drive of the Protestant tradition which is the soul of British and American democracy; to get, if possible, at the roots of that religious intuition.

That involved also the political aspects of the Protestant tradition. It could involve and, in actual life, would involve the aesthetic ideas evolving in the same period. But it was impossible to deal with them because they would have made the book not only too long, but too complex. For a book, like every other form of art, is the communication of an experience. That experience must have form in order to be coherent, in order to be an experience and not merely a confused succession of feelings. It must, that is, like a symphony, have a certain definite consequence, a meaning.

The great problem before a writer is therefore to convey, in one work of art, one formal conception, a significance which is simple enough for immediate apprehension by the feelings of a reader, and yet not false to the immense complication of actual life. Reality is one whole. Religion is full of aesthetic feeling and political action; politics uses aesthetic and religious appeal; every man is born into a society which is at once constant in its primitive natural elements, the natural family relationships, the needs, passions, and ambitions of all human nature; and highly flexible in its larger groupings of tribal, national, and moral organisation. The relations of the simplest character, the implications of the most elementary story, are as wide as you like to make them, and the difficulty is to know where to place your limits.

The second great problem of form is in the construction. When you have cut out your subject and decided its limits, how are you to give it expression?

Each art has its different sphere and its own limitations. Music has a far more powerful and immediate effect on the feelings, but not so precise a one as the poem or the novel. For the poem or novel has significance not only for the feelings, but for the judgement.

I write 'judgement' because, of course, all arts appeal to the mind as well as the feelings. You cannot separate mind from feeling. All thoughts have value; all feelings move the mind. The form of a symphony provokes delight in the mind as well as the feelings; it is not merely a collection of noises hitting directly upon the sense; it is an intellectual structure exciting to the mind. It is a complex of sensuous and mental feeling which is called 'beauty' when excited by a symphony, a picture, a piece of sculpture; and, in a novel, sometimes 'significance', sometimes 'unity', sometimes 'greatness'.

These different adjectives probably express different mental attitudes. The mind delights in the structure, the form of the symphony or the cathedral, but without judgement or reason. It does not say, 'This is true,' but, 'That is right, that is well done.' The reader of a book therefore is continually using his judgement; and novels appeal to what might be called conceptual feeling. To do this they create what is called an illusion of life itself; characters, who, it is said, seem to live in a real world.

This is not strictly true. Hans Andersen and Walt Disney do not trouble to give an illusion of life, but they are highly effective artists. They convey both feeling and meaning with great force. And all great literary art partakes of the fable. But it is true to say that in the pure fable, like 'Jack and the Beanstalk' or 'Puss in Boots', the appeal is to the simplest, most rudimentary judgements of feeling. And that in such a book as Tolstoy's *Resurrection*, which is a religious fable in the sense that the characters have been chosen and the incidents arranged to point a moral, the fabulous element is skilfully dissembled. Tolstoy uses every device to make us feel that the characters are real people in a true story. And we do so; we are moved as by the adventures and sufferings of real people we meet every day. Tolstoy, that is, having to give a moral lesson, knows it is useless to say, 'This or that is wicked'; he must make his readers *feel* the wickedness, and he does it by playing upon their natural human sympathies for others.

Many people do not like *Resurrection* because its moral purpose is too obvious. It does not move them because they see Tolstoy at work trying to instruct them. And the result is not only resentment against the instruction, but a failure to be moved by the book. For it becomes a piece of propaganda, a marionette show. Such readers would prefer, very likely, the newspaper reports of some tragic affair to which they can provide their own judgements. And they draw the conclusion that an author should not have what they call a message; he should write yarns and leave instruction to the professors.

But the real situation, I think, is not so simple. Art can and must be used for any kind of communication, including instruction. Tolstoy's fable of the three old men who walked on the sea moves us powerfully even though we don't agree with its religious object. It is great art. It is a powerful and meaningful experience.

An experience which makes us realise for ourselves the religious climate of another soul, however different from ours, is one of the most valuable we have. Thus the failure of *Resurrection*, if it is a failure, is due not to its carrying a message, but to bad art. It fails to communicate an experience. To me, *Resurrection* is successful, but I agree that Tolstoy only just succeeds in saving his work. And few other writers could have succeeded in his place. For the moment a writer begins obviously to instruct, he ceases to move. His characters become, not real people in a real world, but ventriloquists' dummies speaking with his voice from a stage.

Yet a book must have a meaning for the judgement; it must add up; it must have unity within itself.

The problem of construction, then, is to design a book in which all the characters and incidents form parts of one coherent experience for the judgement; and at the same time to give it the vitality of a narrative from actual life—which in itself, of course, has no meaning, or such a confusion of meanings that it adds up to nonsense.

And this is really the most difficult and troublesome part of the work because there is no end to it. When a critic wrote lately that I had no form, but plenty of life, in a book which had been under construction for several years, I was highly complimented. I would much rather be accused of wanting form—that is, meaning—than life; I suppose because I am so strongly aware of my own meaning. In the same way, critics who, years ago, complained that I was too objective gave me pleasure. For I had tried to be objective; and this is not always very easy when one is entirely convinced that the world is such and such a kind of reality, and not at all what some character believes it to be. One is always in danger of thinking, 'But if I allow such things to be said, and to happen, the reader will suppose that they are true, that they ought to happen, and so make nonsense of the book.'

The unity of a book, so much talked about by the critics, is a unity of experience, of impression. And this, of course, is much easier to attain in a book which aims at one simple and limited impression.

Flaubert's 'A Simple Heart' has the most exact and powerful effect; it achieves precisely what it sets out to do. But it is very short, and its purpose was very simple and also easy.

Sympathy for a peasant girl, a servant, in her devoted service, is universal.

Flaubert's *Bouvard and Pecuchet* was such a failure that Flaubert himself could not finish it. It has form—that is, a meaning—but not only is the meaning feeble, it is expressed in endless repetition. We see Flaubert manipulating his puppets throughout, and simply to express a contempt for the petty bourgeois, a contempt both ungenerous and ill-founded. Contempt for any class, race, people, as a whole, is stupid and the mark of a mind either stupid or rancorous. The smallest experience of life shows that individuals within any one class or race differ far more than classes or races as a whole. One duke may differ far more from another than from his butler. An Indian engineer has much more in common with an English engineer than with one of his own professors of archaeology, who would be happy all day with his opposite number from the U.S.A. *Bouvard and Pecuchet* has a mass of good detail, but its unity is that of a rubbish-chute.

But take a masterpiece of Flaubert's, *Madame Bovary*, a book held up for the admiration of all novelists. It is, however, a dangerous example, for it is very close to the edge of that same constructive error which ruined *Bouvard and Pecuchet*. It is organised to the last degree; it is highly artificial, and the artifices are not concealed. Examine the chapter where Rodolphe makes love to Madame Bovary during the prize-giving at the agricultural show.

And many misguided writers have copied just this artificiality of form, this superficial pattern. Whereas, what saves *Madame Bovary* is not the artifice, but something that apparently Flaubert did not mean to put into the book at all, his romantic sympathy for the heroine. This colours and unifies the whole work; it justifies all the tricks because they are necessary to that unity of impression.

But they are not by any means the only way, or perhaps the best way, of giving that unity. Consider Dreiser's *An American Tragedy*, also a great book, but one that avoids so carefully the least appearance of artifice that it seems to be thrown together by an earthquake. Dreiser is so anxious to make the reader receive his story as true that he pretends to have no art at all, not even grammar. And this itself is high art. It succeeds, it convinces. It gives the book something of the impressive dignity of nature. If *Madame Bovary* is like a monument, *An American Tragedy* is like a mountain.

I am not going to say that I prefer mountains to monuments; I need both, but, as a writer, I am much more afraid of producing the stony mass than the hilly wilderness. The prettiest compliment I have had was from a distinguished English critic who said I improvised. This was of *The Horse's Mouth*, which had been five or six years in gestation and rewritten several times over. But much of that rewriting was intended to hide the construction, to make each part seem to arise out of the narrative.

The world loves its own creation, which is its life. That is to say, not merely the artist, but every man and woman, begins from childhood to create for himself a world to which, as creator, he is deeply attached. Each of these worlds is highly complex and extensive. One man, for instance, does not create for himself only a home, a business, a family, but a religion, a political idea, a nation, a world idea. He creates them in his imagination, and lives in them. Deprived of them, or even of any large part of them, he would wither and die.

I don't know any misery like that of the artist whose work has gone out of fashion. I vividly remember such a man when I was young; his despair, his bewilderment. He had been praised by the critics, admired, he had sold his pictures and enjoyed distinction. Now in his sixties he was not only laughed at, he was despised. And his family was starving. That man suffered more than other old gentlemen whose ideas had become contemptible to a new generation eager to create its own world, because his notion of the world was exceedingly naïve. He could not conceive of any 'good' art except his own academic kind, he was like one of those moralists who nowadays are quite sure that the world is going to the devil on account of easier divorce, or artificial insemination, or women's votes, or drink, or the so-called immorality of the stage and the writers. He had read or at least assimilated no history, and his religion was a reach-me-down; his God was an old gentleman in a fuss.

But his tragedy was real; it was the tragedy also of Wilcher in *To Be a Pilgrim*, regarded from the different angles of family life and moral change. Wilcher is a different man; he has a different response, he did not suffer so hopelessly because he was wiser. As for Sara in *Herself Surprised*, she escaped, at least in that book, from any acute misery, simply by the power of her woman's imagination. Give her for material almost any man and any sort of domicile, and she set about building her nest.

Women are great adventurers in their own lives. A young woman, carefully brought up in some strict school and affectionate, guarded home, having got her man, will cheerfully set out to the other end of the world in order to do her job, which is not by any means in subordination. It is constructive, creative. She builds a society, a relationship, a spiritual world. And for that she must contrive some kind of working partnership with the man. He is at once her necessary partner and her first problem. Her success, like all success, is forever balanced on the edge of disaster. Sara was infinitely cunning in the management of her men, and the only man she loved broke her nose and deserted her. He did not want to be looked after. Yet the everlasting enterprise which was her undoing was also her salvation. She was still making a world for herself, a home, a family, when she was cut off. As for the moral and aesthetic revolutions which had been tearing other people's worlds to pieces during her whole life, she was scarcely aware of them. Her morals were the elementary morals of a primitive woman, of nature herself, which do not change; and she was supremely indifferent to politics, religion, economics. She was a female artist who was always composing the same work in the same style; but it is a style which does not go out of fashion.

But all that had to be left out of the book when I chose to write it in the first person. That is to say, in order to get the life of the character, Sara herself, I chose a means of presentation which, because that character was simple and had to be simple, active, unreflective, could not show the character in depth, as aware of itself, or its significance in the world.

To do that I should have had to write the book in the third person, with a complex plot; to do, in fact, what I did in the second and published version of *The Moonlight*. Whether I was right or wrong cannot be said as no other version of Sara was written, and it does not exist for comparison. That, in fact, is the kind of question which drives writers into an early grave—the technical problem. Every single method has its own advantages and its own limitations. The first person has great narrative force, but is exceedingly limited in scope, in contrast and content. The third, in its classic form, is immensely flexible and revealing, but by the very fact that it allows a writer to be everywhere, to see everything, it loses conviction and force.

Each technique has a further disadvantage, known only to professionals. The first person imposes not only limitations of character, place, and time, but of event. Everything that does not happen to the narrator must be related by him and is therefore further removed from actuality than a story told in the third person. For that story is related by a real person, the author, and this one is told by a fictitious person, the character. Thus such a technique is suitable only for a narrative in which the hero's adventures make up the tale.

In the third person, on the other hand, since there are no limits of time, place, and character, it is so easy to invent incidents and people that the problem is one of selection. This is a real problem for any writer who aims at significance. It took Flaubert five years to write *Madame Bovary*, it took James Joyce seven to write *Ulysses*.

A third method, of course, is to combine the two, like Conrad with his Marlow, to have the story told in the first person by a fictitious character. This way seems to have all the faults and none of the merits of the other two techniques. It has only one advantage: it enables the writer to describe the narrator. I have never yet used this device, but I am not going to forswear it. I may some day pull one of my dossiers out of a drawer, some bundle of character, incident, and suggestion, which has been waiting years for the technical method which will give it expression; and discover, to my surprise, that this one is the answer.

As for what laymen call plots, they grow on trees. Anyone can write a plot; the oldest are probably the best. A plot is the last thing I think about, and it is never fixed until the story is finished. I may make fundamental changes of plot in my last draft. The right and significant form of any work of art is not in any plot, but in a final character of being. This is true of a building, a piece of sculpture, a picture, and a frock, as well as a book. Frocks lead us into aesthetic metaphysics; we have no time just now to ask why one frock is admired and another detested; why even in a sphere considered so irresponsible and fantastic as that of women's fashions, some are forever called beautiful and others forever found ridiculous. But it can be seen that in the most beautiful forms of dress, however different—the Moorish, the Indian, the different peasant costumes of Europe, the eighteenth-century panniers, the Regency muslins, the crinolines, even the bustles—each has some relation to a woman's nature; not only her physical nature but, by implication, the whole range of her special activity, her special powers as a woman. Thus the art of dress and its unities, its rules, arise from the nature of things. So, too, do those of sculpture; and, in still more complex relations, of architecture— a truth dimly apprehended and crudely expressed by the cant about machines for living.

The form of a book, therefore, is not in some artificial pattern, some formula, but in its relation to ultimate truth. I say this because so many people think they can buy the art of writing from some correspondence school. An artist does not start with literature, but life, and the deeper he can go into life, the better. He would also be well advised to suspect any ready-made answers, whether political, religious, or psychological. Where are the Freudians of yesteryear? Where are the Marxists, the behaviourists? All of them have a little bit of truth wrapped up in a mass of nonsense. What you want to do is to dig out the truth, or as much of it as you can pry loose. The fact is that the process of education after one leaves college is complex and obscure. You read, you talk, you meditate: and writing a book is always an exploration as well as a setting forth. It is an adventure in which you survey a new part of your world.

Above all, keep away from the easy analogy, from the kind of criticism which praises Benjamin Constant's *Adolphe* as the most 'perfect of novels because of its sculpturesque simplicity of form'. This notion involves two profound fallacies. One is that sculpture has a special beauty because of its compactness and limitations of form; whereas its beauty, like the beauty of all art, is in the emotional response of those who apprehend it, and this may be very complex. The other is that *Adolphe* is a great novel because it is limited to the exploration of a simple situation; whereas its form is good not because it is limited, but because it is adequate. It is the right method for its author's purpose.

Tolstoy's *War and Peace* is far from simple. It is vast and complex, with scores of characters. It brings in every kind of discussion, every kind of problem, that can trouble humanity. Yet it is not a slice of life; it is not a mere yarn, a collection of events. It has the unity of a great work of art, presenting life not as a confusion of nonsensical accidents, but as a scene of moral struggle, moral achievement, in a world of evil and folly.

Thus the everlasting conflict between what is called the French school on the one hand, and the English and Russian schools on the other, is stupid. There is only one good school: that of writers who find the right form for their material, for their purpose as artists.

Harper's Magazine, CC (February 1950), 87–93; reprinted in *Adam International Review*, XVIII, 212–213 (November-December 1950), 3–11.

Tolstoy's Theory of Art

Tolstoy is one of the few great artists who have written a theory of art. He was not a philosopher, and he had, as we know from his book *Youth*, a poor education. Yet I think that his theory of art, if we try to understand the ideas that lie behind it, is more adequate than that of many philosophers. By 'adequate' I mean closer to the facts. Tolstoy's definition of art is this: 'An activity by which one man, having experienced a feeling, intentionally transmits it to another.' And he adds: 'The sign of art is that it carries an infection.' That is to say, it is something like a fever. Art is not escape from reality, or contemplation of an imaginary world. It is an experience that happens to a man, for good or for evil. And this experience is *intended* by the artist. It is deliberate and designed. The artist is not a mere recording instrument; he is a creator with a definite object. His whole activity can be studied in the diaries and letters of Tolstoy and his wife.

We see the beginning of *Anna Karenina* when Tolstoy one day went to a post-mortem on a woman who had committed suicide by throwing herself in front of a train. He was horrified first by the sight and then the idea of this poor woman, deserted by her lover. And again, we read that one day, looking at the sleeves of his dressing-gown, carefully stitched by some woman's hand, he was suddenly struck by the quality of women's lives, going on among the lives of men, so different in essence, even in occupation, that they live as if in another, inner world. He thought, 'How terrible it is for a woman to be cut off from her own familiar world, where her heart and her mind are at home with the sympathies and the lives and anxieties of other women!' And soon afterwards he was writing *Anna Karenina*, the story of a woman who lost that world, for her lover, and committed suicide at last on the railway.

We have here a complex act which began in a dozen intuitions, confused, vague, powerful, like those of music—the sense of horror at the mangled body which had been beautiful and honoured; the idea, 'This woman suffered beyond telling—there was no one to comprehend her despair'; and then the intuition of women's lives, so close to the man's world and yet so separated in essence. And from this crowd of powerful impressions, among the thousand others which filled his life, he made his book. He was at once an interpreter and a creator.

If we understand this, we can see why Tolstoy uttered his first great heresy against the current theories of art. He separated content from form. He said, 'Art is entirely formal.' And he quotes the critic who said, 'Great art begins with the little difference.' Form, that is, gives the infection of art; and it can carry any content. The critics objected that form cannot exist without content, or content without form; that a word like 'love' or 'hate' is nothing without its meaning; and the feelings themselves, the content, cannot be recognised except under the name or symbolic form. Their whole aesthetic philosophy was based on this, that we know our intuitions only by their forms or symbols; that is, in philosophic terms, their expression.

But Tolstoy's mind was not logical; and his conviction was that life had a meaning, a purpose, if only we could discover it. In practice, this meant that experience did not seem to him an aimless confusion, from which the mind selected what had interest for it. It had in itself a significant character due to the character of being. He himself, as a very young man, believed that this character was such that men could only be happy in loving one another. He said, 'We are intended for brotherhood. Our only happiness is in love. Life is designed to that end, and evil arises only when we ignore that end.'

Tolstoy simplified too much. The spiritual character of life, if it has such a character, is obviously very complex. But I venture to suggest that this creed of Tolstoy's was not only of profound importance to his art, but has support from fact; that experience, intuition, does actually have a character before it is expressed in words. A word is, of course, a symbol. But children have definite feelings before they find speech for them. They love, they fear, they carry out often long and complex trains of action before they can express, in words, the simplest need. If this is so, it means that experience can exist independently of expression; that life has at least some definite forms of mental action without the verbal symbol, a character not imposed or expressed by the artist.

Content therefore can exist independently of a verbal form. And by the word 'form' Tolstoy meant precisely the *symbol*, the technique of art. But the real importance for his art, in this assumption, is in his attitude towards experience. A man who thinks that experience, his own and another's, has a meaning, attends very closely to his intuitions, and afterwards, as artist, subordinates technique to sincerity. In Tolstoy, meaning rules technique; and therefore his technique is extremely flexible. It fuses completely with his matter.

It is, I suppose, a standing temptation for every artist to put technique first; especially if he be a good technician. Nothing gives so much pleasure to an artist as the successful fusion of his sense and form. And it is easier to take a form and give it some significance than to find a form for your meaning.

I sometimes think that Flaubert, that famous technician, suffered from choosing his form first. We know, in fact, that his friend George Sand protested against his manner of writing as if, as she said, he lived only for words. 'Your whole life is full of affection. You are the most convinced individualist. But no sooner do you touch literature than you become a wholly different man, a man who wants to annihilate himself.' She meant that Flaubert had the wrong theory of art, that he wished, as we should say, to live in an ivory tower, and devote himself to technical perfection; and his technique, clever as it is, sometimes seems to detach itself from his intention. For instance, in the scene of Madame Bovary's death, where the priest sprinkles holy water round the death-bed of the poor woman, who has poisoned herself; and then the chemist Homais, the atheist, sprinkles a little chloride of lime. The chapter is brilliantly written and managed, but to me the gyrations of priest and chemist, so neatly constructed, are a little like a pattern in filigree stuck upon a granite column. Death, even the death of a poor wretch, has too massive and formal a dignity for such jewel work. I prefer even Zola's handling of the death of Gervaise, or of Coupeau, in that tragic master-piece, *L'Assommoir*. There, as in Tolstoy, the matter has dictated the form.

This, of course, is the common case of what is called the natural story-teller. His matter dictates his form, because he has no idea of technique. And he may in consequence fail to give us any strong, coherent experience. But Tolstoy was not of that kind. He was a conscious master of form, like Dante, Shakespeare, Milton, Goethe. And to that list Tolstoy himself would add Dickens. He says of Dickens that he is a master of construction. *David Copperfield* is among the list of four or five books which had decisive influence upon his mind and art. And we read in the Countess's diary, 'Lev is reading Dickens. So I know that he will soon be at work again.' To Tolstoy, Dickens was an inspiration on both grounds: of his humanity, and of his masterly handling of a story. Tolstoy could appre-ciate that mastery.

The next point in Tolstoy's theory which affronted the critics of that time was his treatment of beauty. He denied that art was necessarily beautiful. I don't suppose he would even have understood the idealist theory in which art is described as intuition; all intuition is also expression, and all expression, since *ipso facto* pleasing to the expresser, beautiful. So that all art is beautiful at least to the artist.

Like every artist, he was conscious of using two quite different ingredients in his construction, which we may call, if we like, beauty and ugliness. Artists do not talk of 'beauty' and 'ugli-ness'; but they use words like 'discord', 'contrast', 'breaking the line', which mean the same thing as 'ugliness', and are the opposite of ingredients like 'harmony', or 'balance'. Tolstoy does not despise beauty; he defines it, like the old scholastic philosophers, as 'what pleases the senses'. For him, beauty is simply one part, and not the most important, of the total experience which he seeks to give. That is, he does not seek to give only pleasure by his work—by 'pleasure', in this context, I mean a sensuous, comfortable or harmonious feeling. He strikes at the whole man. He excites at one instant feelings of pity, wonder, and, if you like, disgust. Look at the scene in *War and Peace*, of Princess Maria with her father, the old Prince Bolkonsky, drawn from Tolstoy's grandfather. We see the shy girl's plainness and fear. It is a real plainness. We see the rough old man, and we know the stuffy smell of his clothes, his stale tobacco. I won't quote the scene. But notice, when you read, how these strokes of repulsion, mixed with the rest, make the depth of your experience; how they give truth and power to your sympathy. So that at the end of the scene you seem to have lived through a piece of life, at once ordinary and tragic.

I say, you seem to have lived through a piece of life. But in fact, life does not come to anyone in that ordered form. It is confused, a mass of insignificant details. The reason why you feel so deeply in that little scene the tragedy of youth and age is because Tolstoy has meant you to feel it. It is his intuition, expressed for you in a thousand touches of genius, which makes you feel, 'How true this is, and how tragic!', which gives you perhaps a new idea of life itself. And in giving that experience, as I say, Tolstoy uses two different and contrasted elements, which we may call the beautiful or pleasing, and the ugly or repulsive. Each has its place in art, because both are in experience. So that to complain that Tolstoy, or any other writer such as Zola or James Joyce, deliberately shocks, is not valid criticism. The critic's business is to judge of the whole effect intended, and to say if the artist has achieved it by the best means. For as we find the ugly in life, so it must be in art. It is art's function to gather up the experience of the time, always new and always confused, and to give it coherence and meaning. The critic who forms taste, the historian, the philosopher, the scholar sharpening the tools of the mind, the scientist exploring the primitive consistencies of real being, all these are makers of a time, they create the new experience; but when they seek to harmonise that experience and, above all, to convey it as experience, it must be by art.

It is the artist who in every age sums up the times and interprets them to the nations. He deals with a real material, but he moulds it to a form. It is not true to say that great events produce great art. Great art, in the widest sense, that of scholars, philosophers, theologians, produces great events. Luther made history. The Renaissance, the liberation of creative art from the tyranny of dogma and worn-out formulations, made way for the Elizabethans. Scott and Byron and Hugo were world powers. Napoleon himself reaped where Rousseau sowed. Schiller and Goethe made one Germany; Hegel, Fichte, Schopenhauer, Nietzsche, made another. And this influence was largely personal. The great Romantics, Rousseau, Scott, Byron, produced different effects, because their art and their ideas were different. Tolstoy and Dostoevsky, in their several ways, were among the forces which brought revolution to Russia. They not only interpreted widespread feelings of their time, they gave them form and therefore force.

Tolstoy knew very well, and felt deeply, the power of art to realise its creation in men's souls. It was this knowledge which made him say that art and science were the two chief forces which governed men's lives. It led him also to his moral theory of art. Tolstoy was quite clear that art was always art if it carried infection. But it might be bad art. Art, he said, was bad if it appealed only to the educated minority, rather than to the mass; good art was what reached the greatest number of people. He was led into this position by his religious dogma, which was itself a consequence of his divided and unhappy soul.

Tolstoy's moral theory, at first sight, is absurd. But his hatred of what he calls 'art for art's sake' is simply another expression of his feeling that art has an important function in the world: to give to man the experience of truth, which is greater than art. That is to say, he is all against Croce and the expressionist school. I have to admit that for all Croce's brilliant argument, I think his theory fails to meet the facts. I suspect also that it has been disastrous to artists who have attempted to believe that all intuition is expression, all expression art. For if intuition is expression, how does the artist know anything but his expression? He is cut off from reality by his own act. He can't ask himself, like Tolstoy, 'Does this expression fairly represent this intuition?' because for him intuition does not exist objectively. It is to him like Kant's thing-in-itself. He knows it only by his own expression. He is compelled, that is, to accept the word for the thing. He is isolated in his own ego. And in practice he falls back upon expression for the sake of expression. This, I think, is what Tolstoy meant by 'art for art's sake'. But of course he was wrong in condemning what he called exclusive art. Almost all great art has begun as exclusive art, and every great artist has been received with suspicion and called obscure, immoral, or eccentric. The first duty of an artist is to find the right form for his intuition. This was the greatness of Scott and of Hardy. So also of James Joyce, among the greatest.

But if Tolstoy, we think, was wrong in his moral theory, he does us good service by the courage with which he states it. That is one of the greatest services any thinker can do, to make himself and his case perfectly clear. Tolstoy says that science for science's sake is in the same case with art for art's sake; that the man who pursues some line of investigation for the fun of discovery, and not for the public good, is just as bad as the exclusive artist, and ought to be discouraged.

But it is easy to see that science must be free, that if any government had said to Mme Curie, 'You shall not waste money and research on an element so scarce as radium, so completely useless to mankind,' it would have behaved foolishly. Science must be free, because no government can know what value its discoveries will have. Without pure research there would be no science at all. All sciences began in the speculations of Greek philosophers and mathematicians who had no object but seeking the fact. Yet all material civilisation derives from their work. In the same way, all great religions, all new arts and philosophies, begin with the individual creator. And often a long time passes before he has even one follower, one who understands what he is saying and doing. Yet all our spiritual life, whether in art or science or religion, except in its elements, is the construction of such lonely thinkers.

We see, with Tolstoy, that art, like science, has great power: it can do evil as well as good; but it cannot be regimented or you kill it at the roots. Your remedy is not censorship, but education. Let the moral teachers, the critics, attack what they think evil. That is their duty. They must be true to their religious convictions, their ideal concept, as the artist must be true to his intuition, and his idea.

It is because Tolstoy was so completely sincere, so utterly scornful, like the aristocrat he was, of popular judgement, that he stands before us one of the greatest men and greatest artists of the world. His faults were enormous. But he showed them to us. He gives us every step in his feeblest argument. And so, through him, we know the weakness as well as the powers of the human soul, and understand better, by direct experience, by the closest sympathy, that world spirit of our time in which all of us are at once partakers and creators.

University of Edinburgh Journal, XII (Summer 1943), 91–96.

A Novel is a Novel is a Novel

The old lady at the zoo didn't believe in the giraffe; it wasn't her idea of what the creature should be. And a good many people will disagree with every definition of the novel. If you say it is a long story in prose about fictitious characters they will ask, 'What about any historical novel?' If you answer that all the characters need not be fictitious, they ask if Harrison Ainsworth's story of Jack Sheppard, a highwayman who was hanged, or Carlyle's *French Revolution* can be called novels. Both are factual throughout, but all libraries catalogue the first among novels, the second as history. And so the whole theory and practice of labels is derided.

Critics remember Boileau, whose rules bedeviled literature for two centuries. They quote Shakespeare's Polonius with his analysis of plays: pastoral-comical; historical-pastoral; tragical-historical, and so on. They remind you of Boileau's solemn ukase that an epic which does not bring in gods and machinery is not an epic; that John Dennis of the same critical school laid it down forever that tragi-comedy was a monster, that is to say, an unnatural and horrid abortion; a thing that should not be allowed to live.

They quote that great scholar, Rymer, on Shakespeare, when he declared that Iago was a character not to be permitted on any stage; an impossible character for art because 'philosophy teaches us that it is in the nature of man to be grateful, and philosophy must be the poet's guide.'

Yet we all do understand what sort of thing to expect when we read in the advertisement of a play, that it is comedy, tragedy or farce; and these definitions help us to plan our evening. Labels, in fact, are necessary, not only to booksellers, librarians, and critics, but to readers. And when we look at Polonius' celebrated speech, it seems, at least to me, that

Shakespeare was laughing at the old man not as a fool, but as a bore.

Polonius was Shakespeare's Norpois. Proust makes fun of Norpois in *Remembrance of Things Past*, with his diplomatic cant, his *démarches* and *détentes*, but it is not suggested that Norpois did not understand his job. French diplomacy has seldom been stupid. And Polonius's advice to young Laertes before his travels is very much the advice given in official pamphlets to young soldiers nowadays when they go overseas. I have no doubt that Polonius, like Norpois, was an excellent bureaucrat; and as a bureaucrat he had to use labels. He could not have done his work without them.

Definitions are so necessary that they arise by themselves; we have the division of plays even to such a fine distinction as musical comedy and comic opera. We have the historical novel, the romance, the whodunit, the thriller, the Western. All these names, advertised on a poster or a title page, are significant. Nine-tenths of novels are defined to everyone's satisfaction, and nine-tenths of novels answer our definition of a long story in prose about fictitious characters.

The trouble, therefore, is with the giraffes, the monsters, novels which do not answer to the common expectation. This, however, is a real trouble because it is precisely in the neutral ground between definitions that original masterpieces are born. A writer who has something new to express is always likely to seek a new form or expression. *Erewhon* was such a form, so were *Ulysses* and *Finnegans Wake*. The complaint against Hersey's *The Wall*—that it is documentary—is simply another way of saying that the writer has sought an original technique.

This is an age of definition. The prestige of science which leads to suppose that everything can be measured and analysed, the reaction from an age of freedom, the expansion of government, new censorships, a new growth of dogma (political, religious, economic)—all encourage the definer.

The natural and eager desire of every student is for definition, ready-made and easily-remembered. The professor is asked every day, 'Is Whitman truly a poet; is Thomas Wolfe a real novelist?' And if he forgets that every student mind is full of unrecognised assumptions and predigested labels, he is apt to

answer as if he were talking not of labels, which are merely a
convenience, but of works of art; that is, of things real and self-
consistent in their own right.

It is especially and perpetually tempting for the analytic
mind to classify art under strict heads because art appears to
all analytic minds as a realm of ideality and free invention,
where nothing in nature prevents a systematic allotment of
regions: this to the novelist, that to the poet.

Every professional artist has met the questioner who asks of
some detail: 'Why did you do it so clumsily like that, when
you could have done it so neatly like this?' And smiles, as on
a poor dreamer without logic or understanding, when he gets
the answer: 'It might have been better your way, but I couldn't
do it because it wouldn't have belonged.' The notion of a work
of art possessing, developing, and imposing its own laws, of its
being, in fact, not an ideal construction, but a real creature,
would appear to the sober amateur merely fantastic.

But, he says, does not the artist create? Certainly the artist
creates, but not out of nothing. He deals in the profoundest
sense with a given material: not only given words and meanings, given forms of character, given shapes of culture and
morality, but given feelings and a given fundamental order of
relations in feeling; that is to say, in being itself. He explores
and develops a vein of ore which pays no more regard to made-
up distinctions than the main reef on the Rand pays to boundary lines drawn on a map.

This, of course, is why men like Horace and Boileau, who
were not only students of literature, but themselves artists,
set out to make laws for art. They learned in practice that
there are rules of construction, mysterious relations in technique, which exist apparently in the nature of art itself, and
which oblige the artist to respect them.

Painters who have written books on the line of beauty, or the
golden section, had the same intuition. Any architect will tell
you why such a building is right in glass and steel; this other,
say a garden house, needs brick. He will criticise the proportion
of horizontal to vertical, profiles, the light and shadow of a
façade; that is, he will appeal to innate categories of the visual
imagination.

Boileau, by his criticism, abolished the old absurd romance in the style of *The Arcadia*. He laughed Madame de Scudéry literally out of court. That he also tried to destroy the English drama was proof only that he did not understand it. Nor, indeed, did he understand his business as a critic, which was not to make laws but to discover them—to explore the structure of each work by itself and show, if possible, where it succeeded, and why and where it failed; not to define from outside but to clarify from within.

Definitions, like every necessary useful thing, just because they are necessary, because they save trouble, are dangerous. They may check a rich development. There is a comfortable belief in the world that genius, real genius, will always fight its way to recognition. This is certainly untrue; some genius that has fought its way is tough, but most of it has only been lucky. How often have we seen an artist snuffed out by indifference, or forced out of his art into some popular imitation. It happens to a man before he knows it.

How often have we met some sensitive and intelligent person who confesses, usually with good-humoured resignation, that he or she has tried to write a novel but, like Katherine Mansfield, in her celebrated attempt, has seen it turn out something so unlike a novel that it has had to be abandoned. That is to say, it has grown into a creature for which the literary zoologists could offer no cage.

When poor Baron Corvo, whose real name was Frederick William Rolfe, described his *Don Tarquinio* on the title page as a 'Kataleptic Phantasmatic Romance', he was not amusing himself. He, who had been so nearly labelled out of existence as man and writer, was trying to find himself a private label; and Corvo was extremely lucky to get *Don Tarquinio* into print. His masterpiece would have gone for waste paper long ago if that other strange genius, A. J. A. Symons, long after Corvo's death in misery, had not, by as much luck as persistence, succeeded in tracking it down and finding a publisher for it.

Labels belong to the mechanism of society, but we have to keep mechanism out of our thinking. See what it has done to the students of science; the Fuchses of the laboratory; the

pedants and Boileaus of the Party. Since we must have a definition of the novel, let it be the simplest possible, and let us be
careful to pay no serious attention to it.

New York Times Book Review (30 April 1950), 1, 34.

A Novelist and His Public

The best idea of a novelist's public that ever I heard came from a reader who told me he hated my new book and knew he would hate it. And when I asked him why he had read it, he said in a melancholy way that he was one of my oldest public.

A novelist's public, in fact, is people who read everything he writes even when they hate it. They are like those friends who come to see us even when we have bad colds or are in a bad temper. They are almost like wives and husbands who marry for better or worse. Because the relation is essentially mutual, a relation of two persons, the reader knows more or less what to look for in that writer—he has, so to speak, got his wavelength and can tune in. And what he gets is the writer's meaning, or at least the meaning that writer has for him.

How does a writer get a public? He has to write and go on writing, as long as any publisher will publish him, and he has to mean something. If he does really mean what he writes and manages somehow to put it over, he will, in the end, find himself with a public. Usually it will be there before he knows it. It may amount only to a dozen or two, for, if they are really his public, they usually imagine that he has thousands of readers and would not dream of writing him a letter. So it may be years before he discovers that he has what publishers call a public, that is, a certain number of people who read whatever he writes and who, if he does chance to meet one of them, will talk about his characters as if they were discussing actual living people and will even argue with him about them. I have been told, by such a reader, that I had not been fair to a certain woman, a woman invented by myself—that I did not really understand her. And what that reader had to say was not only extremely interesting to me, it was important: the most valuable kind of criticism.

This is exactly the intimate mutual relation of friends who discuss a common interest. It is just the same relation for every kind of author, Ethel M. Dell as well as Henry James. I know that many people make a sharp distinction between the best-seller and what they call the serious writer. The idea is that the latter writes in order to express his own serious feelings about the world, but best-sellers start with the intention of being best-sellers: they say to themselves, 'We'll give the public what it wants and make millions.' Of course certain writers do just that. But what I do not believe is that it can be done in cold blood, as a commercial proposition.

A friend of mine was staying in a hotel abroad where a celebrated best-selling woman novelist was also staying. She was a nice woman. My friend made friends with her; they dined together. One day she came down to dinner sniffing and blowing, with swollen eyes and a red nose. He sympathised with her for catching such a fearful cold. She answered that it was not a cold, she never had colds. But she had been working out a big scene in her new novel, where the hero, owing to a misunderstanding, had broken with the heroine. The scene had been difficult; it had taken all day and she had been in tears most of the time. As she spoke, the tears rose to her eyes all over again. She apologised, she was amused at herself, but they were genuine tears. And we know that Dickens wept freely when he killed Paul Dombey, not to speak of Little Nell.

In fact, I doubt if anyone can *set out* to be a best-seller. I know some best-sellers take a careless tone about their own works as if they meant nothing by them; as if they did them just for fun or wrote them with their left hands in the dark, while thinking of something else. But I do not believe any author ever gets a public unless he writes what he believes. He may, of course, put up some kind of false front, to catch some section of what he thinks is popular taste. But this will certainly come out in the book. No writer can hide behind his book. And people who want the feel of complete honesty and conviction in their books will dislike that author. They may read him, but they will not join his public. Every writer has readers, casual readers, who do not belong to his public and never will; just as every one of us has eaten mousetrap cheese when we cannot get Stilton.

The only people I can think of who get a public and make money by writing as a purely commercial job are detective-story writers, and detective stories are a special box of tricks, just that. After all, murder is a fairly serious matter if it happens to real people, even in a book. The detective writer therefore cannot, from the start, believe in his own people: his murderee, like his murderer, is simply a move in a game. He does not want the sympathy of his reader; he has actually to avoid it. But the novel writer must excite sympathy—never mind if he is writing satire, the reader must feel for his characters.

How does a young writer fail to get a public? The only way is to be a bore. And he is warned every day that the best way to be a bore is to write a novel of ideas. It is true that a novel, like all art, is aimed at the feelings. It has to be an experience. So far as it deals directly in ideas, they must be ideas that convey feeling. Of course most ideas, in real life, do excite a good deal of feeling. Political ideas start wars. Religious ideology, as we all know, is the very devil for making trouble in the world. But there have to be politics and religion to give some form to that world. We need not swallow the whole of a party's politics or the whole of a church's creed, but they have to be there to give that party and that church a form, otherwise they would not exist, and it is good for us that they should be there to define our own position. They make sense and order in the chaos of actual events. We need them to make sense of our own lives. And a novelist is no different from other people, in this respect. He has to have ideas to write at all, to make his characters act like reasonable people, to make sense of his plot, to give the whole book a form. Meaning is form, and form is meaning. When people damn a novel of ideas they are really complaining that the ideas stick out on their own account, that they do not have enough influence on the lives of the characters. So that novel is not a story about people but mere propaganda, and therefore a bore.

Another thing they say to young novelists is: 'If you want a public, do not moralise; because morals are a bore.' But in fact all good novels, and especially popular novels, are about morals. We can see that in the case of Miss Dell. A good novel is about what people do, and why they do it, and how it succeeds in making them happy or otherwise; and these are all moral questions. The idea that there is something aloof and dull about a novel that takes morals seriously is completely wrong: the truth is the other way round. Popular tales, the folklore of simple people, of people who never saw a novel, of primitive tribesmen in Africa, are always highly moral. All gossip is about conduct; that is why it is so fascinating. Listen to any two old charladies conversing together—their talk is all about people, and it is full of judgements about right and wrong, what people ought to do and feel: for the good reason that it is intensely important to them and their happiness that people should have some standards of right and wrong. The novel-reader may belong to Ethel M. Dell's public, or he may prefer Conrad, James, and Lawrence, but what he is interested in first to last is conduct, that is, morals. The greatest writers of the world are just those who take the greatest interest in morals: it is because of that they are so exciting to read. Think of Dickens, Tolstoy, Hardy, and Conrad.

These writers knew that moral theories are nothing by themselves, they are only significant in action, in character. They do not preach. If they did, they would bore. Everyone is on guard against the preacher and the propagandist. He says to himself, 'I'm not going to be knocked off my base by a lot of hooey from a chap who's paid to hand it out.' He has terrific resistance to preaching. But he is not on his guard against the novel. He chooses it himself, and he actually wants it to knock him off his base. He lays himself wide open to the thing. He will ask a librarian, 'Is it my stuff?' as he might ask a doctor, 'Has it got enough kick for me?' and the librarian will say, 'No, it's a bit mild for you,' or 'Yes, I think you'll like it,' according to his view of the reader's temperament, age, etc.

Librarians are always being asked, 'What shall I read?' and the result of the advice is often surprising, even to them. The discovery of reading as a pleasure can change a life. For it is the keenest, the cheapest, the most lasting of pleasures, and it needs no co-operation. The most lonely people can have company in a book; the most god-forsaken soul on earth can find some peace there. And no one knows his own reach of imagination. We had at school a tough of my own age, whose only joys were beer, girls, and football. He was also a very good-natured fellow, open to the worst influences, born stooge to any crook. But he met in the fourth form a great teacher whose passion was Shakespeare—and in Shakespeare this young tough met a lot more toughs, as rough and tough as himself but much more interesting. And that tough carried Shakespeare about with him—the little old *Temple Shakespeare*—for the rest of his life. He did not go to the top of his class: he was too stupid, or idle. He did not cover himself with any kind of glory; he did not even become a Cabinet Minister, although he had been so nearly sacked from school. And he died young in his forties of a hobnailed liver. But he lived a useful life: he became an adult, a responsible and, what is more, an interesting man. You had to agree that his life had been a success. And at sixteen it had every chance of ending in total failure, if not gaol.

Half juvenile delinquency, that is, most of crime, starts in boredom. Boys and girls of twelve to eighteen have terrific energy and too little to do with it; they also have the most lively and eager imaginations, for which almost nothing is provided. If they show any imagination in dress, for instance, like the teddy boys, they are promptly marked down as rebels and nuisances, and respond very naturally by rebellion. If they show any interest in reading, it is odds on that the books will be labelled obscene and thrown on the fire. And then it is highly likely that they will stop reading altogether, and simply get on with gangsterism.

To prevent anyone on earth reading what he wants to read, what he chooses for himself, is a pretty serious responsibility for any authority. The most significant thing about young criminals is that so many cannot read and do not want to begin. They have been put off. You wonder if books were ever read to them in childhood, and what kind of books, to make the very idea of reading a bore to be dodged. All children adore to have interesting stories read to them. They are almost all potential readers, and reading for a good many of them is their only chance of any real education. It is the only kind that goes on for life, among all classes of readers. Most people, by the age of twenty-five, are impervious to any kind of teaching. But if they have the reading habit, they will read for amusement, they will even spend money on a book. And they will often go on from simple yarns, sex stories, thrillers, suitable to their age, to the greatest writers.

It is completely wrong to think the public of a serious writer consists of university graduates and what are called the white-collar men. There are no university or class distinctions among readers. Ask librarians. Ask writers. They get the most penetrating, the most intelligent letters from people who certainly never went to a university; from struggling housewives writing on the kitchen table between the stove and the wash-tub. A book is an experience; a great book is a deep, a powerful experience. Why should not people whose lives are hard-lived and hard-felt understand what Tolstoy or James mean for them? I know a docker and his wife who read James, who read all the classics, and enjoy them intensely. They live in a pre-fab but they are on intimate terms with some of the most interesting, the most exciting minds that ever existed. A novelist's public is not a class public. Great scholars often read tripe, and very simple people enjoy the masters. What is more, they can enjoy a variety of masters: they can belong to many different publics. Reading, like appetite, is a matter of mood. I have a shelf full of masterpieces specially chosen to be completely different in character: Peacock stands beside Melville, Proust next *Genji*, Compton Burnett beside Svevo, *Brighton Rock* and *Middlemarch*, Mark Twain's *Mississippi* and Chekhov, and so on, all opposites. I have read all this shelf so often I can open almost any book anywhere and know where I am in the story and what the people are doing and feeling. And I enter at once into the author's private world, the world he has created for himself. I meet him again in this world, in his own character, his own meaning.

In fact we do not know anyone as well as we know some of the great authors, because they are all people with a special power of expression and they are all trying to give us an experience which has been important to them: they are trying to make us see and feel the world as they have felt it. When I join their publics I form at once a close relation of mutual

interest that I could not get anywhere else. Even my best
friends are not always at home or free to see me when I most
need to see them. But a book and its author are always at hand.
I can be happy and excited with them alone, anywhere in the
world. In fact they are such good company they can make being
alone an actual advantage to be sought for. I remember a woman
leaving a bridge four and going back to the solitude of her
room because she wanted to hear a broadcast-reading of *her*
Trollope. She spoke of this engagement as one that could not
possibly be missed. I still remember the irritation of the other
three bridge players—not, I suppose, members of Trollope's
public—and her apologetic tone. But also her look of joyful
anticipation. She went to her Trollope as to a lover.

Listener (30 September 1954), 521, 522; reprinted in *Saturday
Review* (27 November 1954), 11, 36, 37. Originally a radio-talk
broadcast on the BBC Home Service (22 September 1954).

On the Function of the Novelist

It has been said of Trollope that you can walk about in his books with your hat on. The notion is that his world is more real than that of Dickens. He thought so himself, and so misled a great many innocents, who concluded that a writer's job was to copy life, and got nowhere. For to copy life would be to produce nonsense.

Trollope found in life what we all find, a mass of detail without meaning, of useless cruelty, stupid evil, blind fate, fools doing accidental good and well-meaning saints doing immense evil; what he did was what every writer does, even those modest writers who frankly work for the pay: he created a work of art to give a certain kind of experience.

He said in effect, 'This is the shape of things under the confusion of appearance; these are the forces which really move people to action.' His whole story, however complex, was designed to illustrate and develop a theme. His essential task was the same as that of Dickens; he used only a different method.

As it is a philosopher's job to make sense of life to the mind, to present it as a rational unity, so it is a novelist's job to make sense of it to the feelings. And this means that we must have a consistent point of view. For it is only from one point of view that experience, like landscape, can be ranged in any kind of order.

It is dangerous perhaps to say that a book must have a moral, so let us call it a meaning. What, then, does *Tristram Shandy* mean? To read it is an event, like the first hearing of Stravinsky's *Petrouchka*, and it remains a memory, as of a single experience, like a meeting of which one says, 'That meant a lot to me.' We can't define the effect in words, but we know that it was definite and lasting.

The objection, in fact, even to books that convey morals,

is not really to a form of art, but to bad art. Critics who find fault with Zola in his *Nana* for moralising and driving his moral home with crude means should have protested against a crude moral. If Zola's forte was in brass, he had every right to compose for brass, but not, after he had stunned his audience into attention, to offer them a platitude or a fraud.

When at the end of the fable Nana dies of what Zola calls the small, but was, I fancy, originally the great pox, just as the French mob of the Second Empire is shouting in the streets 'A Berlin', we are revolted by the cheapness of a device which suggests that there is anything in common between the dissolution of a harlot and the crisis of an empire. We see behind it the vulgar illusions, or suspect what is worse, the claptrap, of a mind fed on party politics.

Zola was not a time-server. He fought for justice in the Dreyfus case at the risk of his life. But he was not a profound writer. He made a world rich in characters, but they moved on a surface. He was blind to all the large dimensions of history or morality. He could add intensity to old impressions, but he did not give a new intuition, much less a great one, if we mean by 'great' rich in scope.

A great writer in this sense, whether poet, historian or novelist, is one whose world of organised experience harmonises into one coherent impression the largest area of actual confusion. Tolstoy's *War and Peace* is a deliberate attempt to make sense, both to mind and feeling, of the whole realm of human action and inhuman fate. He did not succeed. For various reasons, both technical and real, no one is likely to succeed. But *War and Peace* is still one of the great achievements of art. And men live by art, greatly in great arts or cheaply in small arts.

Yet writers who, like Zola, give intensity to a common and superficial idea of the world are doing a useful work. The reason is that a very large number of people cease when quite young to add anything to a limited stock of judgements. After a certain age, say twenty-five, they consider that their education is finished.

It is perhaps natural that, having passed through that painful and boring process called, expressly, education, they should suppose it over, and that they are equipped for life to label every event as it occurs and drop it into its given pigeonhole. But one who has a label ready for everything does not bother to observe any more, even such ordinary happenings as he has observed for himself, with attention, before he went to school. He merely acts and reacts.

For people who have stopped noticing, the only possible new or renewed experience, and, therefore, new knowledge, is from a work of art. Because that is the only kind of experience which they are prepared to receive on its own terms, they will come out from their shells and expose themselves to music, to a play, to a book, because it is the accepted method of enjoying such things. True, even to plays and books they may bring artistic prejudices which prevent them from seeing *that* play or comprehending *that* book. Their artistic sensibilities may be as crusted over as their minds.

But it is part of an artist's job to break crusts; or let us say, rather, that artists who work for the public and not merely for themselves are interested in breaking crusts because they want to communicate their intuitions.

Painters, for instance, had used impressionism in their sketches, made only for their private record and pleasure, during hundreds of years before Turner and Constable in England, Monet and his school in France, seized upon the sketch technique as a means to convey their new intuition, or vision, of nature as a play of light.

Of course, since they were born into a world which was accustomed to see nature as classical landscape, poetical objects composed in formal recession, they were not understood. They were labelled ignorant daubers or mountebanks, because these were the only pigeonholes then available for them. There was as yet no Impressionist pigeonhole into which new and often original painting could be thrown and forgotten.

But the new school was resolved to be understood. It insisted on exhibiting its work. And since it had a brilliant technique and bold invention—since, too, it early attracted young and independent minds as well as smart dealers—it did finally break through the crust and give to the world a new and rich experience of permanent value, a new realm of ideal appreciation.

Great writers have done this over and over again. Richardson astonished Europe with his new world of sentiment; Rousseau followed hard upon him with his *Émile*; and the crust which they broke was the crust of the feudal society. Its foundations were washed away—chiefly by sentimental tears.

Rousseau and Tolstoy have had direct revolutionary effect on history. But I am not proposing them as great artists only on that account. All art makes history but most of it by indirect and obscure means.

Jane Austen was a great artist, and she is more read now than any writer of her time. Her influence on minds has been enormous but subtle. It springs not from the novelty but the comprehension and balance of her idea of life and the technical power with which she conveys it. Her world is limited in surface but deep in content and, as far as it goes, more self-consistent than either Rousseau's or Tolstoy's. And she breaks the crust of a dry imagination not by a violent assault but by a series of light taps.

It is her style, her humour, that penetrate. And this, of course, is the means appropriate to her purpose. She was not going to open a tea party with a maroon or a blast of trumpets. She had too much of what Henry James called 'taste', meaning 'sense of proportion', both aesthetic and moral. Much of her greatness as a novelist is precisely in her clear understanding of her job, which was to make a complete thing and have it felt.

The function of the novel, in short, is to make the world contemplate and understand itself, not only as rational being but as experience of value, as a complete thing.

New York Times Book Review (30 October 1949), 1, 52.

Morality and the Novelist

We are said now to be recovering from a period of atheistic reaction. Writers, having abused and derided the churches for forty years, are turning once more to religion. Waugh and Graham Greene have become Catholics. Aldous Huxley cultivates Indian mysticism and venerates the *Bhagavad Ghita*.

It is true that there is a general return to the churches, or, at least, a general reaction from crude atheism among the public. Mechanism, nihilism, are discredited. Students everywhere are demanding a more comprehensive, a more satisfactory, idea of life. They go even to theological lectures and, if they cannot accept Christianity, they take to some philosophy; they set up some theory of moral obligation which at least implies the numinous.

But in this counter-revolution it is the case of the writers which is most interesting, simply because, as writers, they reveal it so plainly. And it has provoked already among critics the sharp judgement that novelists would be better to stick to the objective description of life, and leave philosophy and theology to the professors. A novel, they say, is not a treatise. It is at the opposite pole from the treatise. It is a work of art, it is intended to communicate experience and not argument.

But it seems to me that this is as crude a statement as some of the novels criticised. For an author cannot do without a morality, and morals cannot be harmonised without some principle, an idea.

In the final resort, all novel-writing is moral. It is impossible to give form to a book without some moral creed. It may be confused, instinctive, founded on crude assumptions, but it must exist if only as a principle of choice. The writer is obliged to choose between alternatives of word and action, and his only criterion is moral value. This is true even of Pater, Huys-

mans, or Wilde. For their aestheticism was a creed, a morality.
Restif de la Bretonne, in every line of his work, refers to some
moral principle. He gets his effect by shock. He draws, as it
were, in black on a white ground. Without the whiteness of the
ground, his characters would lose their sharpness, their impact.
Waugh, Huxley, Céline, began as satirists. They revolted
against the bourgeois morality, the easy optimism which had
ruled in the world for half a century, before the '14 war.

This was the common reaction of the time against the whole
civilisation of the generation before, against 'the old men who
made the war'. The young hated and despised even the men
who despised that culture. Galsworthy and Wells had been
attacking for years the complacency and materialism of society,
but also they had promised easy reform, they had offered a
formula for progress, Fabian socialism. They believed that the
world could be saved by act of parliament. They too were opti-
mists, and in the 1920s, among the graves of the war which
had been ruinous to the victors as well as the defeated, the
young were enraged by these confident promises. They had
been deceived and that is what the young cannot forgive.

The revolt was moral. It was founded in hatred of the lie.
And in Waugh, Huxley, in Céline and his like, it was purely
defeatist. It offered no policy, no creed, no hope. It expressed the
despair of millions who afterwards wandered into Communism,
for something to believe; into Fascism; Nazism; or simply
carried on from day to day without any coherent notion of
what the world was about; any principle of good or bad, right
or wrong, in conduct. They lived by routine, by habit; by
prejudice; their minds were full of contradictions; they were
lost souls, borne along by events that they could not understand, towards a destination that they could not imagine.

Some of these, of course, especially those not constrained into
the routine life of the worker, the professional man, took to
drugs and drink, or went mad. The suicide rate was high
among those who had time to think. But the greater number,
without leisure to realise despair, under pressure of need, of
family responsibility, continued from day to day, like Anatole
France's clerks in The Isle of Penguins, to catch their trains, to
go to their offices, to pursue, by a kind of compulsion that

was neither instinct nor reason, the complicated lives of insects. They had no clear notion of anything, no faith that made sense of the chaos about them, they were merely odd feelings and vague assumptions wrapped up in a suit of clothes and pushed about in a crowd of similar packages. It was only the clothes that gave them the appearance of cohesion.

But a writer cannot drift on a stream; he is a man of action. He has to create. He cannot even put words into the mouths of others without some grasp of the values implied by the speakers. Read bad dialogue and you will see when the writer has faltered because he does not know what his character ought to say, or is afraid to let him say something that implies a moral conviction. He dodges the issue because he is not sure of it. His dialogue becomes trivial and his characters lose their integrity.

And the impossibility is forced upon a writer's notice. No one so quickly discovers his own inadequacy of thought or faith than the novelist. He is perpetually inventing people and setting them in action. He is always faced with their moral problems, their reactions, and he has to know not only what they will do in a given case, but what they ought to do. He has to understand the whole situation in which they live and act. And he knows very well that if he runs away from any of their questions, if he dodges an issue or fakes the event, he is not only a fraud, but he will do bad work. There will be a soft spot, a meaningless passage in his composition; mere connective tissue.

Even the satirist needs a faith. In order to give unity and form to his hatred, he must believe that his victim, the society or the individual he attacks, is totally rotten. For if he admits the smallest merit in that victim, then he ceases to write satire, his book becomes an analytical study of the whole truth, and he cannot give it shape merely by the formula of hatred.

Satire can be unified by rage, but it is a narrow field. The satirist rarely continues in it. His very genius as a writer, hatred and revolt, implies strong feeling, a moral obsession, feelings that demand a positive expression. He wants to analyse the world he hates, to diagnose its sickness. That is why even the satirist finds himself driven to seek a philosophy of life, a religion; that is why Waugh, Graham Greene, and Aldous Huxley, having damned the world they knew, sought desperately for a faith. They could not afford to live from day to day, on a set of assumptions. They had to have some integrating idea of life and value.

I shall be told that some of the greatest writers have been deeply divided men, split personalities, whose idea of life, when they had one, was wildly confused. What was Dickens's integrating philosophy, how far did Léon Bloy or Kipling succeed in rationalising their fears and their passions?

The notion of a frustrated generation seeking a philosophy of life may be true, but it is only the outside of truth. What really happened to the generation of '14, at least to those who reacted so fiercely against religion? They were deceived in a facile optimism which had surrounded their childhood, and fled into the idea of negation and defeatism. But a very large number of them, in all classes, preserved a steady and untroubled faith and never doubted that life was worth living, that affection was worth having. They founded families and their children about us now are a sober, cool-headed but energetic generation.

Those grandfathers of our day, in short, received the disasters of war, the collapse of liberal optimism, only with some grumbling, and an energetic will to get better governments, and to establish a peace. Their faith was too deep and strong to be knocked out even by the bloodshed, the fearful tragedies of those long years of slaughter. It was stronger than death or reason, its roots went deeper than any argument, and nothing men could do would throw it into despair.

Wittgenstein has said that everyone has his own world. I should rather say that men are together in feeling, in sympathy, but alone in mind. They are born almost without instinct and are compelled therefore to form their own idea of the world, their working map. The process begins in earliest childhood, long before the child can talk, and it is logical, conceptual, even in the infant mind. It has to be.

The infant possesses, indeed, by nature, if few instincts, certain powers, of affection, attachment, but it is with his imagination that he grasps and synthesises experience.

At first, this world of the infant is entirely egoistic, and self-centred. It is founded in illusion, its faith is entirely emotional and foolish; it will be destroyed at the first check. But it is quickly supplemented even before he can speak by impressions of consistency, permanence, of reciprocal liability. And as soon as he has a clear conception of himself as a person, and therefore of what is over against the person, the rest of the world, he is capable of forming the idea of powers that stand above and outside both: goodness, law, Jesus, God. These are no doubt in the first place only words expressing abstractions. But ready at any time, as the child's experience grows, to take an active and concrete form as people who are good, the police, the man in the Bible who loves all children, and the master of all, the ruler of the world.

And these impressions, these ideas, come to him when he has discovered his own isolation and weakness; when he has begun to realise something of the instability and danger of life. He has no doubt felt his weakness before, but he has not realised his solitude.

This first idea or impression of some benevolent personality in the world, received young, is, within our own experience, very likely to become so much a part of the mind of a child that it is indistinguishable from his first reactions to life. It becomes part of that nature to which it has given shape and coherence.

Indeed, to a small child an idea is much closer to an experience than a concept. It is grasped rather by the desire and feeling of the mind, than the mind of feeling; it is barely a possession before it is half-way to a prepossession, a characteristic.

Later, of course, the growing boy, the adolescent, forms perpetually new ideas, an elaborate aesthetic and political structure. These may or may not be in accord with the fundamental assumptions; especially in times of revolutionary change, they are very likely to be in conflict with them. So we had the frustrated who, after a serene childhood in the old naïve world of the 'tens, formed in the post-war 'twenties the idea that there is no goodness in the world, no law, no truth or unselfish love, and, clinging to that belief which alone, for them,

could explain their own sufferings, or express and give issue to
their rage, were involved in a perpetual contradiction between
their words and their conduct.

On the other hand, one who has had a miserable childhood,
who has no deep faith, may grasp at some philosophy, some
political or religious dogma, and desperately assert a creed in
which, actually, he cannot believe.

We all know men who profess, let us say, behaviourism,
which is the modern form of nihilism, and yet have the
strongest feelings about government, about morals. That is to
say, their minds are in a muddle; there is a deep unresolved
conflict between what they really believe, between their fundamental sympathies, and their idea of life.

But unless they write novels they do not give themselves
away. Even as philosophers, they do not disclose their confusion, for they write theses, and neither appear in them, nor
answer for them.

The writer is in a different case. He has to deal with people
in situations. He has to create people who feel, in situations
which are felt; and he cannot write them except out of his own
feelings and sympathies; out of his own character.

But suppose he is one who has seized upon some creed, some
philosophy of life, which is not in accord with his real sympathies, in which he believes merely by will, then he must ask
himself all the time, 'What ought this character to do, to feel,
to say, in order to illustrate my theme?' We all know the consequence, we have read the Communist novel, the Existentialist
novel, the novel of the religious convert who is anxious to be
orthodox, who looks up the canon to make sure he's got it right.
He is like a man who dances in chains, his clumsy movements
are like a mechanical imitation of life. He is, for himself, and
in his own feeling, a man who follows a narrow winding track
through a wilderness, and fears every instant to tumble into
some bog. His steps are careful and anxious, and, when we
follow his course, we discover, after all, only a track, a superficial direction which is, besides, already worn hollow by millions in the game of follow-my-leader.

Here we have the convert who is afraid to break the least
rule of his newly-acquired faith in case he should lose it, who

propagates it with fervour in order to convince himself. His books have to be narrow, essentially banal, because they must conform to a set of rules. It is not for nothing that converts tend to be fanatics. For many of them, it is a necessity; the alternative would be an asylum.

Dostoevsky was precisely a man who had no deep faith; whose childhood was wretched, who grasped at the orthodox dogmas; who said, 'If truth was on one side, Christ on the other, I should have to follow Christ.' For him, the alternative was certainly an asylum.

The profound division in Dostoevsky is easily traced in his books. Take *The Brothers Karamazov*. This was published serially in the *Russian Messenger*, and in the fifth instalment, 'Pro and Contra', he gives such good anti-Christian arguments to Ivan in his discussion with Father Zossima, 'Pater Seraphicus', that Pobedonostsev, Procurator of the Synod, was outraged.

Dostoevsky, alarmed by the effect of his own work, promised a refutation of Ivan in the next number, at the death of Father Zossima; and spent two months on its fifty pages, more than on any other section. Even then it did not succeed. He had to defend it also, to explain that he could not give Zossima better arguments because he had to stick to Zossima's character.

This is a lame excuse. Why, if Zossima was so feeble an apologist, did Dostoevsky choose him to defend the Christian position?

Professor Simmons, in his excellent book on Dostoevsky, suggests that this is a unique case. But it would be just as true to say that artistic integrity should have obliged Dostoevsky to make his book a whole. His very excuses betray his consciousness of a failure in harmony, in orchestration.

Here is, apparently, the most flagrant case of a convert who does not truly believe, who is not really convinced, who writes to a thesis, and betrays the deep contradiction in his mind.

But no one can call Dostoevsky's works dry, narrow, banal, mechanistic. They are the most explosive masterpieces in all literature.

I suggest that the answer to this conundrum is not simply in Dostoevsky's lack of aesthetic control, but in something much deeper, in the nature of the artist.

I said that the early ideas of childhood rapidly sink into the unconscious; that is to say, they become habitual, spontaneous. But this can also happen with later ideas, especially when those ideas follow a line consistent with the earlier impressions, or rationalise a natural faculty. Dostoevsky had no faith, but he knew the value of love. All children know that, even if they fail to develop those sympathies which enable them to give unselfish affection. They seek for love even when they doubt its real existence; that is the history of nearly all neurotics and their feverish relations with society.

Dostoevsky's Christianity, as picked up in his Siberian prison, was in conflict with his fundamental distrust but it accorded with his needs. He wanted, he longed, to believe; and that longing drew not the dogma but the message of the church, deep into his soul. There was a conflict there between two faiths: the original creed of the nihilist and the acquired hope of the Christian.

And a conflict is not a contradiction. In the conflict of a soul, two elements are locked in battle. Now one triumphs and now another. Dostoevsky's nature was in continuous turmoil, he never had rest; he was never able to put the struggle aside and say, 'Now I am going to be the complete Christian.' Experience of conflict was too violent, too powerful for him, and his only escape was not into creation, but to the gaming table, or some frantic love affair, with Paulina, with his wife.

The Procurator of the Synod had good reason to fear Dostoevsky; he was always dangerous to the church. Ivan Karamazov has converted more orthodox Christians into heretics than the most determined propaganda of the anti-God leagues. For he is the creation of a great artist; he lives for us in the agony of his doubt; he catches our sympathies; we feel the terrible force of his arguments because we are feeling with him.

Dostoevsky did not create Ivan out of theories and theology; out of paper. He himself was Ivan. But he was also Zossima and Alyosha, Raskolnikov and the child-prostitute. He knew them, he lived in them, and they carried his own passions, his own convictions; their conflict was his conflict.

But compare Dostoevsky with Tolstoy. Here too there was a fundamental lack of faith, a grasping at a creed. But that creed, of the anarchist, could never overcome his final pessimism, his terror of death. It could not take him out of himself, into the joy of self-forgetfulness; even his creation was only escape.

Tolstoy was too proud, too disciplined an anarchist, to be carried away by any idea, even his own. Anarchism, for him, remained an idea and did not sink into his subconscious to join itself with his longing, his need for devotion. It was never assimilated into his nature and his experience.

Anna Karenina, his masterpiece, is probably the most integrated, the most symphonic great work we have, since the *Divine Comedy*. Tolstoy did not contradict himself in that work because it was not necessary to his purpose.

He is saying there, as in *War and Peace*, 'Nature is God, follow Nature and you will be happy and wise.' It is man-made law, man-made convention, artificial society, that brings violence, war, discord, misery.

In Anna he sets out to show us a woman who denied her woman's nature which, in Tolstoy's view, was designed by God to make her a faithful and loving wife, sister, daughter, mother. A woman's vocation was the devoted service of the family. This was her primal function, her holy task in the world. And if she turned from it, she would do and suffer irreparable evil.

This is not true of all women. We all know plenty of women who are totally unsuited to be wives and mothers; plenty who have run away from their husbands without either ruining their own lives or causing any serious regret to the husbands. But it was true for Anna. Tolstoy, a magnificent technician, chose a woman for whom we can believe it true. And all the characters in the book are true to themselves as well as the theme. We need not believe that society is hopelessly corrupt because it appreciates a good bottle of wine and a cigar, but we certainly feel that Stepan Arkadyevitch is a selfish, careless, shallow-minded fellow, a parasite on the working world.

It is a different matter in *War and Peace* where the wonderful scene of Borodino is spoilt by the idea, wished upon it, thrust into it, that Kutuzov, a true Russian anarchist, left the issue to Providence.

Here is a contradiction at work: a direct opposition of experience and the idea. Tolstoy, so keen an observer, so brilliant a portrayer, of character, falsifies his own portrait of the general to serve an intellectual fancy.

His theory was never drawn down into his nature to become a conflicting belief, a tension, an experience which was part of his artist's soul. It remained a dogma, a canon, something dry, stiff, and formal, outside the man.

And this is precisely the fate of many of those who, having grown up without a formal creed, embrace one as an idea of life. They are too old or too cold to assimilate it into their nature; into their subconscious habits of reflection. Into, so to speak, the native landscape of their minds.

A landscape does not need to be smooth meadows for men to live with it. It can have chasms, volcanoes, it can be broken by earthquakes. But its natives will find no difficulty in living with it. They will farm the fertile slopes of the volcanoes, and harness the waterfalls on their cliffs for electricity to boil their kettles. They will make bridges, roads, railways, among these precipices, and move freely over the whole surface of the land enjoying its wildness and profiting by its attraction for tourists. They are far from the case of the stranger lost in the wilderness, of which he has no map, who, finding one signpost, follows a track through the darkness. He is not even sure that he is getting anywhere.

No two landscapes of the mind are the same; it is safe to say that other people's natures, if we could know them fully, would be more fantastic than the drawings of Doré or Hugo, Fuseli or Blake.

But laws, dogmas, philosophies, are not made for individuals. They are maps, guide-books, they cater for an average, for an abstract of man. And writers are individual persons or they are nothing.

How can a man, seeking his own way through the unique world of his individual experience, walk on the party line? He must be true to himself, or he will not give truth to others: the only truth he can give, his own experience.

The most brilliant Russian novelists of the new régime, men like Kataef, have long been suppressed. They were Communists but they could not stick to the Communist dogma. They were too individual, too sincere.

I hesitate to write about the Catholic novel, but I have heard both Mauriac and Graham Greene called heretical, by the orthodox of their faith.

It would not surprise me if this were true, because both have the power of men who write from the deepest conviction.

What of Claudel? He too has power and authority, and he is highly orthodox. But we are not suggesting that a sincere writer must be unorthodox. He may, like Tolstoy in *Anna*, choose the themes that are true both to his feeling and his creed.

Or he may be one of the lucky few whose creed, whose idea of life, long assimilated, has become the organising principle of his whole nature. Then, so far from being hampered by its machinery, he is enormously strengthened.

But even where ideas are in conflict with earliest impressions, and with each other, as in Dickens and Dostoevsky, and are assimilated, they do not frustrate the man. For they produce not contradiction, but conflict; and conflict is not a logical opposition, a deadlock never to be resolved; but a tension which has to be reckoned with, which must be revealed, which, so far from producing frustration and sterility, is a centre of force and power.

Les Nouvelles littéraires (11 August 1955), 1, 2—as 'Le Roman à thèse', translated by Christine Lalou. The text printed here is from a typescript among the Cary Papers in the Bodleian Library; its title has been provided by the editor.

Travels in a Mind

Every few months there is another book about Dickens, Poe, Melville, Tolstoy, analysing their complexes. How far did Dickens's horror of the blacking factory, where he was put to work as a child, affect his social attitude? Why was he so unhappy in marriage? What were his relations with his wife's sister Georgina who stayed to care for him when he turned his wife out? In the Tolstoys' fierce quarrels, who was right? The writers reveal everything, discuss every detail of misery and scandal. And at each new revelation there is an outcry from those who admire the victims and their work. They say, 'This is a racket to satisfy the demand for scandal under cover of literary criticism—and to make it pay.' But we do not hear the same complaints when historians write new lives of Washington, Lincoln, Cavour, Bismarck, Napoleon III. It is felt that they are justified in trying to draw the complete picture of men who have changed history. In fact, any man in politics can be regarded as fair game for the biographer, at least as soon as he is dead.

And public instinct is right. It is important for us to know what kind of men these were who gave themselves to public careers, who appealed for public interest and public support; people want to know everything possible about them, not only from base curiosity but to answer fundamental questions about the way they are governed. For, in the final resort, the problem of government is the problem of human nature; of men who are led, persuaded, ruled, and men who understand and practise the political art.

But it seems to me that public interest in the lives of such men as Dickens, Tolstoy, is just as reasonable. For these were men who appealed to the public interest, and profoundly affected the public mind. And no one should complain if the public wants to know what kind of people they were.

So far as a writer is a public man, he must take the consequences of being a public figure. He may complain while he is
alive, of libel or brutality; but his family, his readers, have no
right to complain, after his death, if biographers seek the whole
truth.

That is one side of the matter; the other is this, that these
enquiries into the lives of great writers are enormously valuable to pure psychology; to the understanding of our own
minds.

The psychiatrist, exploring a mind, asks for confession. But
he knows he will get, from most people, very little description
that is worth anything. He has to collect his evidence from
hints, from omissions. For few people have enough power of
verbal analysis, of description, to make sense of their own reactions. They certainly have not the genius of a Dickens, a Dostoevsky or Tolstoy, in handling words and characters. So that
great writers are better known to us, simply by self-revelation,
than our own closest friends, than ourselves.

It is not only in letters and diaries that novelists give themselves away, but in their books. They cannot help it, for if they
are writers of any quality, they write from conviction. They
are passionately concerned with the real world, with good and
evil, right and wrong. They create their characters to take part
in the world as they see it, and the characters, good and bad,
speak their opinions, and reveal their passions, their deepest
preoccupations. Dickens's villains, men like Squeers, the school-
master in *Nicholas Nickleby*, are drawn with the brilliance of
hatred, and they are punished with the fury of revenge. Dickens,
they say, could be a hard man, impatient, cruel. His heroines,
like Dora in *David Copperfield*, were the fancies of a man at
once dominating and sentimental; the typical he-man of a
modern paperback. He married a gentle, self-effacing woman
and, after she had had children, turned her out in favour of a
young mistress and a clever sister-in-law who knew all the art of
flattery.

But the real man is not in the biographies; he is in the books;
and in all the characters and scenes of the books. He laughs
at Mr Micawber, the feckless waster; he rages against Mr Skim-
pole, the parasite. He laughs at the law in *The Pickwick Papers*.

and his fierce attack on the Court of Chancery in *Bleak House* was a strong cause in reform of the law. The enormous variety and richness of the novels is due to the variety and richness, the contradictions, of Dickens's personality. When we read him we are brought into the presence of an extraordinary person, a great master, a great poet, a keen and ruthless man of business, a great dreamer. Everything in his nature is at the highest intensity. He is wildly sentimental, wildly funny; his miseries were suicidal, his delights were frantic. If he entertained, it had to be on the most magnificent scale; he hired a whole theatre for an amateur play. He dressed like a dandy and strutted like an actor from the old melodrama. His hatreds were as violent and bitter as his friendships were headlong. He dropped dead from his chair, in his fifties, completely worn out. But he had lived the lives of ten men.

The books are a rich experience, but how much richer when we know what lay behind them, in the life of a poor boy of genius, with his strung nerves, his fierce pride, his shame for his family, and his reactions from that shame, his longing for the dream wife, the dream house, where all should be love, peace, gentleness; and his raging, tearing life, where he seemed to fear more than anything else a moment's quiet; where he loved above all things to collect round him the largest possible and the noisiest crowd.

Was it really a paradox that he, a bad husband, an impatient father, expressed everywhere his scorn of Thackeray's cynicism? Thackeray, who was a devoted husband to his mad wife, a father who cared for nothing in the world more than the happiness of his two daughters, writes *Vanity Fair*, about selfish, scheming Becky Sharp who betrays her husband and neglects her child, about the silly Amelia who adores the snob and fool Osborne. Dickens, who turned his wife out and forbade his children to see her, fills his novels with devoted couples, united families. Even his comic families, his Micawbers, his Crummles, are patterns of domestic affection.

But Thackeray was a strong and wise man. When in his letters he describes himself as weak and procrastinating, we have the measure of his strength; in what he expected of himself. He saw and grimly accepted a treacherous and insecure world where indeed there were love and goodness, but no security for either.

Dickens, far greater in genius, as he was more nervous, more passionate, more sensitive, unbalanced sometimes almost to madness, could not accept Thackeray's world and hated to be reminded of its real existence. He had to live in his dreams, his personal melodrama, drugged with glory, in doses that had to be increased every year.

Tolstoy in *Anna Karenina* is not only Levin, the good man, who marries the good unselfish Kitty, but Vronsky, the guardsman who seduces Anna Karenina and brings her to suicide. Tolstoy himself was once a smart soldier who prided himself on his love affairs. That is why Vronsky is so well drawn, why we know him so well, why he can illuminate for us the whole mind of the smart guardsman.

But the account of the simple and honest Levin's love for Kitty, in the same book, is also the story of Tolstoy's love; the marriage of Levin and Kitty is Tolstoy's own marriage. He draws for us not only the bridegroom, overwhelmed with the sense of Kitty's goodness and innocence, of his responsibility to her, but the bride: and both from life—that is, from the inner life of their private emotions. He gives us Kitty as well as Levin.

Tolstoy stands in our imagination as a man with intense virility—he had thirteen children and, as late as his middle seventies, he complains in his diaries that sex will not leave him in peace. Yet in his books he is not only Vronsky, he is quite as much his women characters, Anna, Kitty, the wronged wife Darya.

But it seems to be precisely men of this intense maleness who also have the quickest sympathy with women. And not merely because, being strongly male, they are powerfully attracted by women, and so deeply interested in women's character; but because of something much deeper and stronger, because they have actually certain feminine perceptions.

Read, in *Anna Karenina*, the account of Darya's feelings when she catches her husband in a liaison with the governess; follow the whole course of the quarrel, her despair, and finally the reconciliation with her selfish, gay, good-natured Stepan. No one could have drawn the poor wife's mind who did not share, in some measure, a woman's feelings in her own woman's world.

Perhaps sex is by itself a universal quality, undifferentiated except by its embodiment, as wine takes the shape of its jug, but is still wine. So that men and women who have much of it have automatically more of what belongs to the other; and it is the very male men, the very female women, who most easily enter into each other's feelings.

This does not mean that such passionate and intuitive creatures are necessarily happy together. Tolstoy and his Countess, who loved each other so passionately, hated each other with equal violence. It was just because they each had such power of expression that their diaries give so moving and brilliant a picture of this marriage, so immensely happy, so passionate, so miserable from the time that the Count, already thirty-four, carried off his young bride, aged eighteen, in the four-horse coach which so delighted her childish imagination. And yet the diaries are nothing without the novels. For there we have the story in dramatic form, we actually take part in the quarrels, the jealousies that tortured them both. We are the bride and bridegroom, we live in their happiness, and that is something we cannot begin to get in a psychological textbook. For description, analysis, are not experience. They are in fact the opposite of experience. For while we are learning formulae, classifying data, we are cut off from the essential feeling. To take a building to pieces is not to understand its form, its nature.

Experience can only be known by experience, by feeling. It is only in a work of art, in memoirs, history, diaries, and especially in the novel, that we can feel and comprehend another soul. By 'soul' here I mean the character of mind and feeling which is the essential man; not his reason alone, or his emotional reactions alone, but his whole nature. And it is the whole nature which moves him. Men use their reason to satisfy their feelings, to make a world in which their affections and ambitions can be achieved, but since feelings cannot be understood by description, neither can their minds. The whole must be understood and experienced, as a whole.

Without a basic living experience we understand nothing, not even diaries and novels. But the novels can enormously extend and enrich that basic experience; as a great house can enlarge the appreciation of a village carpenter. And from novels we get something more than the immediate experience —a plot designed to mean something, an ordered psychology. We are presented there with characters in a world of meaning, we see cause and effect: Tolstoy says to us, 'See what happens to these people because of their natures, because of their actions. See what happens to a woman like Anna, sensitive, affectionate, intelligent, when she abandons her husband and child for a lover.'

We need not agree with Tolstoy's moral ideas, but they are common enough. There are millions of people who think with him that life should be simple, that luxury is a corruption, that a civilisation can grow too complex, and in growing complex that it becomes evil and forgets the true ends of life; that men and women each have their own essential functions in the world; that the woman's is to be a good wife and mother, to make a home for her husband and family, and that such a home is the highest achievement open to anyone, man or woman.

Such an idea of life may seem to us too narrow. We may ask what kind of homes a nation will have which has no great arts, no dreams, no adventures; the arts, dreams, which break homes, and bring complexity of life. Only a woman can make a home; but the most successful homes are those that breed the adventurous who go out from home.

Tolstoy was a dogmatic thinker, and he wrote with all the *a priori* prejudice of his arrogant and possessive nature. But because he was a great writer, because he had an extraordinary power of creating and revealing character, he can give us the experience of men and women working out a moral destiny; we feel that since they were such people, this would be their destiny. And this is a moral experience you cannot get anywhere except in a great novel.

Its very difference is important to us. It has been said that the best way to know one's own country is to travel abroad. For how can a deer know what woods are like unless, at least once, he can get out of the woods; how can a fish understand the sea, unless sometimes he goes flying?

This is true, and true not only for comparison of atmosphere, of elements. From Africa and India I brought unique experience

of people who, with exactly the same fundamental characteristics as myself, had formed completely different ideas of law,
of marriage, of religion; and, under the ruling of these ideas,
realised their lives with dignity, order, and meaning. But also,
and perhaps more importantly, I had a new revelation of the
possibilities in life, of a new intensity and richness of living till
then undiscovered to myself. In travelling abroad we learn to
know not only our own country but ourselves in a new relation.

But no foreign travel is so consistently exciting, rewarding, as
travels in a mind. And it is the unique quality of the great
writers that they throw their minds, their souls, wide open to our
exploration. They cannot help doing so. It is by revelation that
they live; they are obsessed with the understanding of people
and the world; and all the people are themselves, the world is
their own world.

Reading is both travel and escape. But it is travel that brings
one back to oneself; escape that takes one out of the familiar
and commonplace affairs of our everyday, to a place from which,
when we look back on them, they appear both new and strange,
and far from commonplace.

Holiday, XX (September 1956), 6, 8, 9—as 'Party of One'. The
title printed here is Cary's, from the typescript among the Cary
Papers in the Bodleian Library.

Including Mr Micawber

Every novelist is taught to make his characters as 'real' as possible, to attempt the illusion that his book deals with actual people. For the reader is an actual person; his living sympathies can be engaged only for another actual person or his simulacrum, and it is only by engaging his sympathies that he can be drawn into the tale and put through the experience which it is the writer's object to give him.

Therefore, we are told, a writer should study 'real' people and their ways; he should notice all those little points which distinguish A from B; he should avoid, at all costs, the type, the caricature. And this doctrine has instructed much modern criticism and most of the writing in the last forty years. Yet, when we read the critiques, and examine the novels which stick most closely to the rule, which should therefore be the most telling, we are left with the uneasy feeling that we have wasted our time.

We remember that Trollope despised Dickens for the exaggeration and falsity of his characters, but that Dickens is an immeasurably greater writer than Trollope; and that it is precisely Dickens's exaggerated and false characters who remain in our memory, who, as it is said, are 'immortal'. We are offered the paradox that 'unreal' characters are among the most effective in fiction and have a vitality that keeps them effective for generations.

What's more, we are obliged to notice that Trollope's most enduring Mrs Proudie has been blamed for being overdone, and that the heroes of almost every 'realistic' novel of the last forty years, so carefully drawn from life, so meticulously described and analysed in their smallest idiosyncrasies and related to their 'complexes', have utterly vanished from recollection. They have died on us so completely that we cannot even remember their names.

You may say, however, that this is not because of a 'realistic' conception of character but some inadequacy in the other parts of the work, and that we find among great writers plenty of 'realistic' characters who are also unforgettable. Admitted that Voltaire, Dickens, and Gogol gave us caricatures, that Pangloss, although he haunted us forever with his ruined nose, is a figment; yet Tolstoy, Aksakov, George Eliot, Hardy, Dreiser, James, give us most realistic portraits, unexaggerated, carefully differentiated.

This is quite true. Yet I declare that Hardy's Tess is not more 'real' to me as a living presence than Dostoevsky's Sonia in *Crime and Punishment* who is, on consideration, a mere angel dressed up as a prostitute. What is perhaps more illuminating is that, in the memory of one's imagination, Tess and Bathsheba, even Daisy Miller, take on the stature of figures in a Greek drama, larger than life.

A still more interesting question is the status of those characters who also live intensely to the mind but do not even pretend to be people, much less real. Consider the little Julia, in Melville's *Omoo*, and at least half a dozen of Conrad's ships; the mine in Zola's *Germinal*; the house in *The Fall of the House of Usher*. These are characters so active and permanent to us in their vitality that we have only to shut our eyes to see them— the dancing, dashing Julia, the terrific mine (I can never forget the writhing arms of its headstock as the creature goes into its death agony), the great grey house splitting open and sinking into the ground. If ever novelist achieved an effect, he made it with these symbols, and we notice at once that all of them are soaked in a moral idea. The Julia is gay Courage, the mine is Industry (the giant which grips both worker and capitalist in its iron claw), the House of Usher is Aristocracy in its last refinement of inbreeding and decay.

And it is obvious that Mr Micawber, and Raskolnikov, Sancho Panza and the Red Queen, belong to the same order of being; they are all moralities, compounds of moral qualities. They stay with us because their dilemmas and reactions have reference to our own. We feel with them not because they are differentiated and unique, but because they are, in some important aspect, ourselves.

It is often said that a great writer seems to reveal to us what we were in some dim and doubtful way aware of before. What I suggest is that Dickens often, even at his most extravagant, does just this; that Dostoevsky, when he draws for us his tortured nihilists, his half-crazy saints, opens to us regions of our own potentiality which we have passed by, as a man in his own house passes now and then the door of some forgotten attic, half aware that it is full of inherited relics that should be examined and put in order, that in it perhaps some richness is going to destruction by damp and rats; but too preoccupied by small worries, too guilty perhaps, or too nervous of what he may find, to venture in. Yet when it is opened for him, he finds there great parts of his own history, a light on his own nature; he is illuminated; he grasps a larger world because he has found a larger self.

And if all characters are in some sort ourselves (or how could they mean anything to us?), then there must be a common denominator of character. The individual must be a fractional compound of the universal, in various proportions. And the great writer is one who intuits fundamental elements of this basic nature and constructs his people out of them.

As for our 'real-er' characters—Tess, Anna Karenina, Daisy Miller—what I suggest, in view of this last consideration, is that they are also constructs, symbols, and that the only difference between them as 'real' characters and the 'caricatures' of Dickens or Dostoevsky is in the nature of the moral problem presented. They are symbolic of more subtle and complex situations. They are, in short, no more 'real' life than Jack and the Beanstalk, or Sloth and Evil Communications in the old monkish plays. Their reality is the reality of the philosophers. They are real because they belong to a world of permanent values; they are immortal because they are, in the strictest sense, members of eternity. The great men who invented them were moralists who had the art to make us feel in and through their reality the everlasting realities of the eternal world, which are ours too, by birth, and, only so, comprehensible to us.

I am not suggesting that James or Hardy sat down to put

characteristics together as a cook devises a pudding. The process, I dare say, was complex and largely intuitive. It was probably analogous to the activity of a poet describing a scene. Wordsworth's daffodils, as they exist for us, are a character from Wordsworth's imagination. However, their reality belongs to that region, and not to the botanists.

I shall now be charged, once more, with a reactionary plot to abolish modern literature and return to the puppet play of *Everyman*. Yet I have never been able to read *Everyman*. I find it too dull. And the charge itself is like saying that Cubists and Expressionists, in their revolt against Impressionism, tried to abolish scientific painting, the analysis of light, the division of colours, and go back to the primitive abstractions of Celtic or Mayan art.

If one wanted to argue such a point, one could say that modern people have had revealed to them a universe, both in science and politics, so much more strange and dangerous than any their fathers conceived of, that they are much more serious persons. And art has therefore turned, both in painting and literature, from Impressionism, the imitation of surfaces, to Expressionism, the exposition of meanings. I do not think this is true. I think art has never departed from the exposition of meanings; it cannot do so. For it deals in symbols which are nothing unless they carry meanings. And so the difference between the real character that remains with us as a powerful influence and the one that sinks away into nothingness almost as soon as it is known is in the force of the significance.

New York Times Book Review (15 April 1951), 4, 21.

The Period Novel

Certain novels have the reputation of being in the spirit of their period. These are not historical novels in the ordinary sense of the word. If we want to know something about the eighteenth century as it was to those who lived in it, we don't read Thackeray's *Esmond*, but Fielding, Smollett or Fanny Burney, and we get more of the atmosphere from Fanny Burney than from Jane Austen. In fact the best period novels are never by the greater writers. Compare Yonge's *Heir of Redclyffe* in 1853 with Trollope's *Warden* of the same year.

The Warden had a very small success compared with that of *The Heir*, a best-seller of its day, and for us *The Heir* brings us into an atmosphere so completely foreign as to seem fantastic. *The Warden* is a book which we completely understand—it engages our sympathies as Trollope meant them to be engaged. Yet, to understand the 1850s, *The Heir* is a far better book. It gives us the High Church angle, the High Church feeling in its full intensity. It is only by reading *The Heir* and books of this kind that we can understand the cruelties, as they now seem to us, inflicted on Victorian children. We read of Hare as a small boy when he was thought to be greedy being kept from his favourite pudding while everyone else at table was enjoying it. We read of penances and whippings, of terrifying sermons, and we are apt to imagine Victorian parents as a race of monsters. This, of course, is nonsense. Parents then were the same as they are now, good and bad, but for the most part affectionate, anxious, deeply concerned for their children. The great difference was in the nature of that concern and the character of education thought necessary for the child's welfare. In *The Heir* you get that intensity of religious feeling, and though *The Warden* is a book penetrated with religious feeling, it does not give us that intuition of difference.

We may remark, too, that *The Heir* was a best-seller and *The Warden* had very moderate sales. That is to say, *The Heir* was accepted by its own generation as valuable and true. It answered the feeling in that generation.

And the reason why, as I see it, *The Heir* is more revealing of its time than *The Warden* is precisely because Charlotte M. Yonge was a far lesser writer. She was a very good writer or she would not be as readable as she is today. But she was a simple person without much power of critical judgement and she accepted her time and its ideas as final truth. That is why she was a best-seller and why she is a good period novelist; far better than Trollope. In the same way Surtees in a book like *Sponge* is better than Trollope. He gives us a different picture from Yonge, of a different kind of life. But it is full of a coarse humour and a brutal judgement which we do not find in Trollope's picture of country life. For Surtees, too, the squires of his time were the perfection of manhood, and girls such as Belinda of *Handley Cross* or Lucy Glitters in *Mr Sponge*, the ideal women. It is from novels like this that we get the real character of a time. I don't mean that Trollope was not contemporary, that he was out of his period. That is impossible. I doubt if any writer has been able to stand outside his time. Scott's novels do not tell us much about the history of the '45, but a great deal about Scott's own mind and the Romantic Revival. Conrad in his stories of eastern voyages belongs profoundly to Europe of 1900. George Eliot in *Middlemarch* is as Victorian in spirit as Yonge, but she is read for what she tells us about our own days.

So Hardy in *Tess* or *Jude* was no less of his time than Kipling in *Plain Tales* or *Kim*. But we do not read Hardy or Conrad as we do Kipling and Wells for a light on their period.

George Eliot, Hardy, Conrad, the greater writers, though they were planted so firmly in their time, were bigger than their time. They stand out of it like towers from a fog, and their minds belong in general ideas, in fundamental judgement, to a universal sky. There is more between the Lady Murasaki in the tenth century and Madame de Lafayette in the seventeenth than between Henry James and his contemporary, Benson. Lady Murasaki and Madame de Lafayette were women of the great world with a strong and sober judgement of the characteristics which have always marked the good and the bad. Henry James, so deep in his period that already his books are classics of a time growing mysterious to us, yet brought to the particular situations of its special society a judgement grounded in universal truth. The typical period writer of his time, or any other, has no better criterion than the latest cliché, the newest label, which because it is new in time imagines itself to be final in truth.

Spectator (21 November 1952), 684.

The Tough World of Surtees

For a neglected master I hesitated between Peacock and Surtees.
I have chosen Surtees only because he is more misunderstood.
His special quality seems to be quite ignored. I dare say this is
because people think of him as a writer only for hunting
fanatics, and, in fact, *Handley Cross*, with all the adventures
of John Jorrocks, is a boring work. It was Surtees's *Pickwick*,
thrown together without any conception of form and with not
a trace of Dickens's genius for humorous character.

Dickens's wildest grotesques live in their own right; we do
not feel that Dickens has invented them; we shouldn't be surprised to meet them anywhere. Jorrocks is a mere invention
and in a vein of humour completely dead; that mid-Victorian
humour which astonishes us in mid-Victorian *Punch*. Who now
could read *Mrs Caudle's Curtain Lectures*, so famous in those
days? Jorrocks is in the same style. Even that episode, so often
quoted, where he is carousing with Pigg, the huntsman, and,
fearing a frost, asks him what the weather is like, has gone flat.
Pigg opens the cupboard door in mistake for the shutter and
answers, 'Hellish dark, and smells of cheese.' It won't really
bear repetition, as you see.

But Surtees after Jorrocks, like Dickens after Pickwick, did
acquire a form, and *Mr Sponge's Sporting Tour* is a masterpiece in its own way. It is the story of a crook. Sponge has an
arrangement with a horse-coper to take from him two thoroughly
dangerous horses and hunt them as his own in the hope of
selling them. He relies on his horsemanship to make them
behave. What is remarkable is the portrait not only of Sponge,
but of the whole society in which he moves.

It is an extraordinarily tough society, without any of that
self-consciousness which belongs to Hemingway's heroes. The
men are tough as a matter of course, yet they are by no

means cut to pattern. Look at that sporting nobleman Lord
Scamperdale, Master of the Flat Hat Hunt, and his toady Jack
Spraggon. Scamperdale is exceedingly tough. One realises in
him one puzzling feature of the Regency—how men of fine
manner and classical education could also be thugs, going out
to beat up aged watchmen for a joke.

Surtees was born in 1803, and so wrote some time after the
Regency, but its manner of thought survived in the country
among squires and especially in hard hunting circles for half
a century after the Regent. A nation does not grow up in one
piece. There are witches in Devonshire, and in many a farmhouse still when a man is dying they open the windows to let his
spirit out.

Surtees's England is a century away from us; its peasantry
are real peasantry and he describes them with the same fearless
honesty that he brings to all his writing. He called them usually
'Chaw-bacons'. They are a poverty-stricken and brutalised race;
he had no idea of romanticising his moujiks. You see them as
Goncharov saw his Zahar and Gogol his Petrushka, those two
valet-serfs.

I don't know anybody except Surtees who gives this picture,
or makes us feel so strongly what a good thing it is that in
England we don't any more have a peasantry. Surtees does
this without any political motive; he is not a propagandist;
we trust him absolutely. Of course, he gives his own picture;
he can't do anything else. *Mr Sponge* is contemporary with
Trollope's *The Warden*, and what different pictures it gives of a
different England; all authentic to a feeling of the time and all
complementary when we allow for the writer's purpose and pre-
occupation.

Surtees is brilliant not only with touts, lags and shysters, he
is a master at the snob and the climber. His social parasites are
inferior only to Thackeray's. In one respect he can be better
than Thackeray. Thackeray's Lord Steyne in *Vanity Fair* is a
common cad; compare him with Disraeli's Monmouth in
Coningsby. Steyne and Monmouth are both founded on the
real Lord Hertford, of that Hertford House where we now see
the Wallace Collection. Monmouth, in *Coningsby*, is as arrogant
and selfish as you like, a complete egotist, but he has the grand

style; he is not a vulgarian, and Surtees's Lord Scamperdale in
his quite different surroundings has the same quality. He is a
simple country squire without any of Monmouth's magnificence, but he is still as different from Steyne as that authentic
nobleman. He is a tough, but he does not smell of the gutter.

Probably Surtees owes this success to that observant eye and
candour of speech which is his chief force as a writer. He has
no cant of any kind; he is sucking up to nobody and no class.
He has his moral standards, but he is not trying to preach
them; there is none of that sense that we have, even in Trollope,
of the moraliser. Trollope's world and Trollope's moralising
were also typical of the time, but Surtees has in pre-eminence
that quality—which belongs also to Michael Scott, the author
of *Tom Cringle's Log* and another neglected master, not to
speak of Gogol—of the *describer*. He writes of what he sees
and knows, with a reckless sincerity especially refreshing in
these self-conscious times.

I should think it would be almost impossible to read *Sponge*
aloud; every second sentence has a broken back or tail, and the
grammar is a mine of howlers. Neither does the man get on
with the work. He stops at every corner, looks over every hedge.
He will take half a page to tell you what some minor character
is wearing, what he ate for breakfast. But this is just the charm
of the work. Even in the great masterpieces of formal art, like
Madame Bovary, or *Anna Karenina*, where the characters are
really alive, and we deeply feel for them, they have the inescapable defect of their perfection as parts of a whole. They are
made to measure. They are part of a grand drama and become,
as representative of fundamental passions and dilemmas, a good
deal larger than life; but they pay the penalty in a loss of
immediacy.

That's why Gogol's people come through so much more
vigorously than Tolstoy's, and why the diary writer, as a
recorder of life, real living life, can beat any novelist out of the
field. Pepys, Creevey, Greville, Kilvert after Tolstoy are like
street and farm noises after a symphony. No novelist can get
Kilvert's effects, where every detail is reported and we are looking at actual life.

But there are two kinds of novelists whose lack of form allows them a great deal of detail which is very close to reporting—which often, if we knew it, is almost certainly from direct observation. One is the slack novelist, filling out a chapter when he has run short of invention. Sergeant Bumptious in *Handley Cross* is such a piece of observation, and, for me at least, he is better than Dickens's Buzfuz, founded on the same real person, a certain Sergeant Bompas, renowned for bombast. Bumptious is a rougher sketch of a cruder man, but he jumps out of the page and the scene, while Buzfuz stays where he is put, as a comic character.

The other kind of novelist who achieves *real* real life is the picaresque—Le Sage, Gogol. *Gil Blas* and *Dead Souls* are full of people so real that if you put them into a novel of formal construction it would have to be built round them. As secondary characters, if you fitted them in at all, they would steal the stage.

Surtees is not only a slack novelist, in *Sponge* he is also picaresque. He's licensed to stop anywhere and describe anything, or anyone, from a country-house bedroom about 1850, with half a dozen different kinds of bath, to a spa dandy and his waistcoats. I defy any writer to beat Surtees on clothes. He gives us not only cut and colour, but fabric and quality, the very sewing. He takes a page to give us Sponge's hunting coat, with lapped seams on the outside, and it's not a word too much. That coat is more real to us than our own, for the good reason that it is not only an historic coat, but a moral coat. It expresses Surtees's moral idea, his hatred of sham, pretension, the shoddy in man or clothes, with a force all the more telling in that he is probably quite unaware of it. His eye is on the coat, which certainly existed, and even the fact that he likes it has to be inferred.

Like the true picaresque, he does not deal much in admiration. Sponge is a swindler without a single redeeming virtue except perhaps his clothes and his nerve. Surtees gave him the clothes as the proper equipment of a swell mobsman and also a superb horseman. He could not bear to dress such a horseman in anything but the best. But the clothes are almost the only virtue he allows him and only Surtees would think of clothes as a virtue. Even Sponge's courage is the worst of its kind, the desperate gamble of a con-man. He is not only a crook but a mean crook who will cheat a servant. Among Surtees's gallery of lags, touts and shysters he is surpassed only by Facey Romford in *Mr Facey Romford's Hounds*, who is an oaf as well as a crook and does not wash.

In this respect Gil Blas, even Gogol's Chichikov, is inferior to Sponge. He is done, in Henry James's phrase, to a turn. And this is Surtees's great virtue as a novelist. He never softens to a man; he never tries to catch a reader's sympathy for his worst, his meanest hero. He is objective to the last, like Flaubert, like Proust, and very unlike the later Thackeray.

It is again typical of the picaresque writer that his dialogue is so good. He is in no hurry to make it serve any purpose except the revelation of character. All Surtees is full of good dialogue in its special kind, like reported talk. Scamperdale and Spraggon are at their best in their smallest talk; it is as though we overheard them. We feel the very stuffiness of Scamperdale's den in their yawns and starts.

Surtees was himself a country squire from the deep North, the M.F.H. of a scratch pack. He had all the prejudices of his kind. He hated the fashionable places and people and smart society, he was suspicious of any kind of cleverness. He was prickly and hard, he had little compassion except for dogs and horses. He is pitiless to his victims. When Sponge and Spraggon unite to swindle and bully a wretched youth called Pacey, he records every detail of the latter's humiliation with the zest of loathing. Pacey was silly and weak and so despicable to him. Surtees prefers crooks to fools, because they are hard, because, as he thinks, they have no illusions.

Sponge is not a book for the sentimentalist, but for the man who likes to understand something of human nature in both its strength and weakness, especially in its power of creating, each man for himself, a complete ideal world, social and moral, and living in it.

Of Surtee's other novels, *Mr Facey Romford's Hounds* is not much inferior to *Sponge*, and Sponge reappears in it. The rest are tedious and flat to the general reader. To the social historian, on the other hand, they are of unique value. *Ask Mamma* and *Plain or Ringlets?* record mid-Victorian life as seen by a highly critical contemporary eye at a time when all the other novelists, even Thackeray, were sentimentalising it.

Surtees lived through the biggest social revolution in this country between 1066 and 1938. He was born into the Regency, Pierce Egan's London and the horse age; he describes the three days' journey from his home in Durham to London. He lived to see the railways everywhere, to travel as fast and easily as we do now, and to know a society for whom the Regency buck was not only a brute, but, more significantly, an aberration, a monster.

In Surtees's eyes, probably the most striking change was the beginning of the family holiday for the middle class; tens of thousands on the move instead of the few hundred who alone, before the railway age and the excursion train, had been able to afford to travel farther than the country town or the village fair. He records the more superficial consequences: spas crowded with husband-hunting girls and city fops, town-bred rich men playing squire and sportsman, usually, he tells us, with a typical twist of prejudice, in the wrong clothes.

What struck him was not only the complete change in the character of fashionable seaside places like Brighton, but in the manners of the visitors. The place set out to cater for the crowd, and the visitors had quite other notions of amusement than the Regency bucks and their Harriette Wilsons, for whom the seaside was simply an Alsatia in which they could live openly with mistresses who had to be more discreetly entertained in London.

Surtees had not loved the bucks, but he still more detested the mobs, which seemed to him all that was vulgar. No doubt they were. Newly prosperous and newly emancipated people usually are so. They keep the competitive habit of mind which has brought them up in the world and think of society in terms of rivalry. Especially on holiday among strangers they set out to impress. In these mid-century years leading up to the Great Exhibition all industry was booming and the whole country was full of new rich. Surtees describes them, in mass and in detail, with the particularity of his disgust. But he also jibes at the smart gentry, and in their despite makes a hero of the grocer Jorrocks.

He was the typical provincial Tory magistrate who values himself as a plain countryman and is, in fact, a much more complex and involuted, thin-skinned and incalculable, person than his compeer in general society who hunts with a smart pack; some genial snob like Apperley.

Mr Sponge's Sporting Tour is solid Surtees; he comes through in every line. The reason is that he has no idea of striking any kind of attitude. He has no self-consciousness, as man or writer. He is not afraid of anybody and rolls no logs. To read him is to escape for an hour or two from eyewash and cant into an atmosphere as brisk as one of his hunting mornings, sharp and raw, highly unflattering to everything in sight, faces, hedges, trees, nibbled pasture and greasy plough, but thoroughly bracing.

Sunday Times (14 April 1957), 8—in the series 'Great Writers Rediscovered'; reprinted, with minor changes, as 'Introduction', R. S. Surtees, *Mr Sponge's Sporting Tour* (World's Classics Edition), London, Oxford University Press (1958), pp. vii–xii.

III

The Heart of England

There are at least a dozen countrysides in England, that is, landscapes with qualities of ground, building, and crop as distinct as Maine from Texas. But probably the most famous nowadays, since their discovery in the last twenty years, is the Cotswolds. It has been said of these limestone hills in Middle England that they carry, packed together in about fifty miles square, more beauty of hill, wood, and farm, and especially of architecture, than any other area of the same size in the whole world.

Stratford-on-Avon to the north, Oxford on the east, Cirencester to the south, Gloucester and Tewkesbury on the west, with their great Norman churches, are boundary cities and themselves Cotswold towns. Oxford lies low, on clay, but it is full of Cotswold building, the honey-coloured stone which gives to the smallest village of the wolds its peculiar beauty. For the traveller from London, going west by north, Oxford is the best point of entry. The distance by road is under sixty miles, and from Oxford one mounts straight into the hills. They are not big hills; the highest, the famous Cleeve Cloud, near Cheltenham, is not much over a thousand feet. They are wolds or downs, with soft curving lines—all the better for the Cotswold landscape and the Cotswold explorer. For the roads are never steep and yet they carry one perpetually to some long summit from which one sees miles of the vale, with its hamlets, manor houses, towns, hedgerows, woods, and small winding brooks, laid out to the horizon, as in one of those Dutch pictures which are half topography in their careful detail, but more than half a keen enjoyment of the detail itself—the individual shape of every tree, cottage, field; each twist in the lanes. So that the total effect is not the accuracy of drawing, the skill of imitation,

but the affectionate sincerity of the artist, who loves every
shape, every turn, of his homeland.

I use this image with reason because the Cotswold country
is essentially a homeland; it has nothing grand, nothing to be
called a mountain or a gorge; nothing like a big river or forest.
Everything about it is delicate and gentle, it is full of small
streams, as clear and pretty as their names, Windrush, Coln,
Evenlode, which wind among small valleys with contours so
subtly modulated that the eye is never startled but perpetually
engaged. It is the chamber-music of landscape, a quartet where
the brook sings to the two-acre field, the cottage above is a
note that takes its meaning from both of them, and the whole
is enclosed by a sky shaped by a stone roof, a smoking Cotswold
chimney, a fan-edged clump of beech, and the long curving
lines of knolls that echo each other within this horizon like the
counterpoint of a fugue.

There are not even great houses here. There is but one palace,
at Blenheim, and Blenheim is not Cotswold, it does not belong,
even in name, to its village of Woodstock. Blenheim is a piece
of world history and world architecture, planted in a land
whose history is simply a tale of shepherds and farmers, of
woodmen and local masons, whose architecture, so characteristic, so unpretentious, so beautiful, so long enduring, has
grown out of the same fields and needs as the sheep. Take a
village like Burford, as I saw it last week just below the high
road to Cheltenham and Tewkesbury. It is a show-place, and
like most show-places it deserves to be shown, but like few show-
places it has not yet been spoilt by the tourist trade, or by the
bureaucrats and antiquarians who, once they get hold of anything fine, at once proceed to turn it into a museum-piece,
done up with concrete props and iron signs, for the approval of
archaeological professors.

Burford belongs where it is and nowhere else. Not only the
houses but most of the roofs are out of the local ground, they
are stone tiles from some local quarry. Burford grows out of its
valley as if the field walls, made to keep the beasts, had grown
a little in the course of time, to keep the men. And this is the
history of the place from the first hut of the Anglo-Saxon serf,
which also held the cows, pigs, and chickens, to the two-storey

cottage of Tudor times, when Burford grew rich, like other Cotswold towns, on wool. The manor-house again, rising a little higher still, seems the natural consequence of the same rising ambition which made the squire. The church, overtopping all, might be the temple of some Cotswold god. And that, in truth, is what it is, always has been, with its prayers for rain or good weather, its banns for country weddings, its harvest festival, its graveyard full of local names.

It is typical of this peaceful domestic land that church, manor-house and cottage should lie so close together. The Cotswold squire rarely chose to set up a lordly mansion in a park; he built close to his neighbours. And his manor is often not much bigger or more adorned than a farmhouse, as the farmhouse is simply an enlarged Cotswold cottage. Burford Church, for all its Norman tower, is essentially a wool church, built, you might say, by the Cotswold sheep.

The Cotswolds have always been a wool country. Their limestone pastures were good for fleece. English wool has been famous in Europe from Roman times, and the English Lord Chancellor still sits upon a sack of wool in memory of that rich trade. But it was not until the fourteenth century that the general improvement of commerce and transport enriched a whole new class of merchants and filled the Cotswolds with their manor-houses and churches. These fine churches, especially the later ones, with their high perpendicular towers, immense windows and delicate columns, have been called empty of true devotion, cold-hearted, the guilt offerings of rich men who knew how much they owed to luck. But it is quite as easy and truer to see in them the beginnings of the new European spirit, that change of mind which was doing its secret mysterious work long before the Reformation; to bring light and air into the fortress-jail which had been for so long the medieval idea of the only viable human society. And to call these churches cold is to forget the destruction done by Puritans, the smashing of the magnificent glass which filled the great windows, the whitewashing of painted walls, the tearing away of brasses. A modern critic complained to me that the great church at Cirencester was 'too fantastic', its famous two-storey porch was 'like a wedding cake'. But I think it rich and gay, and I don't see why gaiety should not have its religious moments as well as fear and self-abasement.

And these later centuries did not forget their mortality. Go to the Tanfield monument in Burford, the magnificent Renaissance tomb of Elizabeth's treasurer. It speaks of all the deference which then was claimed by the great officer of state, by all rulers and masters in that hieratic world; claimed and given. But if you look below the pompous figures in their robes, laid out as on a bed of state, you see a skeleton most delicately cut by the same sculptor, to remind you that even royal treasurers must die, that within the most stout and pompous body are the bones of a grave.

But it is a skeleton, not a rotting corpse eaten by rats, worms, and toads, such as you will find depicted in St Dunstan's Chapel, behind the high altar of Tewkesbury Abbey. The Renaissance let light even into the body of man. As its anatomists first made accurate reckoning of his bones, so its masons carved them for a trophy of his end, as clean in line, as sweet in touch, as the logic of their physicists. For them death was an event to be understood and ranged in the due order of its weight; not a horror to terrify.

Reconcilement is everywhere the local note. The Tanfield tomb stands in a church where Norman and Medieval live with each other and with it in the happiest confraternity. The Cotswolds, as they stand, are an unequalled record, in stone, of a history developing so consistently, so gradually, over thousands of years, that it is impossible to say of any point that here is where the centuries divide. You do not pass, as elsewhere, from Gothic to the Renaissance in one jump; you do not even get completely out of the Neolithic age, five or six thousand years ago, till the 1600s. Till then the Cotswold shepherds still used the underground sheep-folds built by their ancient British ancestors, with the dry walls, made without cement or lime, for which the Cotswold mason is still renowned.

You say of a cottage, a village, 'typical Gothic', and at once you see a door-hinge, a panelled chimney, which is as certainly Renaissance. One age slides into another, and makes a harmony, like history rendered by a single master spirit, growing with time but still in the same character. And that character is gentle, modest, domestic. What revealed itself elsewhere in the exuberance of mansions seized with a fever for the classical orders, rediscovered in Italy, is here seen only in the moulding of a doorway, the delicate pilasters of a house front, which belonged indeed to some millionaire merchant, but a Cotswold merchant ready, like William Grevel of Chipping Campden, to live among his fellow townsmen, in a dwelling no higher than many of their cottages and grand only in the solidity of its walls and the number of its rooms.

William Grevel, dead in 1401 and buried in the great church, is named on his epitaph, 'Flower of the wool merchants of all England,' and Chipping Campden is called the flower of Cotswold towns. It has certainly many fine things, the Market Hall, the church with its graceful tower, its many ancient brasses, the famous almshouses; but the whole effect is more important than any detail, and the effect is of a balance in society, a tempered ambition, a concord of work, of religion, of public office and private concern, which is the characteristic sense of all this middle land.

I thought to find some evidence of this sense of community by visiting a pub—not a tourist hotel but a real pub, preferably off the main road. There are hotels now in most of the towns, even in the larger villages, where the food is good and cheap; enormously improved even in the last twelve months. You won't find regional dishes, because there are none peculiar to the district, but the common English fare of roast, fried, and boiled, where excellence depends not on elaborate sauces but on the quality of materials. These are now better, in most places, than they were even before the war. But you don't go to a hotel for company, you go to the pub. As a friend of mine remarked the other day, in a pub, of a woman patron who sat talking steadily and confidentially to a neighbour, 'She thinks she's at a sherry party, which is meant for duets—she doesn't understand that pubs are for orchestral effects.' Everyone in a pub, certainly at the bar, is expected to play his part. So you get talk like this, as I had it one day in a wayside pub on the road to Chipping Campden.

The pub itself was a typical Cotswold cottage, or two cottages, with the mullions knocked out of one window, a Georgian bow patched on, and a gallows sign. There was also a new corrugated-iron garage at one end which, just after I came in, suddenly engaged the attention of the bar.

The talk before had concerned the fearful weather of the year, throughout Europe. A large, heavy man, with a purple face and bright-blue nose, in a heavy twill waistcoat, a man whose temper, at first sight, might have been guessed as steady rage modified only by fear of a stroke, was telling the company that he had lost half his hay and would be ruined for food that winter. His tone was loud and wrathful. But he added unexpectedly that the Danes and Germans had had it worse. And if it *was* worse, well then. He stopped at this mysterious point. But Alice the barmaid, a handsome woman of sixty or so, said unexpectedly, in the act of drawing my beer, that she knew what he meant, well, we were all in it together.

While we were pondering this suggestion, a sports car with a loud engine exploded up to the door, and a young man in a beret and that kind of suit affected by businessmen who drive sports cars, in grey check, at once a little too tight and a little too horsy, came bustling in. A commercial traveller or agent of some kind, who talked like a Londoner. He ordered a double whisky, looked round at us and remarked, 'I see you been making improvements since last year.'

His tone accused us all of some crime, and we waited. He took an angry pull at the whisky and exclaimed, 'That nice tin garage.'

'Ah,' said Alice. 'Well, there we are.'

'You get a real nice old place like this—the real genuine thing, and you jam a tin can up against it. All right, you know best.'

'Well,' said Alice, 'I see what you mean—but it's the price of building.'

'Price of building—that's the tale everywhere. And what's the place worth if you ruin it? You got something unique. Your only asset. And you proceed to chuck it away. All right. It's yours. Go ahead.'

'Garages,' said the farmer in the same reflective tone, so unexpected from a man of his violent aspect.

And again Alice seemed to understand him. She nodded and

murmured, 'Well—they're special, aren't they?'

'What I *might* have asked,' said the Londoner, 'is why you couldn't put it behind, out of sight. You got enough ground for half a dozen garages. But why should you? Who cares? Might ha' cost a few shillings more for gravel.'

A small labourer, in a corduroy waistcoat and canvas leggings, with a very small dirty cap on the extreme back of his head, now remarked, slowly and cautiously, in the tone which one uses to a dangerous dog, 'That's true, yes. But then ground can be awkward too—the wrong shape or in the wrong place.' This man had a dark brown face, which set off brilliant blue eyes, and a nose which I always think of as a medieval nose, thin, enormous, aquiline, shiny as a bird's beak. The man's whole look remined me of a picture in some old history of the battle of Crécy; he could have stood model for one of Edward III's long-bowmen—the tommyguns of those days. But he spoke with an air far removed from that extremity of cocksure violence which belongs to the medieval idea. 'That's as I see it,' he said. 'As I see it, you have to do what you can with what you got.'

'But I been behind,' said the Londoner, 'last year and year before. And there's plenty of room. Come off it. You people don't care, that's all about it.'

'There's room,' said the labourer, 'yes, but then there's the chickens.'

'Chickens,' said the Londoner, with a contemptuous fury that, for the moment, silenced the whole group. Up to now, they had taken the critic calmly—his view was one heard pretty often nowadays in the Cotswold country. A lot of visitors, who have suddenly gathered notions of aesthetic unity from some article in the evening paper, blow up about vandalism in the country. And often they are right. It is easy for one bungalow teahouse, one hoarding, to ruin the finest view. There is plenty of commercial exploitation in the worst taste, but, as it happens, very little in the Cotswolds, where councils and landlords have strong views on the matter. The danger there, up to now, has been from the other side, the pedantry that freezes growth, the vulgarity that builds a petrol-pump in Olde English style.

But the Londoner's cry came from the heart, he was really

shocked. It surprised and shocked the rest, unused to such extremes of feeling. The labourer, standing farther down the bar, cautiously turned his nose until he could bring both eyes to bear on the Londoner. The farmer, after long meditation, appealed to Alice: 'It's quite a problem, ain't it?' and he took a deep pull at his mug, that is, at the half-empty mug in his hand. For he had in front of him, apparently by custom, another full pint ready for use. 'Of course,' he said, 'you could put a bit of trellis on it—and some ramblers. Doll Perkins. She's a ramper.'

'Ah,' said Alice, 'that's an idea.'

'It's an idea,' said the labourer, 'but then—well—you know how tin rusts. Weeds along round the bottom.'

'You got me there,' the farmer agreed.

The Londoner made no response. He did not deign to argue with these oafs. He brooded over his whisky with his beret down to his eyebrows.

'The thing is,' said Alice in apology, 'it's just temporary.'

'I don't go for it—myself,' the farmer declared unexpectedly. 'Give me stone or concrete and make a real job of it. It pays in the end.'

'What about your Dutch barn?' said Alice.

'The way I see it, Dutch barns are different. A Dutch barn is a nice-looking thing—nice round top and those long legs.'

The Londoner, suddenly revived, ordered another whisky and blew up about Dutch barns and tin windmills, and I left them arguing or rather discussing the aesthetics of Dutch barns.

The Cotswold men were not prepared to argue; their keynote was Alice's 'I see what you mean,' uttered with a polite reserve which said plainly, 'But I have my own opinion too.' That is the art of discussion, to exchange opinions without offence, without that direct contradiction which kills talk.

My sympathy was with the farmer who defended his Dutch barn. The ancient Cotswold barns are famous even among the great barns of England, those vast stone buildings, with their magnificent timber roofs, which are found everywhere, often as the last relic of some great monastery. As big as churches, as solid as castles, and possessing also all that special beauty which belongs to things of primitive use, the plough that opens the field for grain, the mill that grinds it, the tools that man needs simply to keep himself and his family alive. English barns are better worth study than half the more pretentious buildings in the guidebooks.

Anyone who finds himself within reach of Bradford-on-Avon should go to see the tithe barn there. Probably, if he is interested in architecture, he will be looking for the Church of St Laurence, a Saxon work remarkable because it is the only complete stone church of pre-Conquest times. It is charming, it has the deceptive air of rustic innocence which goes with primitive construction. But the barn is a noble thing. And yet it is not so noble, so huge, so lofty, as that at Great Coxwell, near Faringdon, on the Oxford-Cheltenham road. This splendid work, built about 1250, is sixty yards long. It is on the edge of the Cotswolds but pure Cotswold in plan, in wall, and in roof, made of split-stone shingles from the ancient quarry of Stonesfield, near Witney.

Great Coxwell Barn is still a barn. After more than seven hundred years it is still serving its turn. You can't say this of the castles so elaborately cleaned up by the Board of Works, or the black-and-white cottages turned into Olde English tea shoppes in show-place villages. Coxwell Barn is not a vulgar fake, it has the dignity of every creature, man, horse or beast, that earns its living.

So have the Dutch barn and the silo, both made of corrugated iron in riveted strips. They fit in as harmoniously, as truly, with a traditional Cotswold farm and its stone walls as the car that takes the farmer to market or the tractor that ploughs his fields. For they belong to a deeper accord than the matching of styles, that of daily work and common need.

Even the railways fit in now. When they first came in, what an outcry from landowners, coach-builders, horse-breeders, and those who loved the beauty they knew, the unspoilt beauty, as they said, of the English land. Oxford at first refused a railway altogether. Finally it agreed to a station, provided that no train came nearer than a mile from the University.

Last spring I was upon an expedition to the fields near Oxford. We walked along the Thames below Godstow, on the towpath opposite Port Meadow, the great town common of Oxford, which is older even than the University, older than anyone knows. It was the town common before Edward the Confessor. The day was cloudy, with a gusty wind, but the town sailing-club was out on the river, here a broad slow stream between the great plain of the meadow and the towpath, lined with willows, hawthorns, and a row of enormous poplars. About twenty boats were out, beating up towards the lock at Godstow, running down at speed towards Medley Weir.

Behind their sails, all of the new Bermuda cut, the common with its three-hundred acres was still so yellow with buttercups that in the distance it looked like a field of ripe mustard. In hayfields the buttercups had disappeared behind the high grass, already in flower. But in Port Meadow the grass was still short—it is grazed. The freemen of Oxford have a right to pasture their beasts there, and there were two grazing herds at the moment, cows near the bridge-end and, far off, a drove of ponies, keeping close together. Cows and horses do not mix when they graze. As if by mutual consent they keep more or less a hundred yards apart.

By car, over the old hump-backed bridge at the Trout Inn, we were three miles from Oxford, by footpath probably not more than a mile. But the scene was deep country. The city, to the west, appeared only as a line of roofs and spires making an edge to the horizon: to the east, Binsey hamlet with its cluster of ancient cottages, its winding lanes, its little spireless church, its old graves, its stone floodwalk, half in ruins, its wishing-well, were half-hidden behind thickets of may trees in flower.

Colour everywhere was so intense that it would be hard to render it, or even believe it, in paint; intense even in its darker shades. The river was a deep lead-blue with, here and there, a bright glittering patch like lead that had been cut. Or rather, this deep dark blue reminded me of the blue I saw once, in some foundry, in a red-iron pot full of liquid metal; and the glittering streak was like silver fire.

Two swans, rising and falling in the curling waves of the last race, looked so white that they seemed to shine by an unnatural light coming from their feathers. The great level flat of green, the yellow streak on the horizon, the blue of the spires and towers in the city behind, light but not pale, seemed, in the same way, to be giving out rays and vibrations of colour.

And as we stood admiring, a train came along the far edge. We could not hear or see the engine, but its steam made a long white trail among the trees, a moving trail among those still colours, a lively white cloud below the immense grey clouds of the sky. And we all agreed that this was a crowning beauty; nothing was more right in this English landscape than the train. The very shapes of its steam, in its rounded masses, echoed the forms of the trees.

The railway that was an alien intruder has stayed to be friend and a native. Already I hear people lament that diesels are coming in and they will no longer see the steam puffing in gay white clouds among the trees. They see the diesel as a mere machine; the steam train is a part of the countryside. Turner painted it, we have grown up with it, it recalls to us our earliest exciting journeys, on holiday, on some visit to town for shopping and a play, the zoo or the conjurer.

A landscape is not only a gathering of objects, it is, like all beauty, a state of the mind. That is why we speak of living beauty and the dead things of the museum. The imagination can play about a mummy, or a wooden plough, the Wright brothers' aeroplane or a Viking ship, but these things are relics, they have been put aside by the rush, the tumult of new creation. And even among the relics, what touches us is the sign upon them of their use by living beings.

At Chedworth, near Cirencester, you can see the ruins of a Roman villa built about the year 180. Chedworth Villa is one of the finest in Britain, showing the whole plan of a Roman manor-house. Placed on a magnificent site high among the woods, it is built around three sides of a quadrangle, with bedrooms, public rooms and farm buildings, including a range of tanks as used by dyers, all clearly distinguished.

The dining-room has a fine floor of mosaic, warmed like the walls through hollow brick ducts. This central-heating system, conveying hot air through floors and walls, was probably more efficient, and certainly neater and cleaner, than the dust-collecting and wall-blackening radiator of today. The furnaces, still almost complete in the cellars, heated also the water for the elaborate bathrooms.

But what I found most revealing, most evocative, was the hollowed step from the sweat-chambers to the cooling-room and the cold plunge, the rounded steps of the plunge itself, worn down by bare feet and bare bodies over centuries of use while this pioneer house of the second century became an old mansion full of the memories of a long past, enriched by the marriages, the child-bearing and the rearing, the anxieties, the struggles and griefs, the triumphs and the deaths, of eight or ten generations.

Looking at those steps I could hear the housewife of A.D. 400 saying to her husband, 'My dear, the bathroom steps are really a disgrace. I know they come down from old times and of course I agree that it would be a crime to spoil this ancient place with cheap modern gadgets. But this is a question of safety. Some day one of the children will slip and break an ankle.'

To the Roman-Britons of 400, as highly civilised as any people in the world today, it was difficult to imagine the destruction of their whole world by savages so brutal that they could not find a use even for the crafts of the land they overran, much less its comforts. Or that a thousand years and more would follow while those crafts were painfully recovered, the comforts only partly restored.

Even now, the Cotswold manor-house, as we know it, has barely climbed back to the standards of its ancestor in the time of the Caesars. The earliest settlers at Chedworth, under Marcus Aurelius, would probably have reason to complain, in a Cotswold winter, of today's heating; they would find the modern bathroom primitive beside their sweat-chambers and cold plunges. But they would recognise the building at first sight for Cotswold work, like their own.

Chedworth Villa is off the main roads, but it is reached easily from Cirencester or Cheltenham. Anyone who wants to feel the long reach of family life through time, the persistence of the Cotswold type, should go to see it. A museum-piece maybe, but look at the bathroom steps and it will come alive.

There must be museums to preserve the unique fragile thing, and matter for scholars; but preservation itself, the setting aside from the wear, the changes of a living world, kills it as dead as a butterfly on a pin. The moment some council or department sets out to preserve, to fix a village on a point of time, to polish up its old walls, cut all the weeds, bury all the rubbish, paint all the doors, mend all the roofs, banish corrugated-iron and hide the petrol-pumps behind thatch, the place begins to die— it will soon be a painted corpse. That's why I liked the tin garage, and why I like the Dutch barn, among the old buildings of a Cotswold farm. They are proof that, like Great Coxwell Barn, the farm is still doing its proper work in the world, that it is still alive.

And you can say that—at least for the present—of all the Cotswold country: it is a living community. Go off the main roads almost anywhere and you find hamlets that have never seen a tourist bus and do not want to. And there are few of them without some special beauty. There is no countryside so rich in the unexpected, from the dovecot at Naunton in the Windrush Valley, to the bridges of Bourton-on-the-Water, and the hundred monuments in village churches. I suppose no one has given even a few days to the exploration of the Cotswold byways who has not seen many fine and delightful things, un-recorded in the books and unrecommended by any guide. Yet the whole area is so compact that it can be compassed easily in a single day.

Last week I went driving with a friend to see Tewkesbury Abbey. We left Oxford after eleven and were back by six. Yet we did not hurry and never had any sense of hurry. We went out to see one thing well and take our time by the way. We travelled by Witney on the Cheltenham road, by Burford, Northleach with its splendid church, Cheltenham, which we explored for its Regency façades, past Deerhurst with its Saxon tower, to the Abbey. And after we had seen all there, we still had plenty of time for a visit to Gloucester Cathedral, in order to confirm our suspicion that its nave was finer than the Abbey's, and to come back by Cirencester, Fairford, and Faringdon.

On the way out we turned aside over the old toll-bridge at Swinbrook to see the Minster Lovell and its ruined manor, lunched on the grass at the roadside, and even had time to stop at an inn nearby for beer and conversation.

The day was as good as a month's holiday for it had, in concentrated form, all the essentials of holiday—boundless leisure, because we had too much time, complete peace, because it did not matter what we did with it, and above all, escape, the only true escape, which is from one occupation to another. For we were never without something of new interest to see, to discuss, to enjoy. And we had always our objective to make sense of the whole enterprise—Tewkesbury and its chantries.

Psychologists may tell us, probably wrongly, why the miniature thing, the model, the doll's house, the lamb, the kitten, has such fascination, but for me, none of these is so charming as the miniature church known as a chantry. Though it is but ten or fifteen feet high instead of a hundred, and holds a total congregation of half a dozen, it is not a toy. On the contrary, it is a place of special use and devotion. It is also, to the architect and mason, an opportunity which they have used to the limit. Since they have no weather to fear, no heavy lead roof to think of, they can indulge every fantastic dream, carve canopies like lace, make pinnacles as tall as the whole nave below.

In Tewkesbury Abbey you will find a work that always seems to me the most beautiful and fantastic, the most moving of all: the chantry built for the Lord Despenser who died in 1375, that Masses might be sung there forever for the repose of his soul.

The chantry is on the south side of the Abbey, but if you cross over to the opposite side and look at it from there, you will see that it carries on its roof another, smaller chantry, probably the smallest, and for its size the tallest, in existence. It consists of a single crocketed spire and it has room for only one worshipper, Edward Lord Despenser himself, in full armour and painted surcoat, kneeling there, century after century, with his face to the high altar.

Tewkesbury is a famous abbey, its western arch is over sixty feet high, its tower is called the finest Norman tower in England, its Norman nave has that massive dignity which belongs only to the high plain columns of the Romanesque, but this Despenser chapel is the treasure of the place. It is also in perfect accord with the Cotswold land, and the Cotswold imagination which has expressed there, over a few hundred square miles of rolling Midland landscape, an idea of life centred steadily upon the simple and permanent needs of human souls, to work, to love, to pray, to know and achieve some dignity of existence, to find some goodness, some beauty in which man can be renewed in the experience of fundamental truth.

These hundred or so villages and hamlets so rich and various in grace, so perfectly in harmony with themselves and with their surrounding fields, have avoided the loud and pretentious by actual intent. They are the masterpieces, produced in all innocence, of home-loving, house-proud people, of neighbours in a workaday world where every class has for centuries not only understood its duty to, and dependence on, the rest, but seen it in everyday practice; where the cottage is next-door to the manor-house, and the manor to the church, where the ricks of the farmyard, full of the new grain, throw their shadows on the churchyard, full of farmers' graves. And the effect is not the *memento mori* of that Tewkesbury corpse, built by some fanatic obsessed with the terror of life and disgust of the flesh, but a calm and tolerant acceptance of a fact neither good nor bad, that dying is as much a part of man's fate as the family love, the daily achievement, which makes his life worth living.

Everywhere about this countryside, one is wholly, confidently assured that these countrymen, for over a thousand years, knew how to live as well as to die. You may say they were wanting in grand ambition and the showmanship that goes with it, there was nothing Napoleonic about them. But Napoleons come only by violence, revolution, and general misery. Change in the Cotswolds has been too slow and peaceful for Napoleons. They had their William Grevels instead, who knew what to ask of the intense, deep Cotswold life and had, for answer, a Cotswold fulfilment.

Holiday, XVII (January 1955), 27, 28, 30, 76, 78, 79, 81.

Westminster Abbey

If a visitor had only two hours for all London, I should tell him, go direct to Westminster. There he will find, within a few yards of ground on the banks of the Thames, the Houses of Parliament with all their recollections for the history of democracy, Westminster Hall, chief court of England, and the great Abbey which records and illuminates so vividly the growth and revolutions of freedom through a thousand years.

I went into the Abbey yesterday by the little door that leads to Poets' Corner. The path to it runs from old Palace Yard. You find it by turning your back on the Houses of Parliament and the Thames, and going under one of the great flying buttresses which support the Chapter House.

My first visit to the Abbey was about sixty years ago, as a child, and I have been there often enough since, but on this occasion I was struck for the first time by the really bizarre contrast between the magnificent nave, which is pure early Gothic throughout, and the confused mass of statuary that covers the lower walls and floor.

The reason why I was so strongly and immediately impressed by this violent clash was the remark of an American friend. I had told him I was to write this article and asked him what had struck him most forcibly at the Abbey, and he answered unexpectedly that he had found it all mixed up.

And now I saw very much what he meant. The Abbey, for instance, is completely different in effect from the Pantheon in Paris, with its ordered dignity, its carefully selected and arranged memorials. It was not built or set aside as a memorial church, it was simply an Abbey church where anyone could be buried by leave of the Dean. And the Dean of Westminster still has sole power to decide who shall be buried there. In 1824, the Dean of that day refused Lord Byron.

There is not even so much order in the tombs as a stranger
expects. He has heard that the poets have their corner; that
scientists like Darwin, Wallace, Joule, Huxley, are together;
that the North Aisle of the Choir is called the Musicians'
Aisle, with the graves of Purcell, Blow, Gibbons; that St Edward
the Confessor lies in his Chapel surrounded by kings and queens.
But he finds Crusaders and soldiers among the poets. Handel
is not with the musicians; his grave slab is next to Dickens,
in Poets' Corner, and on his other side lies a General Campbell
who fought in the Indian wars.

Still more strangely, you find here, within a few feet of Brown-
ing, one Thomas Parr, an ancient Shropshire farm-worker who
claimed to be 152 years old. He died on his first visit to London
in 1635.

A Crusader lies in the pavement beneath Dryden's bust. He
was murdered in the Abbey, where he had taken sanctuary.
And the Abbey was closed for four months until it could be
reconsecrated and confirmed once more in its rights of sanctuary.

It seems to me now that this very mix-up gives the Abbey its
unique quality. How that Crusader, murdered in some savage
political struggle, gives depth and meaning to the names of
poets and novelists about him. Here is the life they wrote about,
breaking in among the cold records of their fame and affirming
its own tragic magnificence.

Not all the tragedies of the Abbey are magnificent, or even
dignified. Everywhere you see the tragicomedy of fame itself,
which so often comes by luck and disappears by a change of
taste; which is no more secure than a soldier's life and does not
make so picturesque a death. Who hears nowadays, except professors, of playwright Shadwell, or even of Prior, whose drawing-
room verses amused the courtiers of William III? But Prior's
monument, in Poets' Corner, is the biggest of all. It over-tops
Chaucer, Shakespeare, Milton; it weighs perhaps fifty tons of
stone, while Thomas Hardy's heart lies under a single slab two
feet square.

The variety of monuments in the Abbey gives richness not
only of fancy and art but of feeling. Read some of the epitaphs;

this in Poets' Corner to Gay, who wrote those brilliant satirical farces, *The Beggar's Opera* and *Polly*:

> Here lie the ashes of Mr. John Gay, the warmest
> friend, the gentlest companion, the most
> benevolent of men; who maintained independency
> in low circumstances of fortune, integrity in
> the midst of a corrupt age, and that equal
> serenity of mind, which conscious goodness alone
> can give, through the whole course of his life.

And this from the magnificent tomb of the Duke of New-castle in the North Transept: 'The loyall Duke of Newcastle and his Dutchess.' What pride and humility in that 'loyall'. The duke spent a fortune in defence of Charles I, and went into exile at his sovereign's death.

And on the tomb of Anastasia, Countess of Kerry, at the end of the North Transept, we read her husband's testimony of gratitude to her:

> ...hoping that his merciful God will consider
> the severe blow which it has pleased his divine
> will to inflict upon him, in taking from him the
> dearest, the most beloved, the most charming, and
> the most faithful, affectionate companion that
> ever blessed man ... as an expiation of his
> past offences.

But the great Abbey is not simply a pantheon for the great and famous. It is full of simple memorials to people whose only claim to remembrance is that their names are recorded there. Here are a few words of one from the Cloisters, recording that Albany Charles Wallis was drowned at thirteen, 'being his father's only hope'. What heartbreak comes down to us still in these words.

And from the dozens of inscriptions to local tradesmen, servants or churchmen: 'Elizabeth Atkinson, body laundress to Queen Anne.'

And from the Cloister pavement: 'Here lyes the body of Philip Clark, plumber to this collegiate church, 1707, in the forty-third year of his reign.'

The Unknown Warrior's grave lies just inside the great West door, between the towers of the West Front. He represents a million British dead in the 1914-18 war. He is a powerful symbol, but the power is in the fact of his mystery. As symbol he is more than any man, but for that reason he is less than a person. The unknown soldier does not represent for me the real people, who still have names if only on the Abbey wall, whose lives, whose tragedies, were so ordinary, so unglamorous, so much in the common run of lives and fates, that they are forgotten, except here, in the Church of the British people.

And there is a particular fitness in their memorial. For the church has suffered along with them, through a thousand years of history, the same common fate: virtually every kind of accident, neglect, sudden glory, and undeserved outrage, the magnificence of coronations, the grand robberies of kings, of petty crooks; the spite of fanatics.

St Edward the Confessor, whose Chapel is still the centre of the church, whose shrine was a place of pilgrimage throughout the Middle Ages, was robbed by Henry VIII at the dissolution of the monasteries in 1539, and again by the Puritans. You can still see the structure of the shrine, but it is a shell. Yet how much more telling is this ruin than the splendour of Henry VII's tomb, in the middle of his lovely Chapel. The world has robbed its saint. It has always robbed its saints. But how little the saint needs the magnificence, the gilt bronze of Henry's monument, which brings crowds from all the world to admire a renowned masterpiece of the Renaissance—but only the masterpiece. Without his tomb, Henry would be forgotten except in the history books. Amid the wreck of his shrine, Edward is still more nobly the king of our imagination.

Whatever space of time you allot to the Abbey, spare at least some minutes for the museum in the undercroft. This crypt, the last surviving fragment of the Confessor's Abbey, is itself beautiful. But no one who has not seen them can imagine the effect of the effigies that stand there. These were the figures made in old times for the funerals of kings and great persons. And made to the life.

Here is Charles II as you might have met him in the street; and the famous Duchess of Richmond, his mistress, La Belle

Stuart. I do not know anywhere a more telling portrait of a great courtesan than this, in all the form and colour of life, with its arrogant pose, the mischievous smile, at once aloof and provocative, of the conquering beauty. She wears her own dress, as made for her in life; even to the underclothes and the stockings, two pairs, one of silk, one of wool.

Here, too, is the wooden effigy of that queen who makes so charming an appearance in Shakespeare's *Henry V*—Katherine of Valois, daughter of the French king, married to Henry V in 1420. Her life was not charming. She died in childbed at Bermondsey Abbey, where she had taken sanctuary from political enemies, and this figure faithfully reveals the sufferings of a woman still young and lovely.

Her tragedy did not end with her life. She was buried in the old Lady Chapel. And when it was pulled down to make way for Henry VII's magnificent new building, her coffin was placed beside the tomb of Henry V. No doubt the intention was to find her a new grave. But for two hundred years nothing was done about it and she lay in the open. The coffin rotted and every casual visitor could look at the mummified body within. Pepys, the diarist, in 1669 was allowed 'by particular favour' to take up the lid, and he writes, 'I had the upper part of her body in my hands, and I did kiss her mouth; reflecting upon it that I did kiss a Queene, and that this was my birthday thirty-six years old.'

One might despise Pepys for such an act of silly and mean brutality. But the queen, poor woman, if she could have seen her body exposed helpless to this fat-bellied busy little go-getter, what would she have cared? It was not she who was diminished, but little Pepys. Her tragic dignity was beyond insult.

Pepys's life was easy and prosperous. He enjoyed his profession, his whores, his books, and his success. She was a princess born to be a queen; and destined from childhood to be a pawn in high politics. She loved her second husband, the Welsh squire, Owen Tudor; but he was taken from her and ended on the scaffold.

Royal history is a tale of high tragedy from first to last. And it is these royal tombs of Westminster which give it most significance. Kings and queens are, for the most part, ordinary people;

genius is as rare among them as in any simple family. But they are called by destiny to a work which is the hardest, the most demanding, and the least rewarded, in the world. They are condemned for the least mistake and receive no thanks for a lifetime of duty. They are exposed to the impertinences of every fool, bore, and crank, without right of self-defence, and a good proportion of them are murdered.

How lonely these kings seem even now, in their tombs in Westminster Abbey among the statesmen who, by one lucky turn or another, achieved the triumph of office; the scientists who were permitted to spend quiet and peaceful lives in some chosen research; the poets who could follow their dreams.

Here is Henry III, chief rebuilder of this splendid Abbey; he died bankrupt and despised. Here is Richard II, deposed and starved to death by his rival. Here, in one small stone box at the east side of Henry VII's Chapel, are the bones of Edward V and his brother Richard, the royal children murdered by their uncle Richard III. Mary, Queen of Scots, beheaded in 1587, lies in Henry VII's Chapel; and opposite her, in one grave, Elizabeth, the queen who could not marry because marriage for her was a political impossibility, and her sister, who imprisoned her, and who died in despair, hated by her subjects.

Here, too, is Saint Edward in his ruined shrine. And Katherine of Valois: political wife, political widow, political refugee.

These kings and queens do not belong among that crowd of star-blessed notables that crowd the aisles of their magnificent Abbey; they are with the mass of those ordinary humble people whose fate is to endure a narrow destiny as chance has dealt it to them; with such as old Parr, Elizabeth Atkinson the laundress, and Philip Clark, 'plummer to this collegiate church'.

The Abbey is a mix-up of values as well as reputations. But for me it is just this mix-up, brought in from the living world and its conflicts, that gives Westminster the very richness of life and makes of it the most fascinating, the most touching, of all London sights.

Holiday, XIX (April 1956), 62, 63.

Britain's Liberal Influence

Britain is profoundly a liberal state. Its dominating mind has been liberal for more than a century. This liberalism had a long and complex history; extending far back into the Middle Ages. But as we know it today it has two main sources: the Protestant tradition, and the Whig revolution of 1688 with its ideals of toleration and individual right.

The Protestant tradition is part of the Christian tradition of Europe. It should be noted that the Catholic church was itself a source of liberal opinions long before the Reformation. It was for centuries the only house of learning; and it offered to men of learning, men of a reflective turn, the only secure refuge open to them. It was also the nursing mother of saints.

Men of learning are essentially explorers and discoverers; they live, despite themselves, in a free world of the mind. True, they may attempt to make their discoveries, their reflections, agree with dogma; they often succeed, like Aquinas, in doing so. But in the very act, they breed the spirit of enquiry; the methodology of the critic.

It is safe to say that Aquinas has fathered more heretics than bishops. And the church taught Christ; charity between man and man; the forgiveness of sins; the love of one's neighbour; and even tolerance. The story of Martha and Mary is a reproof to the legalist. And it was the saints of the church like St Francis, the poor friar, who first taught charity for the poor and dispossessed; who founded hospitals, nursing orders, things unknown in the rest of the world.

Many of the saints have been an embarrassment to the church. They denounced her wealth and criticised her government. They became heretics and went to the fire. But the church, however rich and conservative, still preached Christ; and the revolutionary Christ of the Bible, the man who rebelled against the Pharisees, again and again escaped from their control and turned upon them.

Wycliffe, in England, the first English reformer, was born in 1320 and became Master of Balliol College, Oxford, about 1356. He was a famous scholastic and based his criticism of trans-substantiation on Aquinas's own doctrine of substance and accident. He translated the Bible into English, the first English Bible, and proclaimed it as the supreme authority in all moral and religious questions.

This, of course, was a direct challenge to the tradition of the Catholic church. It was an appeal from the church to Christ. And the church at once recognised the danger and denounced Wycliffe.

Wycliffe's writings reached Bohemia and were the inspiration of the Hussites. His influence died down in England. But his rebellion followed a pattern repeated throughout the history of every Christian church; not only that of the mother church. The faithful and devoted servant of the church, brought up to love Christ, revolts from the church in the name of Christ. Thus one of the most conservative institutions known to man breeds continually the most extreme revolutionaries.

This of course is true of all churches. The Anglican church has produced plenty of schismatics, and in the early days these were extreme not only in religion but in politics.

The church of Laud, in the early seventeenth century, begot the anarchist and republican sects which killed the King, and afterwards fought Cromwell. But Laud's church was founded in the old principle of one church, one state. It was oppressive and intolerant. And it is a truism to say that one tyranny begets another. The Bourbon monarchy begot Robespierre and Napoleon; the Czardom begot Stalin.

It was the good fortune of England that she escaped early from this conflict of absolutes. I am not going to argue whether this escape was more due to luck or to an early development of parliamentary institutions which were, by their very nature, inclined to set up the law against the king. And that law a constitutional law securing certain rights to the estates of the realm. For the existence of the parliamentary tradition was itself a lucky fact.

But the certain fact is that it was the revolution of 1688, conducted so politely, without a life lost, that was decisive in English history. It established toleration as a principle, and asserted the rights of the people.

Locke's famous *Epistola de Tolerantia* was actually published in Holland, in 1685; his *Two Treatises on Government* some time later. The treatises, asserting 'the ultimate sovereignty of the people', were intended to 'establish the throne of our great restorer, the present King William; to make good his title in the consent of the people'.

This William III, of Orange, had, of course, no legal right to the throne. His grandfather was Charles I of England and he had married his first cousin Mary, daughter of James II; but he was not the heir. He was merely the nearest Protestant of royal blood available to the revolutionary party.

Locke's treatise has been described simply as a party pamphlet meant to secure the revolutionary Whigs in power. And it could be said that religious liberty in England, like her free institutions, arose so early simply by chance, and not from any wise far-sighted principle. It was, for instance, a Catholic bigot, James II, who forced upon an unwilling people the first act of toleration, in the interests of his own Catholic minority.

No doubt there was luck in this event; but it was not all luck. James II seems to have had a true belief in toleration as a principle and Locke was a liberal philosopher who had learnt much from Spinoza during a long exile. His friends were philosophers who looked far beyond the immediate political settlement. They were truly concerned to establish general principles of government.

And it is difficult to say, in the long run, and in the confusion of actual politics, whether the practical consequence of the settlement, or the indirect working of the theory, has been the more important. The theory has produced in every generation, not only in England but in Europe, convinced liberals. The settlement established the freedom of religion, with the unforeseen result that dissenting bodies since have rarely taken the extreme revolutionary position, that there has never been, in England, a strong anti-clerical or atheist movement, and that the Protestant monarchy has survived to give still a unique rallying point of sentiment to the whole commonwealth; a sentiment which is itself as much religious, in the largest sense of the word, as patriotic.

True, the revolution of 1688 was not democratic. Those who describe it as the successful plot of a few great peers, to seize the chief power and diminish the king, are, on the face of things, perfectly right.

But though its main purpose, undoubtedly, was to secure the liberties and power of the Whig lords, who kept power for almost a century and a half, their party cry was still civil and religious liberty; and just as the old conservative church of Rome bred prophets of free thought, so the aristocratic party of the old Whigs produced continually apostles of democracy.

And the party had still its idealists, its philosophers, like the great Burke, who sincerely loved justice and liberty; not only the liberties of the English people, but those of America.

It was here that the classical tradition had its effect. The Whigs, always at war with the king and his party, loved to quote the Roman Republic as their example. Burke's own adored master was Cicero, whom he studied throughout his life. Byron's theory of liberty was thoroughly classical, republican and Whig.

The Whigs were not democrats. Indeed they despised the masses. But the Reform Bill of 1832, the second great revolution in British history, which did open the way to democratic government, was a Whig measure, proposed by a Whig aristocrat and founded in the ancient tradition of the people's rights. The theory of Locke had at last produced its logical fruit, power to the people.

This power was not as yet very extensive. The Liberal Party, first known by that name in the early 'thirties, represented the new middle class of manufacturers; but it contained, from the beginning, radicals who truly sought the welfare of the masses. Palmerston, during his long life and long office as Foreign Minister, was a typical Whig: a great landowner, a steady enemy of the court party, a convinced supporter of colonial emancipation in the Empire and of every liberal movement in Europe. But it was a radical, Lord Durham, who gave Canada representative government; who is the chief founder of British colonial policy, in establishing the daughter states which now form the British Commonwealth.

Durham demanded the widest extension of the franchise and was hated by the old Whigs as an extremist and a demagogue. He was in front of his time; but not very much so. There was now a permanent demand for votes by all who had not yet got them, and every new franchise bill meant a further devolution of power. Parliament became steadily more democratic; until, in this century, the Liberals were displaced by the Socialists with their programme for free social services, the abolition of poverty, redistribution of wealth; in short, the Welfare State.

This immense extension of government control, and the bureaucracy required by the new service, is already causing anxiety to those who believe in liberty. But it has not yet restricted liberty in any important degree; and the Socialist Party have lately gone back from the extreme policy of nationalisation as advocated by Shaw and the Webbs.

It is, at present, still a liberal party; while the Conservatives, having accepted the Welfare State, are no longer, in the old sense of the word, reactionary. They have absorbed at least half of the old Liberal Party vote and all their younger ministers are liberals, in their public pronouncements. British government, at the moment, is perhaps more strongly liberal than at any time in its history.

What has been the influence of this history in the world? During the eighteenth century, it was the fashion for liberals abroad, such as Voltaire and the Encyclopaedists, to admire the English constitution as the model of a free state.

That constitution was misunderstood. Attempts to reproduce it, with various local adjustments, in the United States, France, Germany, and Italy, always had unexpected and disconcerting results. Constitutions cannot be transplanted; the most important effect of English Whiggism on Europe was simply in its inspiration of liberals everywhere who were able to say, 'In Britain there is religious toleration, liberty of thought, and publication, and yet Britain is a prosperous and formidable nation.' In the next century, the policy of the old Whig Palmerston, in power down to his death in 1865, was to support everywhere the liberal and the liberator against absolute power.

These filibusters disgusted the orthodox conservatives of Europe. For Metternich, for the Czar Nicholas, the British were anarchists who were tearing Europe to pieces. But the British saw themselves not only as liberators, but as the one reasonable people in Europe. For them, absolutism, repression, were supreme follies which perpetuated disorder.

I am not going to say that they were right. I do not suggest that the wars which have done such enormous damage to Europe might have been avoided by a more liberal policy in Russia, Germany, France, Spain. The political state of Europe in the nineteenth century was far too complex for anyone to dare such a judgement even now. It was far more complex than English liberals supposed. They were often naïve, almost as naïve as such great Russians as Herzen and Tolstoy, in their political assumptions.

They did not realise that votes and popular assemblies are not the cure for every political and social ill; that they do not even begin to cure ignorance, and that they are very likely to increase poverty. Democracy is not a constitution, it is a state of affairs; the end product of a long process of industrial and social development. It is a balance of powers between forces all capable of fighting the central government; but held in some kind of unity by a common history, common ambitions, especially common fears. And such a balance of force is not possible in a primitive community. It does not possess the trade and professional orders that can stand up to the government; it has not the education to foresee the consequences of its political actions. It either obeys and endures in blind patience, or revolts in blind rage. For good or evil, it has to have strong central government.

The early revolutionary liberals did not understand this; the Russian idealists of the nineteenth century did not realise that if they destroyed the Czardom, they would make way only for another, more efficient and more ruthless, despot.

But they had grasp of a deep truth, the deepest truth in politics: that man seeks freedom; that he hates every kind of restraint.

He will accept control only for some good reason: fear, conscience, or to gratify his own will and ambition. This will may be a good will, it may spring from family affection, patriotism, religious devotion; the most important ruling agent in the world is self-control induced by some such motive.

But self-control is still restraint against which all men chafe; from which many must break out from time to time or they could not bear their lives.

This is the fundamental political condition of the individual soul: dynamic energy of imagination, ambition, curiosity, more or less restrained by private interest, private ideals and the police. It is the fundamental free energy that keeps the world alive, in creation.

All men of government are deeply aware of this situation, but they are divided in their remedy. One set say, 'Since man is by nature selfish, cunning, and lawless, since even in his best moments, he aims only at the benefit of his family, class, or country, he needs the strongest kind of control or he will wreck society and destroy himself with it.' The other set say, 'Since man is by nature intelligent, affectionate, idealistic, ready to sacrifice himself for his family or his friends, controls are quite unnecessary and only serve to exasperate his temper and corrupt his morals. He learns violence from the police, and hatred from the law.'

These two sets of political philosophers have always been at war. For each has much reason on his side. The truth, in fact, like all political truth, does not lie in abstract generalisation about mankind, but in a concrete situation.

The liberals, for instance, made one capital error, which still haunts their thought, when they defined freedom as absence of restraint.

Absence of restraint is an abstraction, an empty concept. No doubt it describes the sensation of a child released from school, but it does not contain the essential fact, that the child leaves school by its own volition, with its own muscles. It exerts a power. Freedom is power, the power to do what you like. Free will is dynamic in every man, incessantly seeking some enlargement; more scope; more freedom.

It is the power which has brought the world from primitive tribal communities governed by the most absolute traditional law, to modern democracy. In the primitive tribe, there was not even the concept of liberty. But there was the will to be free, to break out; the same power that was controlled, instructed, prevented from breaking out, by the tribal law.

As I have seen in Africa, that will, that power, even among the most primitive, is incessantly seeking liberty. The children, of course, fight against authority. They have not yet been disciplined. But also grown-ups, especially the young men and women, break the law. They will even defy the law. There are always a few, who, for one reason or another, will rather die than obey. And there are always plenty who will seize any chance to escape from the tribe.

The primitive tribe breaks up of itself as soon as tribal authority is relaxed and there is anywhere for the fugitive to go to. Tribal life is too narrow, too boring to stand up to the attractions of the meanest kind of modern state. I have known Masai warriors, members of the proudest and finest of African races, walk twenty-five miles only to gaze in the shop windows of Arusha, under Kilimanjaro.

Ladies' underclothes, costume jewellery, shoes, the cutler's window, the photographer's, these were more exciting to their imagination than cow-keeping or lion-hunting. And they had the power to gratify their curiosity, in strong legs and the English law. They could not be punished by the elders of the tribe merely for going to Arusha.

Freedom is the power to gratify frustrated desires, curiosity, ambition, love, family hopes; and in its instinctive, incessant drive for gratification, its everlasting battle with all authority, it has transformed the political world. Autocracy, where it still exists, among backward or primitive peoples, no longer even dares to call itself autocracy. It borrows the names of the free Western state; it is a people's democracy, it is a republic.

Free men smile bitterly at this hypocrisy, which appears to them as a political racket; but astute politicians do not play such games without a reason. And the reason is compelling: that all the peoples of the world are bent on liberty, and that in their minds democracy is the only kind of government that can secure their liberty.

The belief is naïve, where democracy is merely the label

chosen to hide a police state. But behind the creed there is an immense hope, an increasing pressure. The demagogues themselves, who preach democracy, even with their tongues in their cheeks, increase the hope, the pressure.

That pressure already modifies policy even in a police state; it may well smash any given police state. In that case, if the people are still not ready, by education and industrial development, for true democratic government, revolution will produce only chaos and misery, followed by another dictatorship.

But the hope will remain, the pressure will begin again; and the industrial development will continue, at increasing pace, as politicians seek to keep the people quiet by raising their standards of living.

The liberal revolution of the last two centuries in Europe is not a phase that will pass. It is the symptom of a growth; it is the consequence of a fundamental drive in the nature of things, in human nature itself; of the free creative soul in man seeking power, dignity, and achievement.

Call it what you will, it will continue; and destroy at last not only the name of autocracy, but the thing, throughout the world. The police states, since they are forced to educate, to organise, to develop industry, are digging their own graves. For education is power, technical ability is power, and these powers are in the hands of souls fundamentally and everlastingly free; which are for ever seeking, openly or secretly, for more power, more liberty; more achievement.

It has been the British genius to recognise, however dimly and instinctively, this truth, and to model policy, at home and abroad, upon it. But Britain's influence, and that of her daughter dominions in the States, Canada, Australia, New Zealand, has probably been most effective simply in the contagion of example, the indirect effects of her literature and of personal contacts.

For her very philosophy of the liberal state, of toleration and respect for individual rights, has forbidden her to force her own ideas of government, education, and religion, upon other peoples. If Eastern members of the Commonwealth, India, Pakistan, Ceylon, show such diversity of government organisation and policy, it is because, from the beginning, they were encouraged to develop on their own lines.

This, especially by Americans, and Russians, has now been made a reproach. It is said that great progress, for instance in India, could have been obtained by more definite and revolutionary schemes. That may be so. Old British officials would answer that the only good and safe revolution is a slow one, and they went as far in innovation as they dared. My own comment, as an ex-official myself, is that we followed our idea, which is by now so deep in our nature, as Britons, that it amounts to an instinct. The typical Briton hates the blueprint; he suspects the theorist who offers Utopia by system, he believes that government is not so much a set of formulae dealing with the general as an art working on the concrete particular; he prefers to collaborate with human nature in its known needs, than try to change it into something more amenable to reason and more obedient to the police. He feels in fact, even when he hardly recognises his own convictions or their source, that man is essentially an individual, and that as an individual he has a unique claim to individual consideration.

Comprendre, 13–14 (June 1955), 45–51—as 'L'Influence britannique dans la révolution libérale', translated by M. Bouvier. The text printed here is from a typescript among the Cary Papers in the Bodleian Library; its title is an adaptation by the editor.

The Sources of Tension in America

An American, when he heard me say that his countrymen are more warm-hearted than their European relations, that they show more kindness and express their feelings more freely, remarked in a sombre way that other feelings in America were also warm and very frankly expressed. He showed me a political article and asked me if I had read some of the columnists. And his explanation of their violence was that, though the physical frontier disappeared fifty years ago, its spirit still ruled in the mind. He asked me to notice the tension of American life, the sense of insecurity, the ethic of 'toughness', the bitterness of politics, and he repeated what is often said of Americans, that they are an emotional people, warm and quick in anger as well as friendship. I could have added to that what I had seen for myself, other characteristics of the old frontier, energy, ingenuity, and imagination.

An American professor, lecturing the other day in London on American literature, said the same thing when he pointed out that the heroes of Sinclair Lewis and Hemingway were in the direct line from Natty Bumppo, simple, frank, full of courage and enterprise, ready always for the new adventure.

There may be something in this theory, and also in the reciprocal effect of literature on life. People everywhere do tend to form an idea of their national character out of the national literature and live up to it. The logical Frenchman, the romantic German, are quite as much the products of their own self-portraits as of history. And it is, I suppose, true that the frontier and its ethic had a long and powerful impact on American thought. For the pioneer, life is a struggle, full of danger and the unexpected. He can never relax in security. And in America he had special hardships. As a friend said to me, 'In England you think of nature as a friend, here it is an enemy.' I had

just been grounded in a plane, during a storm, at Burlington,
Vermont, and compelled to travel eighty miles by car round
Lake Champlain (I should like to record the brilliant work of
the driver, with the road inches deep in rough ice and the bliz-
zard exploding in the middle of the windscreen) to keep an
engagement at Plattsburg. 'What you don't seem to realise,' said
my friend, 'is that a slide into the ditch could have made the
affair not quite so amusing. People get frozen for less—at ten
below.'

In fact, as I realised then, northern winters and midland
deserts are always dangerous, even in the car age. And more
pioneers died of frost and drought than in all the Indian
wars.

But I am not going to stake anything on this American suggestion; I must be true to my own impressions or what is the
good of them, if any, and for a visitor to great cities like New
York, Chicago, Washington, New Orleans, San Francisco, there
is no more obvious mark of a spiritual frontier than in Paris or
Rome. In all, people discuss the same subjects in the same way,
and if they are aware of insecurity and danger, it is from a
worldwide sense of worldwide conflict. So that if this is a pioneer
feeling, it could be argued that it has come to the States from
Europe, which has always been a spiritual frontier with the
East. And in the same way, the violence of political warfare in
the States is nothing new or strange to anyone who has heard
political discussion or read the papers anywhere on the European continent.

One is reminded in all the books on the States that they are
continental, but one does not realise how true this is, and what
it means for American ideas and American government, until
one travels, as I did, from New England and New York to the
South and West. One discovers then the difference of climates,
physical and spiritual, the immense contrasts which still obtain
between North and South with their different histories; the
cosmopolitan pressures of New York and the anxieties of
farmers dependent on an uncertain rainfall. One realises for the
first time that states' rights are much more than a relic of
pioneer settlements and their charters; that states have a
measure of real independence, local interests, and much local

patriotism. And their interests are often in direct conflict. The question of water rights in the West is a matter quite as entangled and embittered to half a dozen states as the navigation laws on the Danube or the Rhine to European nations. And in California, at the shore of the Pacific, I felt for the first time what it means to look out towards a thousand million of Asians, and understood why Californians may differ pretty strongly from New York and Washington about foreign policy.

The tension of life in the States (and I agree that I had from the first and everywhere, except perhaps in the deep South, a sense of tension) could, therefore, be explained plausibly enough by their continental magnitude and diversities, both of climate and interest, ambition and danger, the variety of race and religion, the conflict of powers, the everlasting battle (as in Europe) of pressure groups with paid staffs whose only duty is to fight. But I had the impression too (for what it is worth after a visit of ten weeks) that there is another and deeper reason for this tension; that, if it is continental, it is also American.

On the European continent, the insecurity, the political bitterness, have external causes, in class and religious warfare much more savage than any known in Britain or the States, in national hatreds kept alive by fears that are justified by recent history. Frontiers there are real and close. But it seemed to me that in the States, all those qualities given to the old frontier ethic could have an internal cause, that they are steeped in an atmosphere which, though it is shared by thousands who have no declared faith, is in fact religious, with a very strong emphasis on personal responsibility.

It is in such an inherited angle that one could find a clue to the kindness as well as the violence, the idealism as well as the toughness, the ferocious competition and the anxious charity, which between them give (as I think) a special quality to the American tension. Everyone feels that he or she has a personal duty towards society, a personal guilt for what is wrong with it. There is an intense and continuous interest in what are called world problems, like population and standards of living (books on such subjects sell in thousands) as well as the more local and immediate questions of education and morality.

I was told to expect an eager and informed interest in the arts and, in fact, my impression was that more is done to encourage the artist and writer in the States than in Britain. But again I thought (judging from very many conversations with writers and critics, professors and students) that here too there was a special sense of responsibility at work; the sense that the arts deserve study and support not only for their own sakes, but as part of the personal contribution that everyone owes to the world; that the writer, the artist, has a special duty to society in the discovery and revelation of a certain kind of truth. Sinclair Lewis, for instance, is valued as a pioneer who opened up new regions of character to be mapped and mined. He was a great artist because he was deeply concerned with fundamental things.

You may say that this is true of all great artists; what I am suggesting is a difference of angle, the difference between writers like Maupassant and Scott Fitzgerald. Maupassant seems to say in every line, 'These poor devils are human,' and Scott Fitzgerald 'These poor humans are bedevilled.' The first is a Latin judgement, the second, I think, American and profoundly in the American tradition. It expresses that sense of the individual soul in battle with fate, with the powers of evil, which haunts all American letters. Poe, Melville, James, Dreiser, Lewis, Hemingway, Faulkner, all from their different points of view, ask, 'What shall a man do to be saved?' or in Melville's (as in Fitzgerald's) case, 'What shall a man do not to be damned?'

We hear a lot nowadays about the sense of guilt. But a sense of guilt is only the negative half of a sense of duty. Both together are the positive and negative of the democratic soul; the electric tension which, I suggest, is much more in the character of American life than the tradition of the frontier, and goes much further back, to deeper and older resources. One could say that the pioneers were children of that inheritance.

And with this, I had another strong impression of the American idea. Liberty is still a slogan in Britain and Europe. All governments are careful to say that they value liberty and understand its virtues. Controls are always described as temporary and evil necessities—due only to the pressure of circumstances; and it is true that in Britain many have been done away with. But apart altogether from party politics, there is always a battle between efficiency and liberty. A modern state, for reasons that no state can put aside, has to organise. Defence alone means elaborate planning, the allotment of raw materials, the division of functions, and it touches every part of life. States must organise or go under. But organisation needs a bureaucracy, and bureaucracy, by its very nature, is the enemy of liberty. It exists to work the machine, to standardise, and left to itself it finds no room for the individual difference.

It may be said that bureaucracy is only the tool of organisation, which by itself is neutral. It can be the friend as well as the enemy of freedom. It can be the necessary means of freedom. There is very little freedom possible to any state without a common law and a police to enforce it. The manager of a team of tennis stars, by taking on himself the small routine worries of ticket-buying and hotel-hiring and so giving them the time to practise, actually adds to their power of competition in the games where only individual excellence counts. But the same organiser, taking the same stars on an exhibition tour, can say to them, 'No need to wear yourselves out—we'll arrange who is to win and each of you will get his turn.' The result, so much pleasanter for the performers, looks as good or even better to the spectators. Sets can be designed to go the full distance and to provide excitement. Only the game suffers and, at first, imperceptibly.

Life cannot avoid struggle, tension, and tragedy. They are in the nature of things, of a world in everlasting creation and therefore continuous change. To try to make the world safe for anyone or anybody is as hopeless a project (as dictators have often discovered) as to command that everyone shall think alike, or stop thinking altogether; that no one shall get old or sick; that storms shall stop blowing and earthquakes cease to crumple. All one can do is to salvage the victims, and nothing can give a cripple two sound legs again or restore the dead to life. The aim of democracy should be to give everyone his chance, to see that it is a fair chance and that, even if he fails with it, he suffers as little deprivation as the state can contrive.

This was the practical object of Liberal governments when they founded social insurance and the various pension schemes. And the Labour Government could and did argue that nationalisation of coal, power, and transport was an economic necessity to preserve the nation's life and therefore its freedom. But the important question, as usual, is not so much the details of a policy as what is behind it. And a good many people in Britain, a minority but a powerful minority, are committed to nationalisation not as an economic necessity but a moral theory; they think that competition is itself wicked and unnecessary, the final source of conflict and insecurity. This doctrine appeals strongly to the natural longing, which we all feel now and then, for rest, for peace of mind.

But there cannot be permanent rest and peace, except in the graveyard, and competition cannot be abolished. There is a conflict of needs and wills in the smallest family, even in the mind of the solitary individual. The source of tension is in difference, which is as universal as likeness. Both competition and co-operation exist and must exist in every society. If anyone should say that economic competition at least is unnecessary, the answer is that to get rid of it (if that were possible) would be only to replace the struggle for pay, and what it can bring to the imagination, by the struggle for power, and what power can do for the ego: a struggle more demoralising, less easily controlled, and much more dangerous to peace.

The problem for democracy, therefore, is to maintain national defence and guard standards of life, while keeping the essential freedoms—to use organisation for the increase of freedom.

And I came away from the States feeling that the solution is more likely to be found there than in Europe; because in Europe, as I say, State Socialism for its own sake, quite apart from Communist propaganda, has the sympathy, though often the unthinking sympathy, of large minorities. In Britain that minority has diminished very much in the last years. The advantage of practical experiment, in politics, is that it shows the cracks in the dream. But in the States I felt that there is still a much deeper grasp of the danger that belongs to all regimentation. That, too, is in the American tradition, so much more profoundly democratic and individual than that of any other people in the world.

Saturday Review (23 August 1952), 6, 7, 35.

Political and Personal Morality

Almost every great statesman has been described as a crook. Metternich, Cavour, Bismarck, Gladstone, Disraeli, Lloyd George, Roosevelt: history is made up of names at which the moralist holds his nose. In literature, to describe a character as a politician is to rank him with the villains. Political novels, from Stendhal's *Rouge et Noir* to Anatole France's *Ile des Pingouins*, treat the political world as something meaner and dirtier than that of the gangsters; meaner because it is hypocritical.

Yet we all know honest men in politics, we all discuss political issues as if they were amenable to moral law; we all distinguish between countries which have a high standard of political morality and those which are corrupt.

The fact is that the world has got into the habit of talking cant about politics and politicians; so much so that it cannot recognise a political scene, fairly drawn, when it is put before it. And what is odd is that the same men who talk cant about the wickedness of the political world, the corruption of power, and so on, will discuss, acutely and reasonably, some actual political situation— What ought Eisenhower to do about Formosa? What line should he take having regard to Communist suspicions, nationalist anxieties, military necessities, the situation in Japan, in Russia, in Germany? How far should he look forward; how much should he risk, either way? That is to say, they perceive a highly complex and difficult problem, full of blind issues. It is, moreover, always a unique problem. It has never occurred exactly like that before, and it will never occur exactly like that again. And it changes while you look at it; it is different today from yesterday. Some minister has spoken somewhere, some action has been taken, some information has come in which changes its whole aspect. And the ordinary man, grasping this basic fact, is quite prepared to hear that the President or the Secretary of State, faced by a fundamental change in the situation, has changed his mind about policy.

No one was surprised or talked of bad faith when, after the United States was attacked at Pearl Harbor, the U.S. Government abandoned its stated policy of neutrality. This is only to say that political action is always the expedient action; the most honest statesman cannot always keep his promises or fulfil his programme. This is easily accepted in practice, but it raises pretty large questions. When is a statesman entitled to break promises, to change a policy which, often, is the one that he was elected to carry out? And an even bigger and formidable question is this: When is he entitled to deceive? I raise this point here because it is not only closely allied to the other, but because it is precisely deceit which is the major crime charged to the politician, and which has got him his bad name. In Huxley's *Grey Eminence*, Father Joseph is a good man, almost a saint, until he becomes Richelieu's confidential secretary and an intriguing politician. Then at once he is a crook.

We all know that it is often impossible for a statesman to avow his purpose. To do so would be to defeat the purpose. Cripps, when Chancellor of the Exchequer in England, was asked if the Government had any intention of leaving the gold standard. Cripps answered that there was none. But, in fact, the thing was already decided and Britain was off the gold standard within the week. Cripps was a man of the strictest truth, but if he had not evaded that question, misled the House, there would have been a major crisis; and the whole advantage of the operation would have been lost.

No statesman could give away in public all details of policy. If therefore he is questioned, he must often evade or deceive. And often evasion is not enough. By itself it will reveal an intention. This is why all responsible statesmen make use of a special language, so exasperating to newspapermen and so much scorned by the moralisers. They seek phrases that do not commit them; they use a kind of doubletalk; they utter, in public, rows of platitudes. They do not want to be pinned down and they have very good reason. They never know what the situation will be tomorrow; they do not want to have to admit, 'I was wrong that time and I can't, after all, do what I said I would do.'

Practical men of affairs recognise this problem; they meet it every day in the ordinary business of life. But it has led to an idea, unfavourable to the politician, and often very bad for him, that there is a special political morality. It is said, for instance, that Bismarck's action in editing the Ems telegram, although unscrupulous, was justified by the enormous issues involved. He needed war to unify Germany. He needed war then in order to frustrate possible alliances against Prussia. He had to be sure of winning the war. Millions of lives, the destiny of Germany, were at stake.

The double standard of morality, allowing a statesman more latitude than the ordinary private man, is so widely accepted that it is made an excuse for the greatest crimes. Worse, I suspect that it is often accepted by politicians themselves as justifying actions that they would not dream of in their private lives. And it is supported by all the history teachers who point out what great issues hang on a statesman's word; by the general legend of political skulduggery.

In fact, there is no double standard. Lies are always lies, evil is always evil; public and private morals are governed by precisely the same law. The destruction of one life by criminal pride or folly is no less and no more a crime than the slaughter of a million. The quality of an individual is his unique life. And you cannot treat that life as a unit in a mass. You cannot divide, subtract, or multiply quality. Ten Titians are not better in quality than one Titian. Twenty children are not less or more separate persons than one child, and cannot therefore be dealt with as a greater or less responsibility. A mother or father who corrupts or destroys a child's life is in exactly the same moral position as the statesman, the political leader, who corrupts or destroys a people.

Parents, mothers, in their own family relations, act as responsible statesmen. What is more, they practise the same policies. They deceive, they evade; in a word, they manage a situation. What mother would tell a backward child that it is a fool? To do so might well ruin the child's only faint chance of some measure of education. Who has not promised a child going to the dentist's that it will not be hurt? Who has not made promises that cannot be kept; changed his mind to meet some new contingency? All relations between human beings in a free world require continuous adjustment. Every moral situation is unique and needs a special answer.

I shall now be accused, I have been accused already, of advocating universal dishonesty. But this is completely wrong. It is just because the free creative world, in which we live, presents to us a continuous novelty of event that personal integrity is of such enormous importance. It is our only criterion of value. Our trust is given to certain leaders because their honour, their character, are the only things we can trust. We know that they may have to change their minds, to break promises, to let us down, but if we trust them, if we can say of them they are honest men, we do not reproach them. We are sure that if they have broken a promise it was because they could not help it; if they did conceal some facts from us it was not for their own good but ours. That in the final resort they have given their lives to serve what they conceive to be a good end; that they are not in politics for their own advantage or glory.

Ask yourself how far this rule goes in your opinion of a given statesman. Why Washington, why Lincoln had such power over men and make such great figures in history. And why among your own friends and acquaintances the word of one has so much more weight than that of another. He may not be cleverer, but you know he is disinterested; he is not a self-seeker. He will do his best to advise you, regardless, of his own interest. Of course, he may still give you bad advice, as the honest statesman may take a wrong course. Or both may be frustrated by a change of wind, by bad luck. And you may blame him, and break your friendship; and the statesman may be ruined, not only in his career but in history. He may be held up to derision so that his very name becomes a term of abuse. Think of the political reputations ruined by the Depression, something very wise men could not have foreseen in its full disaster, and which needed measures that, politically, it was impossible to make accepted until disaster had arrived. For the politician is not only faced by an everlasting crisis; he is usually so hampered by prejudices of all kinds that he has very little room for manoeuvres in dealing with it. He is like a man sent out to fight a hungry lion in handcuffs. And this is especially true of the statesman in a free democracy.

It has been said that government is the art of making people do what they don't like, since they will cheerfully follow their own inclinations without any instruction; and that, in the final resort, there are only two ways of making them act against their own inclinations: to shoot the disobedient or to wangle them. If you include under shooting every kind of coercion; if you include under wangling every kind of persuasion, such as an appeal to conscience, to patriotic or family feeling, to self-respect or self-interest; then this is true. And it is the last method which is the only one open to the government of a free democracy. They are not allowed to shoot.

Democratic statesmen must be leaders of opinion; they must persuade; and it is a great advantage to them to have the arts of persuasion; an understanding of the popular mind, rhetoric. But this does not mean they have to be demagogues. Lincoln's Gettysburg Address is great rhetoric, great art; it is not the work of a demagogue. The demagogue is the disease of democracy, as the brute is the disease of autocracy, whatever its name.

It is a delusion that democracies are more corrupt than autocratic states. The corruptions are only of a different order. The tricks of a demagogue cannot be hidden; the blackmail of a police state is secret. It is also much more dangerous. It is a rottenness that is not perceived until the roof falls in. Where are the autocracies of last century and how did those magnificent and solid-appearing structures stand against the talkative, the scandal-ridden democracies, with their spellbinders to lead them?

Persuasion is an art, but not necessarily an art of lies. Great democratic statesmen, like great preachers, find their chief power in the truth. But it is a selected, an arranged, truth. And how far they may go in the selection of phrases, in arrangement of facts, in suppression of complex difficulties, is between themselves and their consciences. And it must stay there. For no *a priori* rule, no moralistic sermonising, can lay down in advance what should be a statesman's right course of conduct. And we need not envy him. For though, morally speaking, he is in exactly the same position as any private citizen, or any father or mother of a family, his problems are enormously more difficult.

And his decisions affect millions of lives; as his mistakes destroy whole nations. The private citizen who ruins himself or his family may suffer the anger of his dependents; but the statesman can bring upon himself the hatred of a whole generation. And if he is an honest man this is exactly the risk he has to take. That is why the easy judgements of history, especially popular history, strike us so often as unjust. Before we call any statesman a fool or a crook we should ask what problems he faced, what kind of people he had to handle, what kind of support he got, what pressure he withstood, what risks he took.

But our final question will be still: 'Was he an honest man?'

Saturday Review (31 December 1955), 5, 6, 31, 32.

Clothes as Expression

Anatole France in his *Penguin Island* gives us his idea of the
origin of clothes. A stone-age young woman, dirty, hungry,
naked, and hideous, is wandering on the beach, in search of
dead fish and other garbage, surrounded by men equally starved
and repulsive, who ignore her as they disregard each other. Suddenly, upon some impulse, the girl picks up a piece of seaweed
and wraps it round her hips. At once the men lift up their
noses from the rocks and pursue her, panting with curiosity
and appetite, in a string that continually lengthens.

Anatole France was a cynic and all cynics have the same
fault, they simplify too much. They take their eye off the facts,
the actual situation, to observe a general idea (in this case, an
idea of the nature of woman and love) which is itself usually
derived from some other cynic; and from this general idea, like
any medieval logician, they deduce their local applications.
France's idea was that dress is meant to captivate. In fact, the
moment we look at the real situation, not only of women, but
all mankind, we find it highly complex and interesting. Why,
for instance, did primitive man, when he had acquired clothes,
stick to the same style for centuries? Why do tribesmen and
peasants have a national dress? Why do they abandon it? Why
then a uniform dress for soldiers, nurses, priests? Why a formal
dress for one occasion and informal for another? Why does a
woman grow ashamed of old hats and frocks while men cherish
them? Why is a man who breaks out into a new fashion suspected and criticised while a woman is admired? What, in
short, are the secret forces which have such universal and continuous power over conduct and fill all the newspapers with
their propaganda?

When I was in Africa, I saw the origin of clothes in a different light from France. In our remote station, Nafada, the

District Officer, Carlisle, wished to establish friendly relations with a certain pagan tribe, the Tangale, who had been raiding and murdering among peaceful neighbours. As he said, if they provoked a war, in which they would, of course, be defeated, they would be so embittered that development would be held up for years. As he had managed to get in touch with some of the Tangale chiefs, he showed them some shots at polo, and proposed a game with them, provided they could help in clearing a ground at Nafada; and, just as he had hoped, the chiefs, who were great sportsmen, at once came in with their tribesmen (under a 'guard of honour' which was really intended to protect innocent sightseers on the road) and cleared a ground. The whole party, chiefs and followers, treated the affair as a huge spree. They laughed and shouted all day while they hacked the scrub, and danced or sang all night. But especially they delighted in the goods displayed on the market-stalls. Ours was a very poor market, but these tribesmen had never seen anything like it before. It was Bond Street and Fifth Avenue to them. And when they found that the strange objects, coins, with which Carlisle had paid them for their work, could be exchanged for pots, knives, beads, dried fish, sweetmeats, they had to be restrained by their chiefs. There was something like a riot, or a sale. For they assumed that once the things before them had been sold, there would be no more available, at least for a long time. And while the men were buying knives and beads, their women, who, till this moment, had gone completely naked, except for a bunch of leaves, demanded cotton prints and draped themselves in various fantastic modes. But not, as far as one could see, with any idea of attraction. They were seized by the same joyful excitement which had infected the whole party. All men and women were calling to each other, like children at a Christmas party who show off their presents and paper hats for admiration and approval. It was a feast of the imagination. The culture of thousands of years broke up in a couple of days, under our surprised eyes; and (this for me was the interesting point) it was a spontaneous break-up—from within. These people were fascinated even by the elementary civilisation of Nafada. They wanted all they could get of it.

And looking at them and their holiday gaiety, it struck me for the first time that their lives at home must be exceedingly dull and monotonous. The very idea of tribal life reveals its boredom. The reason why tribesmen and peasants wear the same clothes for centuries is only the presence of an all-powerful social law, from which they can't escape. The elders, the chiefs, the witch-doctors, hold the young in a paralysing grip, until the young cease to be young and also become conservatives, without imagination or enterprise.

Nothing can preserve a national dress in its old form as a mark of subjection. It must disappear or change its nature as a self-conscious expression of a national feeling. It must and does acquire a positive meaning. The wearer, that is to say, uses dress just as an artist uses his art, to communicate a meaning. He or she creates something, the work of art, himself dressed in a certain way, to have a certain effect.

Here then is the origin and sense of uniform, which at first sight seems to deny the freedom and the imagination that exploded so violently in the pagan Tangale. Uniform is an expression of meaning. The nurse's plain dress is saying, 'I am not an individualist, an egotist. I am not thinking of myself or my appearance at all. I am, at this moment, the faithful member of a great profession and you can trust me to remember my duty.'

So you get the tribal position reversed. The tribeswoman, the peasant, wears uniform because the elders say to her, 'Stay in your place, young woman, and do what you are told. Dare to set yourself up to be different and we'll teach you where you get off.' The nurse wears uniform because she willingly expresses her subordination to rule.

This, of course, is the meaning of all uniforms, on soldiers, priests, dustmen, porters; all proclaim a social function. But the uniform of the soldier and the priest go further. They say to the world not only, 'We serve a law greater than ourselves,' but also, 'We are different from the rest of you.' These uniforms, that is, profess a moral principle for which the wearer is prepared to die. And that public profession, as the founders of armies and priesthoods well understood, is of vital importance to the work and the efficiency of the dedicated workers. It is

not so silly as recruits think for officers to pay so much attention to their dress. Neatness and uniformity are not required
merely to give a smart turnout to the ranks; it is a sign of
allegiance, a discipline of the soul. And the dirty soldier is
either a bad soldier or a misfit. His dirtiness is mutiny, or the
dumb protest of some unhappy country-boy lost in strange
surroundings and abused by his comrades or a hazing sergeant.
With him again, clothes express a meaning which the man
himself scarcely comprehends.

But if he is mutinous he wilfully shows his hatred of the
whole system. His protest is against all uniform. And it is often
said of women that their indignation when they meet, upon
another woman, a duplicate of their frock, is the same kind
of reaction: that this is the mark of their difference, to be born
rebels and anarchs, without even a sense of law. The proof is
the everlasting change of their fashions, their everlasting demand for something 'exclusive'.

But again I suggest that the truth is both more complex and
more interesting. For one thing, women in the professions, in
parliament or congress, adopt formal dress just as men do and
for the same reason, to show that they estimate their duties
at a higher rate than any personal advantage. And that they
should do so is still more interesting than that nurses should
be given uniform, at the same time as Florence Nightingale
was giving them professional standards of honour. For this choice
of formal dress is a voluntary act; it is the answer of some
instinctive feeling for what is 'right', to a moral problem which
was not anywhere expressed, which like the instinct belongs to
some fundamental region of morality.

But, it is objected, these same professional women, if they
conform (hypocritically) to the standards of men during the
day, will still, when off duty, follow every change of fashion,
and strip themselves half-naked in the evenings, to gain notice
and distinction, while the men wear the soberest of their uniforms.

What are the facts? Any husband, brother or uncle who has
been made late for a party because some woman can't make up
her mind what frock she ought to wear, should realise them.
The very freedom of woman to be different lays an obligation

upon her. Every party, however simple (indeed the simplest are often the most difficult), poses the question: 'What is suitable?' And again this is largely, in the broadest sense, a moral question. For to be 'wrong' is offensive, it hurts feelings, it spoils the pleasure of others. To be too smart at one party casts a reflection on the rest, and embarrasses the hostess. To be dowdy at another is a rudeness which may be a cruelty, implying that the hosts are not worth consideration. That is to say, the woman who is worrying about her frock is thinking of others as well as herself; she is facing a social duty; and she is different from her husband only in having a different duty. It is his to be as inconspicuous as possible. He is allowed, like the tribesman and the peasant, only some small licence in detail, in the quality of cloth, in trinkets. He is well advised indeed, after the age of twenty-five, to give up even this privilege, and wear studs and links of plainest gold. But it is his wife's duty to be as beautiful and interesting as she can contrive. She is the decoration for which the men provide the background, and the hostess her hangings.

Yet she is limited on all sides by complex considerations. She must judge the fashion for herself and reject that which is, for some mysterious innate reason, vulgarly striking. She must not look like a *cocotte* or a mannequin advertising some dress-designer. She must, like the men, be 'right' for that party, but, unlike the man, whose only problem, perhaps, is whether he dare not wear the enamel studs given him by some relation who may be encountered during the evening, she has to answer half a dozen, of which most are blind. For instance, the first of all, 'What kind of party is this one going to be?', 'Will my hostess wear full dress or a dinner frock?', 'My best frock is made of So-and-so. Will it crush in the car? If so, it will look dirty and Mrs X will think or pretend to think that I am scorning her party, especially as she knows very well I do not like her.'

There is no room here to ask what is the meaning of the larger tides of fashion. We see that clothes become more democratic, less formal, every year; and yet, in spite of all the talk about mass-thinking and mass-activities, more varied and colourful. Out of city clothes which, for reasons we have noticed, are informally formal (less formal than they were, but no longer

of a uniform black or dark grey) men as well as women wear
jackets, sweaters, caps, hats, and slacks that, in shape and colour,
are more extravagant than anything invented by their fathers
for fancy-dress.

Is this a protest against the encroachment of bureaucracy
upon private liberty, or a symptom directly contradicting the
pessimists? Is it in fact a breaking-out of the tribes seeking
always more richness of self-expression, more food for the
imagination? I suspect that it is precisely the latter, a sign
that the people as a whole are thinking and acting less as a
mass and more as individuals than they did even twenty years
ago. It is freedom quietly asserting itself under all the laws, a
freedom that may have unexpected consequences in any election.

It may be said that such serious consideration of mere dress
is absurd. But it is just because we have to deal with such
commonplace and universal factors that they are so interesting.
It is not the immense earthquakes, once in a century, which
are most interesting and important to the geologist, but the
measurement of daily earth-waves, the minute changes in the
earth's surface by which the immense forces at work below
(that is, the normal forces) can be detected and analysed. So it is
precisely the everyday functions and changes of dress which
are most informing. And what is most interesting about them
is just what nobody seems to regard, their moral implications,
the clue they give to moral and social relations which belong
apparently to what is called the region of intuition and instinct.
For that means that they can be trusted. They are not faked.
They are as unselfconscious, in their casual expression, as the
flight of birds or the dance of the bees. And that is why they
are so valuable to anyone who wishes to study character, the
character which underlies and informs all individual and moral
character, in its primary and elemental springs.

Previously unpublished. The text printed here is from a typescript among the Cary Papers in the Bodleian Library.

Joyce Cary's Last Look at His Worlds

We live by our ideas to realise our feelings. The fakir on his bed of nails is as happy as the Texan oilman in his Rolls; possibly much happier. His idea of life is more profound, and more satisfying. But they would not change places. Each looks upon the other with condescension, even some contempt. They serve different ideas of life and they haven't the least notion of what the other's idea means, what it feels like to live by it.

This age derides the idea of service; the word 'servant' is a term of abuse. The old estate carpenter, in Vita Sackville-West's *The Edwardians*, brooding over his store of seasoned timber, is regarded simply as a fossil, or more often as the victim of an idea inculcated to make him the useful tool of a class society.

This, of course, is period nonsense. Subordination is necessary to every organised society; we are all subordinates, from the Queen, who accepts her vocation in duty, to the road-sweeper; and that subordination can find quality, and therefore dignity, only in the idea of service. As for the notion that service belongs to a class society, it is the essential ideal of the Communist Party, which took so much else from the Victorians, and from the old Russian Church.

Service as an idea was far stronger and deeper fifty years ago than anyone today can realise. In Ireland, when I was growing up, our social framework was old-fashioned. Our servants were illiterate and would now be thought of as the humblest of their kind, pitiable in their inferiority. But this would be the stupidest kind of misconception. In fact, they had the strongest feeling of their worth and one completely justified by their sense of service; and with it went a personal dignity that often does not belong nowadays even to high office in the state.

When I was a boy I delighted most to be out with a certain Barney Magonagel, groom and dog-man to my uncle, Tristram

Cary, late of Ballybrack. Barney was illiterate and he had no idea of himself except as a servant to my uncle. He spent his whole life, from the age of twelve, in my uncle's household. But to be with Barney was to realise a new sense of dignity in man and in his work. And this sense of function in society, of the essential dignity of work well done, ran through the whole of the social organism as I knew it. The relation between Barney and my uncle, and myself, too, was a double one, of duty and respect. He was, in the old Roman sense, a member of the family. And this meant that he felt a strong sense of proprietorship in the family. He was quite as deeply concerned as we were in the loss of my uncle's Irish property. I've heard him exclaim with indignation that my uncle's overcoat was not fit for him to be seen in. And it was a personal indignation; Barney felt that my uncle was letting him down, as well as the family, by going out in such an overcoat.

This is a hierarchic relation, where master and servant both know their place in a social unity, which both, if more or less unconsciously, accept as a necessary situation. And such a relation, at the beginning of this century, was common even in factories, especially those small workshops and mills still the commonest type in Britain. Workers felt a personal allegiance to their firms.

I remember, not long ago, an old railwayman saying to me, quite innocently, 'That was *my* railway, the Great Western.' He was telling me about the fate of the broad gauge, with pride and grief. It had made *his* railway the finest in the world. To the modern economist or social historian this old man's talk of 'my railway' would seem pathetic, another piece of period nonsense. But it was not so. It expressed a truth of the man's actual existence, of the way he felt about his work, and his life. And this is a fundamental value. By such values we live. The old porter, like Barney, had the unbreakable dignity of vocation, of conscious and loyal service; the dignity of kings. And this quality, almost ignored by historians, was probably the most important element in the climate of that time. It profoundly affected all relations of master and man, it made sense of rank.

The hierarchic society was dying and had to die, but it was not stupid, it was simply a form of the social organisation necessary and inevitable in all states. It has been replaced by the cruder relation of the boss and the worker; of a battle for power controlled only by fear. Their mutual interests are the same, but that real community of interest is not expressed in the actual relation.

For us the sense of social duty went deep, yet we hardly noticed it. It explained, for instance, the position of women. To woman was allotted a special function in society, as daughter, sister, wife, mother; and this function, like that of a priesthood, carried its own obligation and its own sacrifice. Nowadays women are horrified at what they call the Victorian subjection of their sex. It didn't feel like subjection then. Then, as now, the majority of women married and the Victorian matron had formidable power in the home. She did not feel subjection, but duty, obligation to her task as a woman. And that was also a sacred vocation and a privilege.

It was this sense of vocation, of privilege, that made so many women fight against the suffrage. I remember the gloomy prognostications of wise men that the emancipation of women would destroy that sense of vocation and bring down civilisation itself. They were ludicrously wrong. Women nowadays emphasise their sex as never before. The modern mother is even too nervously concerned for her children. Human nature, the character of the sex, has proved much too strong for politics. Women are probably not happier. They are burdened by new problems of choice and responsibility, new conflicts. But no modern girl could endure the old life again; it is not happiness that matters to her, but power, freedom to act, richness of life. And that new richness is all our richness. The gain to general society is immense.

It is the feel, the atmosphere, of a time which is forgotten, and yet it is the breath of history. You find it in novels, but not unless you are sensitive to fine shades of assumption. Wells and Galsworthy, so unlike in every other way, have the same assumption that good sense will cure all evils. They were fundamentally rationalist and so, I think, they were period novelists.

Hardy, Conrad, and James, with their deeper sense of fate, of the evil will, are greater than their time. They belong to it, of course, but they stand out of it. The period is there, but you won't notice it unless you look for it. It is not in the air, it is in the details, in the dialogue, in the characters. But, with Wells and Galsworthy, deeply immersed in their period, it is a climate that they accept as the natural state of things. And this is their special value as novelists—that they give us the feel of a time with the sincerity only possible to those who do not examine their own premises.

It is in this unconscious rationalism, I suggest, that you find a reason for that extraordinary calmness with which we faced a war that was actually the end of our liberal civilisation. We assumed that the liberal world had the experience and the intelligence to cope with it. After all, it had taken the Crimea, the Italian War of 1859, the wars of 1861, 1870, in its stride. They were all quickly over, they were all localised, and they left no permanent scars. We imagined in 1914 that a new European war would be no worse—even the Germans expected it to be short as well as profitable.

But you won't find this argument stated anywhere in the press of the time, nor even, I think, in the novels. It was an assumption, and assumptions do not get into print, they are deep in the subconscious. They are assimilated by children from their general experience, not only talk and reading, but the behaviour of all about them. The defeatism of the 'twenties, especially among the young liberals, was typical of neurotic frustration— their fundamental subconscious assumption about the nature of the world had suddenly proved delusive.

Personally, I escaped that collapse of faith. As an Anglo-Irishman I had lived from childhood in the climate of agrarian war, the most cruel and unjust of wars. For it ruins just those landowners who have tried to do their duty, the residents who have put their money into their native land. I knew something about violence and nationalist passion. But also I had seen, as I thought, the Irish land war concluded by a reasonable settlement. Home Rule was in sight. Why shouldn't I believe that liberal good sense would deal, in the end, also with nationalist megalomania?

The liberal assumptions were nonsense, but they had some excuse. Every period, as Sainte-Beuve remarked, has its special bit of nonsense, but it does not know its own nonsense, it always thinks itself profoundly wise and profoundly disillusioned about nonsense generally, and it looks with astonishment and contempt on the nonsense of all former periods. So the late Victorians despised the religiosity of the early Victorians and decided that nothing mattered in life but personal relations, complete honesty between man and man, and especially men and women. Virginia Woolf complained that Arnold Bennett had forgotten that man had a soul. This was not true of Bennett, but it is true that he ruined his life for want of a coherent faith. For liberal faith, when it corrupts to a sentiment, is the emptiest of all. It lays down only one duty for man: to be kind to his friends. That is to return civilisation, at full circle, to the tribal hut, or rather to the pygmy family, which does not build huts, but lives, they say, in a pre-tribal but affectionate family relation.

Anarchy is the natural temptation of every liberal; he believes in the perfectibility of mankind. His instinct is against all government, and even Marx prophesied the end of government. He too believed in the automatic progress. I don't think anyone under forty would believe in it today. They are more inclined to talk of the Gadarene Swine and the evil spirits that drove them to suicide. They realise that the evil spirits are always there, ready to take possession at any vacancy. Their modern nonsense is probably to suppose that education and a good pay-packet can fill the vacancy left by faith. In fact, education and higher standards of living at once increase political turmoil. It's not the proletariat which makes trouble, it is the class just risen out of the proletariat; and, since education is absolutely necessary in the industrial development of every state, that class is growing everywhere at speed.

But possibly this faith in aid and education is not the typical illusion of our time. I would not put my finger in the fire for it. When this age is defined, say in twenty years, as a period, it may well seem stupid in quite another way. Our young men will be called fools and blind for assumptions they do not and can not perceive, and their children will have no idea of what it felt like to be an innocent of the 'fifties.

I am sometimes envied for the peace, the leisure of my time, when, as a boy, at my grandmother's home in Donegal, I could spend all day on a book, or wander off on the shore or the mountain and never meet a soul. But I remember very well how, at the sound of wheels on the gravel of the drive, everyone in the household, except my grandmother, would rush to the nearest window. A visit, if only from a higgler with a poached salmon to sell, was an event. Even my grandmother, if she did not get up, would expect to hear of it.

It is true that we were not bored, not impatient. But that was because we accepted our situation, because, to our feeling, it was the normal thing. We would drive for two hours to a dance twelve or fourteen miles away, and think of the time as short, having regard to the hills and the weight of the old carriage. Horse-transport and horse-speeds were as natural to our feeling as to Jane Austen.

Jane Austen does not give the tedium of those journeys to her heroines because she did not feel it. None of the old novelists has it. In Surtees, in Dickens, the horses are always at full stretch, the carriage and the mail are dashing along at eight or ten miles an hour. In fact, even in a gig we were half our time at a walk up or down hill. And in a carriage we were always asking ourselves, on the hills, whether we should get out and walk to save the horses.

What excitement, what emancipation came in with bicycles. I just recall the first arrival of this new machine to an aunt. A special frame was made for it, and it was kept in the hall— the coach-house was held too draughty, too damp. And it was cleaned and oiled after every outing. Of course, it was an expensive property. In that day's value it cost more than a horse. But it was worth a dozen horses to my young aunt. It enlarged her world by at least twenty miles, it enriched her life by a dozen more friendships, by hundreds of hours of gossip, by the latest novels a week earlier. It gave her the power to go shopping when she liked, even if Dan, the groom, wanted to hoe the potatoes that day.

And power is freedom. Power to do, to know, to see, to comprehend. Bicycles were a very important addition to power, in remote country places. Their impact was revolutionary, especially with women.

People of my age have seen bigger changes in the world than

any generation before. They are not only a matter of mechanical inventions, motor transport, aeroplanes, and the wireless, but of idea and the feelings that go with the idea.

I myself, as a government official in Nigeria, saw a primitive Africa, with no idea of racialism or nationalism. For example, about 1920, there were four men in my guard-room. They were murderers, self-confessed, and I put them in the guard-room because they begged me not to remand them to the local gaol, a mile away in the town. They sent for me two or three times a day. But when I went to visit them, they never did anything but give me the ordinary salute. They had no complaints. Finally I asked the sergeant-in-charge what was worrying them, and he said, 'They want to be sure that you have not gone away, as you are the only man they know in these parts.'

These people had come from a village only about fifteen miles away, but they felt themselves among strangers in the town. They looked upon me as a friend because I had been to their village, they had seen me there and knew me as a friend of their chief. They knew neither nationalism, racialism, nor that sense of inferiority which underlies so much racialism and makes it hysterical and psychotic. They felt merely different. But now this relation of trust between myself as an old-fashioned Nigerian political officer and the tribesmen would be described as paternalism, meaning by paternalism something disgraceful to both parties. It is replaced by what is called self-government, where these tribesmen would appeal to a Negro magistrate. And this is not disgraceful but admirable.

Yet self-government is just as false a description of the actual situation as paternalism. In each case, the tribesman is under the law; the real change is simply in the colour of the magistrate and the idea that he represents, African nationalism. Nationalism is the idea that now dominates all political thinking and most propaganda. And it is tearing civilisation to pieces. It is, as I say, merely an idea, but it is based on feelings deep in human nature, of personal pride, ambition, and distrust of the stranger—feelings very easily worked up by a demagogue into arrogance and hatred, fear and revenge.

I say it is an idea because nationalism has no basis in any real difference. All North Europe, from Shannon to Danzig, is the same racial mixture. Africa has much more variety of race and colour, so has India. But North Europe is a dozen national units; Africans and Indians talk and think of their continent as one. It is the name that matters, the symbol, the embodied idea. Men live by such symbols, such ideas, whether political or religious, and die joyfully for a word or a flag. It expresses not only their egotism, their pride, but their love, their love of this strange and romantic idea, a nation, a name.

When I was young, the ruling idea was that of the liberal revolution. Of course, there were national ideals, but they were held to be subordinate, and, as egotism, wrong. Liberals preached nationalism, self-determination, not as sops to local bosses, but as conferring moral responsibility. This was also the idea of rebellious peoples. And the idea gives form to the feeling.

It is true, of course, that the old empires which gave comparative peace and order to the world for nearly a hundred years could not last, for the very reason that they raised standards of life, that they gave education, that they developed their dependencies. They were digging their own graves; they were creating the technical ability and local wealth that, in the hands of the local demagogues, would be turned against them. The devolution of power was inevitable, but it has produced very much the same situation now that destroyed the Roman Empire, abolished a civilisation very little inferior to our own, and brought in centuries of misery and war. The tragic paradox of this situation is that it has been fostered by the very idealism that inspired the immense social progress of the nineteenth century.

I was myself a liberal, like most of the young people of my time. In fact, like so many at that time, I overlooked the enormous power of evil working incessantly to destroy happiness and peace anywhere in the world. I had forgotten how many people take actual pleasure in evil, in spreading lies, and building hatred, and that they are incurable. I had forgotten, too, that the masses of the people everywhere, the great majority, are totally ineffective in short-range politics. Over centuries they have their effect, but from day to day the world is run by pressure groups, by lobbies, by secret societies with their teenage gunmen, by army cliques, longing for war to get them promotion and glory, by groups of frustrated persons seeking revenge on some other group, or even, like Hitler, on the whole world.

And it happens, just now, when the old liberal empire is breaking up, that wireless and television have enormously increased the effect of propaganda, of the lie. Lies are far more effective than truth, because they are simpler and easier to remember. They have the defect of misleading and, in due time, of being found out. But meanwhile, as the demagogue calculates, they have put him in power, and the true demagogue never looks further ahead than next week. Communist, Nazi, and Fascist propaganda have proved the power of the lie, and every ambitious young nationalist politician has grasped it.

It is quite certain that in twenty-five years the present day will seem even more remote than 1900 does now. For the revolution of the free mind goes faster as that mind invents new tools. We live, literally, in the creation, and every year there are more creative imaginations at work. And more, much more, for them to feed on. The world grows more tense, more dangerous, but also infinitely richer in experience. There is no more happiness, perhaps less, but very much more intensity of living, more occupation for the mind and the senses.

I so much prefer the modern world to the one that I was born into. No doubt it has its nonsense too, but it is far more mature. It has suffered more and takes life harder. It begins to look fundamental and everlasting evil in the face and to distrust the sloganeer and the cheap-Jack politician with his snap formula for the golden age. It knows that there will never be a golden age; that everything has to be paid for. Only the grace of God, in love, in beauty, in truth, is freely given, and that's why we don't say thank-you for it.

Vogue (N.Y.), CXXIII (15 August 1957), 96, 97, 150, 151, 153.

EPILOGUE

A Great Author Faces up to Death

An Interview with Joyce Cary by Graham Fisher

At his home among the colleges and spires of Oxford, the distinguished English novelist Joyce Cary is dying. Scholar, soldier, thinker, as well as one of the outstanding writers of our day, his books include 'The Horse's Mouth', 'Herself Surprised', 'Prisoner of Grace', 'Not Honour More', as well as many others.

Now, at 68, he has been stricken with a progressive paralysis. His left arm is almost useless. His right will last out another three months, with luck.

His expectancy of life is about two years. The most he can hope for is five.

How does this reasoning man face up to death? Here is what he told me:

I had always hoped to die suddenly, as with a bullet through the head. But in a way, this illness of mine might be regarded as lucky; I might have had a galloping cancer. This thing gives me some more years for work, is almost painless, and doesn't affect the brain.

Solace? I don't need any solace. I've got my faith and I've got my work. I don't see why anyone should moan when he's had his life. Life is given to us. It is a free gift. We do nothing to merit it.

I've had a good life, a happy marriage, a happy home, devoted friends. I've been a very lucky person and I have nothing to complain of now.

This thing started immediately after the Viscount crash at London airport last year. The Viscount I was on took the wrong runway and hit a lot of building material just as it was leaving the ground.

No one was really hurt. I didn't feel hurt at all at the time and went on by the next 'plane.

I first noticed something wrong while I was out in Greece and Cyprus. I had two small falls, though I didn't pay much attention to them at the time. I was told by my doctors that I had temporary brain damage which would pass off, the sort of thing a jet pilot gets if he pulls out of a dive too quickly.

But when the disability increased, specialists revised this opinion and said that what I had was disseminated neuritis and I must have had it a long time before it began to show its effect. This is a form of paralysis which, at least at present, has no cure. It is progressive, but varies in the speed of its progression.

I had started on a novel in 1954, *The Captive and the Free*, before this thing began. I am going on with that now.

Will what has happened affect what goes into it? The main lines of this novel have been laid down for years and all the chief scenes are already written, so that if recent events affect it, it can only be in detail. The novel is about religion and deals partly with faith-healing, for faith-healing raises some of the fundamental problems of religion; for instance, the question of miracles and of what we mean by omnipotence.

Personally, I do not believe in what are called physical miracles. That is to say, any interference in the natural order of things, so far as it is revealed by scientific research. I know, of course, that science rests on an assumption of consistency in material nature. For instance, the proposition that all men are mortal cannot be proved true until all men have died, but this criticism of the scientific position seems to me rather frivolous.

A fundamental objection to physical miracles is that they make God responsible for all evil not due to evil will; that is to say, for all bad luck. When a child dies in agony of meningitis, its misery is due simply to bad luck, and not to anybody's wickedness. God could not abolish the power of doing evil because if he did he also would have to abolish the power of doing good. The world would be a machine; there would be no evil ... and no goodness; no happiness and no grief, for machines feel neither.

But if physical miracles are possible, there is no reason why any child should die in agony. To believe in their possibility makes God responsible for that evil.

What has happened to me has not changed my perspective on anything. I have had the same religious views from at least the age of thirty, and the same values on life.

Do I believe in God? I believe absolutely in God as the ground of love, beauty and goodness. These are personal things which can only exist in personality; that is why we think of God as a person.

These feelings exist universally in human nature, and human nature is part of a universal nature. As soon as one realises this very simple fact ... that there is personality in nature ... it becomes the most important thing in nature. It is certainly the most important thing for humanity, because men live to satisfy their feelings. They use their brains only to create a world satisfactory to their feelings.

And, again, personality cannot exist in a machine. It exists only in the free world, the free soul, with power of moral choice, power to create its own answer for each moral situation, always unique.

The word 'soul' is highly ambiguous. For me, a man's soul is the character of his personality, good or bad. It is partly inherited, as the fundamental emotions and intuitions of human nature, and partly formed by his education and his own moral choice.

Of course, this free creative mind can also plan evil and does so every day. Also, since it is perpetually at work inventing new ideas, new processes, new politics, the world is always full of insecurity. We live among perpetual changes. Nothing ever stays fixed. This is the price we pay.

We owe what makes life worth living—family affection, achieved ambition—to the same factor of free creative personality as makes for all the injustice, insecurity, and change that infect all existence. They belong together in the free world. It is no good complaining of bad luck for luck is also the field of our freedom.

Do I believe in an after-life? There is no real evidence either way. That is to say, I don't believe or disbelieve. I certainly don't count on it and I can't visualise it. If there is such a thing, it must obviously be quite strange to our ideas. If there is no after-life, then death is final. I don't believe in reincarnation.

At present, I'm finding out what a lot of things you can do without when you have to. I used to live a very active life, enjoying all kinds of sport: sailing, punting. I used to walk three or four miles a day in the country or the parks. I used to go to the theatre. But I don't miss those things. I haven't time to miss them.

My one real regret is not having finished some of the novels I've started. I should like very much to finish some of these, but I shan't look at them until I have finished my present novel.

I don't know exactly how much longer I have to live, but I do know that I've got much more to do in the time than I shall ever be able to do.

I went to art school once for two years. I intended to be an artist. I'm sorry I haven't had time to carry on with it, but this writing job takes up all your time. I wish I'd had time for art as well—I miss it—but I'd have had to have another life for that.

Is there anything I regret not having achieved in life? Not really. I'd have liked my novels to have been rather better. Every book I start I think is going to be wonderful—a masterpiece—and then when it's finished I'm always disappointed. If I'd another life, I'd rewrite the lot.

Language is never adequate to express feeling. Words are just marks on paper, after all. Music is much more powerful in the direct expression of emotion—much more exciting—but not so precise. The novel has to give the fact as well as the feeling, the scene of actual life, as well as a judgement upon that scene.

Would I be willing to barter the books I've written for a few more years of life? No, I wouldn't. It isn't that I think my books are so good, but they're me. They're something I have done with my life.

Has my illness revealed any difference in the world? Nothing very definite except the tremendous amount of goodness in people. I've had letters of sympathy and kindness, sometimes without even an address given. I receive extraordinarily kind letters from complete strangers nearly every day. Friends come in to see me, write to me, send me flowers. So do my children. In fact, I have been rather embarrassed by all the sympathy and to-do.

When the newspapers quoted me as saying that I was ready to die, one of my friends—a woman—remarked, 'Well, we are all ready to die.' And that's quite true. What's more, it's a very important truth.

It is very important that people should realise that any week may be their last ... that next week they may be smashed up in a motor accident or knocked out with polio.

Do I mind dying? Of course. I mind very much. But I look upon the time I have left as a gift. And I am very busy.

Coronet, XLI (January 1957), 41–44.

Acknowledgements

Some essays have appeared previously as follows and the editor is grateful for permissions given:

'An Interview with Joyce Cary', by John Burrow and Alex Hamilton: From WRITERS AT WORK: *The Paris Review Interviews* edited by Malcolm Cowley. Copyright © 1957, 1958 by The Paris Review, Inc. Reprinted by permission of Martin Secker and Warburg, Ltd. and The Viking Press, Inc.

'Speaking for Myself': First published in the *New York Herald-Tribune Book Review* (as 'Joyce Cary' in 'Important Authors of the Fall, Speaking for Themselves').

'A Child's Religion': First published in *Vogue*.

'Horror Comics': Copyright by the *Spectator*.

'Barney Magonagel': First published in the *New Yorker*. Copyright © 1954 The New Yorker Magazine, Inc.

'Cromwell House': First published in the *New Yorker*. Copyright © 1956 The New Yorker Magazine, Inc.

'A Slight Case of Demolition': First published in the *Sunday Times*.

'The Meaning of England': © 1958 HOLIDAY MAGAZINE.

'The Most Exciting Sport in the World': © 1957 HOLIDAY MAGAZINE.

'Africa Yesterday: One Ruler's Burden': First published in *Reporter*.

'Christmas in Africa': First published in *Esquire Magazine*.

'Policy for Aid': First published in *Confluence*. Copyright by Mouton Publishers.

'Unfinished Novels': Broadcast on the BBC Third Programme.

'The Way a Novel Gets Written': Copyright © 1950 by Harper's Magazine. Reprinted from the Feb. 1950 issue by special permission.

'Tolstoy's Theory of Art': First published in the *University of Edinburgh Journal*.

'A Novel is a Novel is a Novel': © 1950 by The New York Times Company. Reprinted by permission.

'A Novelist and His Public': First published in *The Listener*.

'On the Function of the Novelist': © 1949 by The New York Times Company. Reprinted by permission.

Notes

The following notes, keyed to page-numbers, aim to locate or elucidate only those references considered of some importance in their contexts or likely to puzzle some readers.

4. *Barbara Hardy's essay*: 'Form in Joyce Cary's Novels', *Essays in Criticism*, IV, 2 (April 1954), 180-190.

6. *Nimmo*: one of the three protagonists of the Second Trilogy (*Prisoner of Grace, Except the Lord, Not Honour More*). See also p. 14.

6. *Bonser*: a major character in *A Fearful Joy*. See also pp. 111-113.

6. *Wilson*: Woodrow Wilson (1856-1924), President of the United States, advocated the League of Nations but could not carry his country into it.

6. *Charlus*: the Baron de Charlus, a major character in Proust's *Remembrance of Things Past*.

6. *Jimson's father*: His 'papa' is remembered by Gulley Jimson (one of the three protagonists of the First Trilogy) in *The Horse's Mouth*, Chapter 6. The Prefatory Essay to that novel describes Cary's boyhood encounter in France with the outmoded painter; see also p. 125.

9. *Cecil*: Lord David Cecil (b. 1902), Oxford don (Fellow of New College 1939-69, Goldsmith's Professor of English Literature 1948-69), critic, biographer, and close friend of Joyce Cary.

10. *Shaw's tale of life force*: Bernard Shaw adopted Bergson's concept of the *élan vital* as determinant of all nature; see his Preface to *Back to Methuselah*.

10. *novel upstairs*: the unpublished *Daventry* (written during 1919, Cary's final year in Nigeria), whose hero, a young District Officer, is led to his death by a public-school sense of honour.

10. *Proust to Mme Schiff about Swann*: in two letters, speculatively dated July and August 1919 by Mina Curtiss in her edition, *Letters of Marcel Proust* (New York, 1949; London, 1950).

12. *best novel*: *Cock Jarvis*. See also pp. 109-111.

13. *son, a composer*: Tristram Cary (b. 1925), well known for his electronic and film music.

19. *rent strike*: policy of withholding rent from landlords, advocated by the Irish Land League during the 'land war' (see note for p. 34).

19. *driving*: i.e., driving a tandem. See pp. 45-46; and compare the account of John Chass Corner's tandem race in *Castle Corner*, Chapter IV.

29. *Carrig Cnoc*: Gaelic name meaning Rock Hill. This essay is closely related to *A House of Children* (1941), which it may have inspired.

34. *famine*: The failure of successive potato crops caused the Great Famine (1845-9), which reduced the Irish population by at least a quarter.

34. *land war*: Eviction of tenants, withholding of rent, boycotts, and mounting violence in the late 1870s led to Gladstone's Irish Land Act of 1881. This enforced wholesale reductions of rent, and many of the Ascendancy landowners, like the Carys, were unable to maintain their property.

40. *three-decker*: war-ship with three gun-decks.

43. *Gavarni*: French artist (1804-66) whose scenes of everyday life, like those of his contemporary Daumier, were very popular. The picture described here is a lithograph in the series 'Nuances du Sentiment'.

60. *gold-stick*: bearer of the gilt rod which precedes the sovereign on state occasions.

60. *Nat Gould*: English novelist (1857-1919).

60. *Marlborough House set*: The wild behaviour of the Prince of Wales (later Edward VII) and his circle scandalised many in the late 1800s. Marlborough House was the Prince's London residence.

62. *bonbonnière, vinaigrette*: fancy boxes containing, respectively, sweets and smelling-salts.

66. *Prichard*: H. A. Prichard (1871-1947), Fellow of Trinity College (1898-1924), White's Professor of Moral Philosophy (1928-37).

66. *art study*: Cary studied art in Paris (1906) and at the Board of Manufacturers School of Art in Edinburgh (1907-9), before reading law at Trinity College, Oxford (1909-12).

74. *in the 'twenties*: Cary's administrative career in Northern Nigeria actually began in 1913 and ended in 1919. While based at Nafada, in his first few years, he was introduced to polo, and missed it greatly when transferred to the remote district of Borgu in 1917. Compare with this essay the account of a polo game in *The African Witch*, Chapter 7.

89. *groundnuts disaster*: the abortive scheme to develop large-scale groundnut production in southern Tanganyika (1947-51).

90. *Castle of Otranto*: the haunted castle which gives Horace Walpole's Gothic novel (1764) its title.

91. *bariki*: Nigerian variant of 'barracks'.

105. *Eatanswill election*: *Pickwick Papers*, Chapter XIII.

111. *at least three years*: Cary worked on *Cock Jarvis* intermittently for about a dozen years (1924-35), during which he published three other novels set in Nigeria (*Aissa Saved, An American Visitor, The African Witch*). He incorporated some of its material in *Castle Corner* (1938), and seems also to have drawn on it for *Not Honour More* (1955).

114. *novel about artists*: the fragmentary *To sleep in Ulro* or *Hamper*.

114. *Bacon, Frith*: Francis Bacon (b. 1910), Irish-born painter of nightmarish, suffering figures; William Frith (1819-1910), realist portrayer of Victorian life, often in panoramic crowd-scenes.

116. *the other*: *The Captive and the Free*. See also p. 252.

119. *the best chapter*: 'The Old Strife at Plant's'; published separately (*Harper's Magazine*, CCI, August 1950, 80-96).

124. *Rodolphe's love-making*: *Madame Bovary*, Part Two, Chapter VIII.

128. *Adolphe*: short psychological novel (1816) by the French politician and journalist Benjamin Constant (1767-1830).

130. *Tolstoy's Theory of Art*: In this essay, Cary summarises and discusses the argument of Tolstoy's *What is Art?* (1898).

130. *women's lives*: *The Diary of Tolstoy's Wife*, entry for 20 November 1876.

132. *George Sand's protest*: in a letter to Flaubert, 12 January 1876 (slightly misquoted by Cary).

132. *Madame Bovary's death*: Part Three, Chapter IX.

133. *deaths of Gervaise, Coupeau*: *L'Assommoir*, final chapter.

134. *Bolkonsky scene*: *War and Peace*, Book One, Chapter XIV.

138. *Jack Sheppard*: Historical novel (1839) by Harrison Ainsworth (1805-82).

138. *Boileau, Dennis, Rymer*: Neo-classical critics of the seventeenth-eighteenth centuries—Nicolas Boileau-Despreaux (1636-1711), John Dennis (1657-1734), Thomas Rymer (1645-1713).

139. *Erewhon*: a satirical romance (1872) by Samuel Butler (1835-1902).

139. *Norpois*: the Marquis de Norpois; see, for instance, *Within a Budding Grove*, 'Mme Swann at Home'.

139. *The Wall*: novel (1950) by American John Hersey about a doomed uprising in the Warsaw ghetto against the Nazis.

141. *The Arcadia*: prose romance by Sir Philip Sidney (1554-86).
141. *Madame de Scudéry*: French writer (1607-1701), best known for two long romances.
141. *Katherine Mansfield's attempt*: *The Aloe* (completed 1916), a strongly-autobiographical novelette, which was extensively revised as the short story 'Prelude' (*Bliss and Other Stories*, 1920), and published posthumously in its original form (1930),
141. *Fuchs*: atomic scientist (b. 1912) convicted of espionage.
155. *Restif de la Bretonne*: French novelist (1734-1806), seen as a forerunner of Balzac and Zola.
155. *The Isle of Penguins*: *L'Ile des pingouins* (1908), satirical novel by Anatole France (1844-1924).
157. *Léon Bloy*: French writer of violent, visionary novels and essays (1846-1917).
160. *Simmons's book*: Ernest J. Simmons, *Dostoevski: The Making of a Novelist* (London and New York, 1940).
162. *Kutuzov at Borodino*: *War and Peace*, Book Ten, Chapter XXXV.
164. *Claudel*: Paul Claudel (1868-1955), French dramatist and writer of prose-poetry.
168. *Darya, Stepan*: *Anna Karenina*, mainly Part I.
173. *Pangloss*: character in Voltaire's *Candide*.
177. *the '45*: the Jacobite Rebellion under Prince Charles Edward, begun in 1745 and ended in 1746 at the Battle of Culloden.
177. *Lady Murasaki*: author of *The Tale of Genji* (about 1000), considered the greatest work in Japanese literature and the earliest novel; it was owned by Cary (see p. 148) in Arthur Waley's famous translation (1935).
177. *Madame de Lafayette*: French writer of romances (1634-93).
177. *Benson*: Edward Benson (1867-1940), English novelist.
179. *Mrs. Caudle's Curtain Lectures*: very popular series of expatiations on domestic topics by Douglas Jerrold (*Punch*, 1845).
180. *moujiks*: peasants. Zahar is a character in Oblomov (1857), a novel by Ivan Goncharov (1812-91); Petrushka is in the novel *Dead Souls* (1837), by Nikolai Gogol (1809-52).
181. *Michael Scott*: Scottish merchant and writer (1785-1835); his *Tom Cringle's Log*, a series of tropical and sea adventures, appeared first in *Blackwood's Magazine* (1829-33).
181. *Creevey, Greville, Kilvert*: nineteenth-century English diarists —see *The Creevey Papers* (1903), *The Greville Memoirs* (1938), *Kilvert's Diary* (1937).
182. *Buzfuz*: *Pickwick Papers*, Chapter XXXIV.
183. *Gil Blas, Chichikov*: picaresque heroes of *Gil Blas* by LeSage (1668-1747), and Gogol's *Dead Souls*.
184. *Pierce Egan's London*: Pierce Egan (1772-1849) wrote guides

to fashionable London life in the Regency period (1811-1820).

184. *Harriette Wilson*: famous English courtesan (1786-1846), whose *Memoirs* (1825) scandalised the public.

185. *Apperley*: Charles Apperley (1779-1843), English sporting writer ('Nimrod').

202. *Edward Lord Despenser*: member of the powerful Despenser noble family, favoured by Edward II.

208. *Pepys's statement*: *Diary*, 23 February 1669.

220. *Natty Bumppo*: pioneer-scout hero of five novels by James Fenimore Cooper (1789-1851).

227. *Eisenhower and Formosa*: In 1955, tension over Formosa (Taiwan) took China and the United States to the brink of war.

228. *Grey Eminence*: biography (1941) by Aldous Huxley (1894-1963) of Father Joseph, a seventeenth-century cleric and statesman.

228. *Cripps and the gold standard*: As Chancellor of the Exchequer in the Attlee Government, Sir Stafford Cripps (1889-1952) devalued sterling in 1949. (Cary seems to have confused this, to some extent, with the financial crisis of 1931, when the gold standard was abandoned.)

229. *the Ems telegram*: Bismarck precipitated the Franco-Prussian War of 1870-1 by altering a message from Kaiser Wilhelm I to express defiance of the French.

233. *origin of clothes*: *Penguin Island*, Book Two, Chapter I.

239. *old carpenter*: Wickenden—*The Edwardians* (London, 1930), especially pp. 54-56.

242. *wars of 1859, 1861, 1870*: the Italian War of Liberation (1859-1861), American Civil War (1861-5), and Franco-Prussian War (1870-1).